Taking Care
of Business

Taking Care of Business

LuAnn McLane

Patricia Ryan

Toni Blake

A SIGNET ECLIPSE BOOK

SIGNET ECLIPSE
Published by New American Library, a division of
Penguin Group (USA) Inc., 375 Hudson Street,
New York, New York 10014, USA
Penguin Group (Canada), 90 Eglinton Avenue East, Suite 700, Toronto,
Ontario M4P 2Y3, Canada (a division of Pearson Penguin Canada Inc.)
Penguin Books Ltd., 80 Strand, London WC2R 0RL, England
Penguin Ireland, 25 St. Stephen's Green, Dublin 2,
Ireland (a division of Penguin Books Ltd.)
Penguin Group (Australia), 250 Camberwell Road, Camberwell, Victoria 3124,
Australia (a division of Pearson Australia Group Pty. Ltd.)
Penguin Books India Pvt. Ltd., 11 Community Centre, Panchsheel Park,
New Delhi - 110 017, India
Penguin Group (NZ), cnr Airborne and Rosedale Roads, Albany,
Auckland 1310, New Zealand (a division of Pearson New Zealand Ltd.)
Penguin Books (South Africa) (Pty.) Ltd., 24 Sturdee Avenue,
Rosebank, Johannesburg 2196, South Africa

Penguin Books Ltd., Registered Offices:
80 Strand, London WC2R 0RL, England

First published by Signet Eclipse, an imprint of New American Library,
a division of Penguin Group (USA) Inc.

First Printing, August 2005
10 9 8 7 6 5 4 3 2 1

Contents

Driven

LuAnn McLane

For Linda Keller, the best CRM
in the business.
Thanks for all that you do
for so many authors.

Chapter One

"**S**ex is out. I've been trying for hours and getting absolutely nowhere."

"Well, try harder."

Ian closed his eyes and blew out a frustrated sigh. "You're forcing me to do something that just doesn't come naturally to me. I do murder, not sex. I won't do it, Jan."

"I've got a six-figure contract that says you will. Sex is part of the deal, Ian." Her usual soft, southern drawl took on a hard edge.

"Screw the contract." Ian gripped the phone tighter and raked the fingers of his other hand through his short-cropped black hair.

The silence at the other end of the line was deafening.

Ian suddenly felt like a jerk. Jan Davis was one of the best literary agents in the business, and he was damned lucky to have her. He was making more money writing than he had ever dreamed of making as a

PI, and here he was giving her a hard time when he should be kissing her ass. "Look, I'm sorry. This is so frustrating. I just can't make the sex scenes work. I don't want my book to be a wallbanger."

"Ian, your characters, Jack and Margo, have been dying to sleep together since chapter three of your first book. The sexual tension between them crackles on the page. Quite frankly, I think Ian Parker fans will be outraged if they don't—"

"Screw?" Ian began to pace the small confines of his office like a caged cat.

"No, make love, you idiot. God, you're such a *guy*."

Ian paused in his pacing to roll his blue eyes toward the ceiling. "It's a murder mystery, not a romance novel. Give me a break."

"I've given you a fat contract and I'll remind you that you signed it! You have a deadline hanging over your handsome head. . . ." She snapped her fingers. "Hey, wait a minute. I've got a great idea. Oh, why didn't I think of it before?"

"What?" Ian had the sinking feeling he wasn't going to like her idea—just a hunch, but his hunches were rarely wrong.

"Have you ever heard of Maxine Mitchell?"

Ian swallowed a groan. He knew where this was heading and he didn't like it. "Yeah, she's a popular romance writer. Perky little redhead. I met her at a writers' conference last year." She had sat at his table. All smiles, and had never shut up. She was a sexy distraction that he didn't need then, and didn't need now.

"Well, she writes romantic comedy, but she's trying her hand at romantic suspense, and she's struggling with the details. Guess what her hero is?"

"A private investigator," Ian answered dryly.

"Ian—"

"Jan, no—"

"She could pick your brain."

He gripped the phone tighter. "I don't want my brain picked."

"Maxie writes the hottest love scenes in romance. She could—"

"No way!" Ian shook his head, but he could tell that Jan wasn't listening. She was on a roll and there was absolutely no stopping her. This was how he got roped into adding sex to a novel that in his opinion didn't *need* sex . . . but it was also why she was one of the top literary agents around. Damn, the woman could sell. "Jan, I don't want to hook up with Maxine Mitchell."

"She's fun. You'll like her."

Ian groaned. "I'm *not* fun. She'll hate you for this."

"Maxie is already staying at my retreat. This is perfect. You can join her for a few days and brainstorm."

"Retreat?"

"My log cabin in Tennessee." She sighed. "God's country. I've mentioned it to you before, but you pointedly ignored me. It's a great place to write, Ian. Quiet and peaceful, with no distractions. Maxie goes there two or three times a year. It's only about four and a half hours from Cincinnati, so you can drive."

"Can't we just do this via e-mail? You know, send stuff back and forth? I really don't think I should interrupt her vacation." Not to mention, Ian hadn't exactly been friendly to her in Maui. He didn't want to drive all the way to Tennessee to have the door slammed in his face.

"It's a big log cabin, Ian. You and Maxie can both have your privacy. This is a perfect setup. You'd be crazy to turn it down."

Ian frowned. His PI instincts kicked into gear, making him wary. "Does Maxie know I'm coming?"

"Sure."

"And she's okay with it?"

"Why wouldn't she be? This is business. She has as much to gain from this as you do. You'll love Maxie and you'll love the cabin. Oh, and Ian?"

"Yeah?" He swallowed another groan. A damned log cabin? He didn't do log cabins. He didn't do love scenes. He would *do* sexy little Maxie Mitchell, he thought, with a shake of his head. *God.* Avoiding her in Maui had been easy, but staying with her in a log cabin in the middle of nowhere was another thing altogether. One of the main reasons his career was skyrocketing was the fact that he stayed focused. He didn't need any distractions or complications to screw things up.

"Pack your fishing pole and hiking boots. I just had the lake stocked."

"I don't fish. I don't hike. . . ." Ian protested, but Jan either wasn't listening or didn't care. She rambled on about mountain streams, fresh air, and did she say bears?

Ten minutes after their one-sided conversation, Ian's fax machine hummed and then spit out the directions to . . . *Possum Creek?* "God's country?" Ian muttered under his breath. "Sounds more like hell."

He glanced at his computer and realized with surprise that it was well after midnight. Jan might be a night owl, but he wasn't. No wonder his eyes were burning with fatigue. He had been working on that love scene for hours. Ian sat down in his swivel chair and decided to read the scene one more time. Maybe it wasn't as bad as he thought, and the trip to Tennessee could be canceled.

Ian ran his hand over his face. Oh God, it was bad. He just didn't know what to call all of those female parts. Boobs? Tits? And what about all that heaving and moaning? Why in the hell couldn't he just write, "and then they . . . fucked like bunnies"? *Show, don't tell,* his writer's brain answered. He sighed as he shut down his computer. Maybe his problem was that it had been so long since he had actually *had* sex.

That thought conjured up an image of Maxine Mitchell. He remembered a riot of red curls, cleavage spilling out everywhere, and a pouty mouth made for kissing. But then Ian moaned. A pouty mouth that *never* shut up. Perky, endless chatter that would drive him insane.

Ian liked silence. Solitude. That's why the writing life suited him so well. After getting a degree in criminology, he had applied for a private investigator's license, but had soon grown weary of chasing down cheating spouses. He thought of Maxine Mitchell picking his brain and chuckled. A PI's job was much less exciting than most people thought, thanks to television.

Ian pushed back from his desk, stood up, and stretched. He needed to go for a long run and relieve some tension. But it was late, and he was weary, so instead, he headed down the short hallway to his bedroom. Looking at the clutter, the stacks of books, Ian thought once again that it was time to look for a bigger place, maybe even a house. This latest contract meant he could finally do just that . . . which was why he was going to head for Possum Creek, Tennessee, first thing in the morning.

Maxie squealed into the phone, and then jumped up from the front porch rocking chair where she had been enjoying the view of the Great Smoky Mountains. "So Ian Parker is actually coming here to work with me?"

"Don't get so excited," Jan warned. "He can be a real pain in the ass. He isn't exactly—uh, how can I put this nicely?—*social*."

"I know. I met him at the Maui Writers Conference last year. He's one of those strong, silent types, like those alpha males that I love to write about. I know his type inside out. I'll be fine." She lifted her face to the cool spring breeze and smiled.

"Maxie, Ian is a real, flesh-and-blood man, not a character in one of your novels. He might *look* like a cover model, but there's nothing remotely romantic about Ian Parker."

Maxie's smile faded a bit. "You know him that well?"

"I've been his agent for going on six years, and although he isn't very vocal about his personal life, I've never known him to be seriously involved with a woman."

Maxie shook her head. "A guy who has his good looks and is highly successful to boot? I don't get it. . . . Oh, he isn't—"

"Gay? No. I asked him that once."

"You didn't."

"You know me. Anyway, he laughed his ass off. One of the few times I ever got a belly laugh out of him."

"Then what's his problem?"

"I'm part of the problem. I've kept him so busy that he's been in a writing cave for years, going from one book to the next."

Maxie frowned. "Everybody needs a break."

Jan chuckled. "So you like to tell me. Ian is just, I don't know . . . *driven*."

"Oh, that's so sad," Maxie said wistfully. "Maybe he needs—"

"Whoa. Hold it right there, sugar. Ian Parker is *not* a brooding hero who needs to be saved by a beautiful heroine. Switch off your romance writer right brain. This is a business arrangement. He needs to write a smoldering sex scene, and you need to learn about the PI mumbo jumbo. Keep this professional."

"You mean you're not matchmaking?"

"Certainly not! The only matchmaking I do is between editors and authors. You stick to picking Ian's brain and telling him how to *write* a sizzling sex scene. The operative word here is *write*."

Maxie giggled. "But the hands-on approach would be so much more fun."

"Maxie . . ."

"Okay, okay! I'm kidding. By the way, about what time do you think he'll arrive?"

"What time is it there?"

Maxie glanced down at her Mickey Mouse watch. "A little after ten."

"Knowing Ian, any moment now."

"You're joking!" Her green eyes widened as she gazed at the gravel path leading to the main road. "Geez, I've got to go shower. I'm still in my jammies."

"Don't you dare say, 'and shave my legs.'"

Before Maxie could formulate an answer, she heard gravel crunching. "Ohmigod, I think it's him. Gotta go, Jan."

Squinting her eyes against the sun, Maxie looked down the tree-lined path at a black Escalade kicking up dust. *Well, damn,* she thought, glancing down at her Pooh Bear lounging pants and matching tank top. *She really needed to visit Victoria's Secret more often.* Without makeup, and her auburn hair a bed-head mess, she hardly looked like she could pen a sultry sex scene. She had just decided to try and make it to the front door of the log cabin without being seen, when the mean-looking SUV came to a halt.

The dust settled, and Maxie wasn't able to take her eyes away when the shiny black door opened and long, jean-clad legs unfolded. She angled her head when Ian bent at the waist, presumably to retrieve something, and couldn't help but admire his very fine butt. Maxie sighed. She remembered trying to catch his eye at the Maui conference without success. In fact, her many attempts at conversation had seemed to annoy him. Maxie shook her head. Guys like him went for long-legged, cool, sophisticated blondes, not short, perky, raised-on-a-farm redheads.

Maxie gave herself a mental shake. "This is business," she said under her breath. "Trying to get Ian Parker in the sack would be so *unprofessional* and so"—her eyes widened when he straightened up and turned around—"unforgettable."

Chapter Two

With his duffle bag hefted over his shoulder and his laptop case in his other hand, Ian headed up the path to the log cabin. Maxine Mitchell stood on the wide porch clutching a big coffee mug while shooting him a bright, welcoming smile. Ian dug deep to try and conjure up a returning smile, but could only manage a slight curve of his lips.

As he ascended the three wide fieldstone steps to the porch, his eye for detail told him that Maxine Mitchell was nervous. Her smile remained, but her green eyes were open a bit too wide, and her chest moved up and down with shallow breathing. A better man would have said something to put her at ease, but the last place he wanted to be was Possum Creek, Tennessee, stuck in the middle of nowhere, to brainstorm with a doggone romance writer.

When her bright smile dimmed a few watts, he realized that he was scowling. "Hello, Ms. Mitchell." He dumped his duffle bag on the wooden floor and held out his hand.

To her credit, her smile wavered but remained, and her handshake was surprisingly firm even though his hand totally engulfed hers. "Welcome to Possum Creek, Mr. Parker. I can't *wait* to get started. I have so many questions."

Oh great. "I'll do my best to answer them."

"I made a list."

Ian stifled a groan. "That's . . . good." He tried to smile, but it felt like a wince. Knowing that he was totally screwing this up, and that Jan would have his ass, he tried to recover, and then politely said, "And I hope you can show me how to do the sex. I'm told you're extremely good at it."

Her cheeks immediately turned pink.

Okay, that didn't come out right. God, he didn't want to be here. "Writing. Not showing. The scenes, I mean." Ah damn, he sounded like a frigging idiot.

"You *really* don't want to be here, do you?"

Ian hesitated, thrown off balance by her unexpected accusation, but she gave him a pointed look, and he really sucked at lying. "Ah, no, actually."

"Especially with me. I annoyed you in Maui, didn't I?"

He gave lying a try. "Ah, no. I found your company quite, ah—" Damn, he drew a blank.

"Annoying?"

"A little."

Her eyes narrowed. Miss Perky was getting pissed.

"Hey, I didn't mean that. Quit putting words in my mouth."

"Oh, come on. Your body language says it all."

"What?"

"The firm set of your jaw. The scowl."

He made an effort to soften his expression, and she rolled her eyes. This was going from bad to worse.

"And to think I was actually looking forward to working with you."

The disappointment in her tone got to him. "Look," he began. She blinked up at him, but he drew another blank.

"It's because I write romance, isn't it?"

"What?"

"You don't take me seriously."

Her full bottom lip extended into a pout, making it hard for Ian to concentrate. She was getting to him in more ways than one. Unconsciously, he took a step closer to her. "You're putting words in your mouth—*my* mouth—again."

She took a deep breath and blew it out, making her chest puff out, and for the first time he realized that she was in some sort of pajamas . . . and braless. A cool breeze suddenly kicked up, making the braless thing even more apparent while blowing the tumble of dark red curls across her cheek. She reached up to brush the hair from her face, but a strand stubbornly clung to her bottom lip, bringing his attention back to her mouth.

Out of nowhere, a white-hot sizzle of sexual heat had him longing to cup those full breasts, back her up against the log wall, and kiss her senseless.

The perky smile disappeared. "Okay, I have a proposition for you."

"Y-you do?" Damn, he was getting aroused.

"I'll give you a stack of my books to read. That should help you with your love scenes. I'll give you my list of PI questions and you can write down the answers. I'll stay out of your hair, and at the end of the week, we should both have everything we need." With that, she spun on her bare heel and flounced into the cabin, letting the screen door shut with a bang.

Ian stood there for five full seconds, confused, aroused, and unsure of what in the hell to do. Grovel? Nah, he wasn't quite sure *how* to grovel. Apologize? Ian shook his head, and muttered, "For what?" She was just too doggone sensitive. Should he just take her up on her offer? Ian shrugged and picked up his duffle bag. Still undecided, he entered the cabin and gave a low appreciative whistle. The interior was much bigger than he had anticipated and decked out with rustic but beautiful furniture.

"Wow." Ian stepped into a huge great room with cathedral ceilings and a gorgeous fieldstone fireplace. Floor-to-ceiling windows showcased a view of the Smoky Mountains and surrounding forest of tall pine trees. To the left was a galley-style kitchen separated from the main room by a long breakfast bar and high-backed stools. A hallway to the right led to what he guessed was a bathroom and bedrooms. Ian wondered where he was expected to dump his gear when he noticed a spiral staircase that led to a loft area where there were additional rooms.

The spraying, pattering sound of a shower coming from behind a door down the hallway had Ian deducing that Maxine must be occupying one of those bedrooms, so he headed up the staircase, trying unsuccessfully not to imagine her wet and naked body underneath the steamy spray of the shower. He had gotten her mad as hell without even trying, making staying out of each other's way seem like the best scenario. After locating a spacious bedroom with a connecting bath, Ian dropped his duffle bag on the quilt-covered bed, and placed his laptop on an adjacent desk. Two windows let in streams of sunlight filtering through the trees. Opening a window, he inhaled the fresh scent of pine and spring blossoms. All in all, he thought, this was a surprisingly pleasant place. . . .

And then he heard a door slam.

Wrapped in a fluffy white towel, Maxie stomped around her bedroom, mumbling under her breath while getting dressed. Not wanting Ian to think she was remotely interested in enticing him, she tugged on an old pair of gray sweatpants and a plain white T-shirt. She headed back into the bathroom and pulled her damp curls into a sloppy ponytail, but couldn't resist a bit of mascara, lip gloss, and a dab of perfume on her wrists. She would do that even if he weren't here, she lied to herself. With that, she stomped back into her bedroom, and picked up a copy of her latest release and her carefully thought-out private investigator questions. Maxie was about to head back out into the main room, when she stopped and took a deep breath.

"Calm down, Maxie," she chided herself. "You're letting this guy rattle you." She ran a fingertip over the smooth, glossy cover, and silently read the caption underneath her name. "New York Times *best-selling author of* Second Time Around, *Maxine Mitchell, hits the mark again with wit, sass, and steamy sex.*" Maxie sighed. Okay, she'd never be an Oprah pick, but her books entertained. Made people laugh. Her English professor mother might never quite approve of her mass-market appeal, and her conservative father might get embarrassed over the steamy sex, but, hey, screw them all. Right?

She was enjoying life—having fun and making money doing what she loved doing most. Not many people could say that. It was certainly better than walking around with a perpetual scowl like Ian Parker. She remembered from the Maui conference that he was always so tall, dark, and serious. It had been her personal quest to make him laugh, and she thought she had done it, maybe *once*, but she had mostly gotten under his skin.

God, she also remembered what Ian had looked like emerging from a swim in the Pacific Ocean. She had been protecting her fair skin underneath a beach umbrella, and suddenly there he was, dripping wet and rippling with lean muscle. She had given him an enthusiastic wave and a come-hither smile, but had gotten a mere slight inclination of his head in return.

Maxie frowned while tapping her finger on the book jacket, getting angry all over again. Until now, she had forgotten about that particular snub. And she was sensitive to snubs. All through high school, guys had snubbed her when she had been a short, flat-chested, freckle-faced, fuzzy redhead. She had tried to overcome her lack of physical appeal by being the class cutup, and could always manage to get a laugh, but never a date. Her stand-up comedy had landed her many an hour in detention, but had honed her comedic skills, so life had a way of paying you back.

And then suddenly, freshman year of college, she grew boobs. Big boobs. Practically overnight. It was as if the boob fairy had waved a wand while she slept. Armed with this man-magnet asset, and a roommate who could work magic with hair, even hers, Maxie jumped into the dating scene with the enthusiasm of one long denied. Unfortunately, it was where she got most of her material for the chick-lit angst in her books that, unlike her own love life, always ended happily ever after.

Maxie sighed as she headed out of the room. *I want happily-ever-after, damn it. Where in the world is my knight in shining armor, my Prince Charming? I'd even kiss a slimy toad.* So engrossed in her thoughts, Maxie almost ran into Ian at the bottom of the spiral staircase.

"Oh!" Backing up a step, she thrust her book and list of questions at him. "Here is my latest release. There's a love scene in chapter four, um, chapter eight, and chapter twenty-three."

"Okay," he said slowly.

"You can answer my questions whenever you get the chance," she said stiffly, and turned toward the front door.

"Where are you going?"

Surprised that he asked, she stopped in her tracks. "For a walk in the woods," she answered in a none-of-your-business tone without turning around.

"Is that safe?"

Maxie paused to look over her shoulder. "I grew up on a farm. I'm not afraid of spiders and snakes."

"But what about bears?"

Maxie shrugged. "Jan has warned me about the black bears that roam the Smoky Mountain Range, but I've been coming here for years and haven't seen a bear or Bigfoot once." She took another step toward the door.

"So, how long will you be?"

Maxie turned all the way around, facing him with her hands on her hips. "Why do you ask?"

"Well, if I have an idea of when to expect you back, I'll know whether to come searching—"

"Searching?" At first she thought he was kidding, but then she realized that Ian Parker probably never kidded around. "Mr. Parker, I come here several times a year. There is a path at the back of the cabin that I know like the back of my hand. I appreciate your concern, but you can relax."

"Okay," he said, but looked unconvinced.

"Look, you've made it quite clear that you don't want to be here, especially with me, so let's stick to the 'staying out of each other's way' plan, okay?"

He looked at her for a long moment, giving the impression that he was going to argue that point. She tried not to care, but her heart betrayed her by pounding hard in her chest.

Chapter Three

Ian wanted to keep his mouth shut, but the thought of Maxie wandering around in the woods by herself bothered him much more than he wanted it to. "I just don't want you to be breakfast for a bear."

"I can take care of myself."

Yeah, right, he thought. She was feisty, but a little bitty thing. With her chin up and her hands on her hips, she was spoiling for a fight, but he didn't care. "I'm coming with you."

"You are not!" she sputtered.

"Watch me!" *Okay, that was mature.* He narrowed his eyes at her.

Her mouth opened, and then shut. She was fuming. Green eyes blazing, color high in her cheeks, she could only sputter. For some reason, he found this amusing and grinned at her, sending her into orbit.

"I'm leaving and don't you *dare* follow me." With a quick pivot, she hurried out the door.

Ian followed her around the side of the cabin to a trail leading into the woods. She ignored him, and he knew she would try to ditch him, so he stuck close to her heels. By the straight set of her back and her clenched fists, he knew he was royally pissing her off again, and he found this amusing as well.

And tiring. Maxie hiked up the steep hillside with ease, but Ian's long legs had him easily keeping up with her even though he knew she was trying her best to lose him. Luckily, he was in decent shape and found the exercise invigorating. The crisp mountain air smelled of damp earth and spring flowers mixed with the tang of pine. *Maybe this nature thing isn't so bad after all.*

Ian took a deep breath as he followed her, admiring the sway of her hips and the way the sunshine caught fiery highlights in her dark, red hair. He was watching her fine fanny so intently that when she slipped on a loose stone, he wasn't prepared for her to slide backward. She yelped when he caught her around the waist, and the impact of her butt into his gut caused him to stumble backward on the steep incline. Not wanting to crush her, Ian twisted, letting her fall on top of him. She squealed as they slid downward, surprising fast. He grunted when he felt sharp stones and twigs dig through the thin cotton of his shirt.

They didn't stop sliding until the ground leveled out. For a stunned moment they remained that way. Maxie was on top of him, clinging to his neck, while the dust settled. Finally, with an angry squeal, she pushed up with her hands on his chest, straddling him.

"What the hell was that all about?" she accused. Twigs and leaves littered her hair and she had a smudge of dirt on her chin.

"You fell backward, taking me with you!"

"You're blaming this on me? I told you *not* to follow me."

"Well, excuse me for my concern."

She glared down at him.

"You could at least thank me for breaking your fall."

"I wouldn't have been going so fast if I hadn't been trying to ditch you."

"Oh, so this is my fault?"

"Yes!" She leaned over, nose to his nose, and said through gritted teeth, "Why don't you just go home and do the sex scene on your own."

"It's more fun with a partner."

His dry humor was so unexpected that Maxie burst out laughing, and to her surprise, he joined her. When their laughter subsided, Maxie realized with a jolt of heat that she still straddled him and her mouth was almost brushing his. A bit embarrassed, she quickly pushed up on his chest, not realizing that he still held her fast around the waist. This unexpected resistance caused her hands to slip over Ian's shoulders and her mouth landed smack against his warm, firm lips.

Suddenly Maxie was kissing him. The heat of his mouth had her melting against him for a long, hot moment, and then she regained her senses. "Oh, s-sorry," she said against his mouth. Her hands slipped around in some dry leaves on the ground as she tried unsuccessfully to scramble off of him.

"Don't be," he said with an unexpected sexy grin.

"Ian, you s-should let me go so I can get up."

"Believe me, I know. But right now all I can think about is kissing you."

He was flirting with her! God, what a turn-on. Her brooding bad boy had a hidden playful side. Maxie so wanted him to kiss her, and yet she hesitated when her old insecurity reared its ugly head. Ian had made his disinterest quite clear in Maui. Just a little while ago he had admitted that she annoyed him. Was kissing her merely a way to pass the time on Possum Creek? If another woman were available would he still ignore her? Was she just—

"Uh, Maxie?"

Oh, poor thing, he sounded a bit frightened, like he was afraid she was going to turn him down. This unexpected vulnerability was yet another turn-on. Plus, kissing him in the woods was something one of her heroines would do that would lead to something more. Maybe it was time she should take a walk on the wild side instead of just writing about it. "Okay, I'm—"

"Shhh!"

What? He was shushing her already? *Well.* She pushed at his chest, but his arms held her fast.

"Don't move!" he said quietly but with urgency. "There is a bear not ten yards behind you."

Maxie grinned. So serious, brooding Ian had a sense of humor, too. Ooh, maybe this weekend was going to be fun after all. Maxie grinned down at him, but her grin immediately faded. His eyes were wide and she realized that his heart pounded rapidly beneath her palms. *Oh God.*

"Lie very still," he whispered, "and maybe he'll go away."

Maxie's heart picked up speed. If Ian was messing with her, she was going to kick his ass. For a few more pulse-pounding moments, they remained perfectly still. Then, Maxie heard rustling as if something was moving. Ian's arms tightened around her, and he tensed. She *so* wanted to ask if the bear was coming closer. Shivering, she felt all too vulnerable perched above him. Closing her eyes, she anticipated a huge claw ripping her to shreds or a big bite being taken out of her butt angled upward like an offering.

"He's gone."

It took a moment for his words to register. "You're . . . sure?"

"Reasonably. I'm not sure how far, but he's out of sight."

Maxie started to move, but he held her fast.

"Be still for another few minutes, just to make sure."

"Okay." She clutched a handful of his shirt in her fist. Although he felt warm and solid beneath her, all thoughts of sex were taking second seat to survival.

Finally, Ian took a deep breath and then said, "I think it's safe."

"Think?"

"Hey, I'm not Jed Clampett. I'm much more comfortable with concrete beneath my feet. I *think* it's safe."

Maxie took a deep breath and then rolled off of him. Before standing up, she cautiously looked around, squinting into the woods. When she saw no sign of the bear, she pushed up to her feet.

"I told you it wasn't safe to wander off by yourself."

Maxie put her hands on her hips. "I didn't *wander* off. I went for a walk! It's a well-worn trail."

He stood up, towering over her. "Well, don't go for another walk without me."

"Who made you my boss?" Okay, that was mature. She barely resisted sticking out her tongue.

"I'm self-appointed."

"Well, *un*appoint yourself." She spun on her booted heel and headed back down the trail, watching for the bear out of the corner of her eye. He followed close behind her, and she was secretly glad.

When she reached the front porch of the cabin, she sat down on the steps and removed her muddy boots. He joined her, doing the same to his running shoes. When his thigh brushed up against hers, she felt intimately aware of his proximity while pretending to ignore his existence. But when she made a move to get up, he restrained her with a hand on her thigh.

"Maxie, I know I'm not your boss, but please don't go off into the woods by yourself."

She wasn't about to, but she raised her chin a notch and responded, "I've been coming here for over five years and have never seen a bear. That incident was a fluke."

He blew out a sigh. "So, in other words, you'll do as you damned well please."

"Pretty much."

"You're impossible."

She looked down at his hand, and he removed it from her thigh.

After standing up, she said, "I'll stay out of your way, Mr. Parker. Just pretend I'm not here."

He stood up. "Fine. If you get gobbled up by a bear, then it's your own fault. Just don't scream for me to come rescue you."

"Ha. If I needed rescuing, you'd be the last person I'd scream for."

"Then we understand each other."

"Perfectly." Back ramrod straight, chin up, she padded on sock feet into the cabin, paused to grab a bottle of water from the fridge, and then headed to her bedroom for her laptop to write.

Chapter Four

ollowing Maxie inside the cabin, Ian watched her flounce out of the room. *Flounce*, he thought with a grin. Now there was a good word. He had thought of a whole new vocabulary when it came to describing Maxine Mitchell. She flounced; she sashayed. . . .

And he'd bet she would be as hot as a firecracker in bed. Ian grinned. Or in the woods. If the damn bear hadn't interrupted, he might have had her right there in the pine needles. With a sigh, Ian opened the refrigerator and grabbed an apple and a bottle of water. Perhaps it was for the best, he thought, taking a big crunchy bite of the fruit. Jan had sent him to Possum Creek to write a sex scene, not perform one.

While munching on the tart Granny Smith apple, he picked up her novel and headed for the back deck to do some sex scene research.

After easing his long frame into a lounge chair, he took a deep breath of crisp mountain air. The breeze was cool, but the sun felt warm beating down on his head. Picking up the paperback, he bit back a chuckle as he read the title, *For Love or Money?* The bright yellow cover had a cute cartoon couple, the woman with her back to the man, and a building of some sort in the background.

"Take the money and run," Ian muttered under his breath, but was intrigued, nonetheless. He flipped the book over to read the back blurb:

> Marcie Weston and Pete Sommers have been rivals ever since they served on student council together in high school. Marcie always voted with her heart, while Pete was all business. Now, years later, business tycoon Pete is back in town and wants to tear down a historic diner to make room for his upscale restaurant. But Marcie, who is on the town council, still votes with her heart, and is in the way of Pete's progress.
>
> Sparks fly, but when love blossoms, will Pete choose the woman he's always wanted or the money?

Ian shook his head in wonder. "That's the plot?" he mused out loud. "You gotta be kidding me." With a sigh, he opened the book, thinking that reading the insipid book was going to be a real chore, sex or no sex.

Thirty minutes later, Ian turned the page to Chapter Three and had to admit, probably *wouldn't* admit, that he was thoroughly entertained. The dialogue was snappy, and Maxie had captured the essence of the seaside setting. He could smell the sea, feel the soft sugar-white sand and the heat of the tropical sun. But more than anything else, he was waiting impatiently for Marcie and Pete to fall into bed instead of dancing around their attraction. The sexual tension sizzled on the page. By Chapter Four, Ian was hoping Pete would give up the fancy-assed restaurant and let Marcie save the damned diner, so the poor guy could finally get laid. . . .

And then it finally happened. Despite their differences, when Marcie accidentally walked in on Pete as he was coming out of the shower, Ian knew he was about to read one helluva sex scene.

He wasn't disappointed.

Good God, they made love for five pages. That damned Pete was the king of oral sex. Ian felt like taking notes. He reread the five pages, for research purposes, of course, and an unwanted thought crept into his brain. Was this Maxie's fantasy coming to life on the page? Pushing that thought out of his mind, he tried to concentrate on the writing.

But he couldn't. Reading this stuff was making him horny as hell, especially after his interrupted interlude in the woods. And even though Marcie, the heroine, was tall and blond, Ian kept visualizing a short redhead, with a pouty mouth and too many curves, in the scene.

Well, hell. Even though it was barely noon, he needed a cold beer.

Maxie picked up the phone and dialed Jan's number. She was going to tell her agent that this was a crazy idea and she was going to bail. When Jan picked up, Maxie got straight to the point.

"Jan, I'm outta here."

"What? Maxie, what's wrong?"

"Ian's out on the back deck reading *For Love or Money?*" She peeked out the window for the hundredth time. His nose was still buried in her book.

"Wasn't that part of the plan?"

Shaking her head, Maxie stared up at the beamed ceiling. "I never thought about how embarrassing it would be. Jan, that first love scene is page after page of oral sex."

"Yummy, as I recall."

Maxie groaned.

"Oh, come on, Maxie. You're both adults. What's the big deal?"

"I'll never be able to look at him! I'm leaving."

"Maxie, I've worked my tail off getting your editor to agree to let you try romantic suspense. Don't you *dare* leave that cabin until you get what you need from Ian Parker."

Maxie sighed. That was the real problem. She knew exactly what she needed from Ian, and she had almost gotten it in the woods.

"So, have you helped him with the sex? God, the man needs it."

Maxie frowned. "We *are* talking about writing, aren't we?"

"Of course. I wouldn't *dream* of trying to hook you up with such a sulky bad boy. This is purely business. Now, go to it. You need each other. This a great opportunity—don't let it pass you by."

"But we are such opposites. His writing is so intense, and I'm pure fluff."

"You are not pure fluff. Don't sell yourself short, Maxie. You're much more talented than you give yourself credit for."

Maxie sighed. "Jan . . ."

"Do this for me. Ian has a huge contract riding on this, and between you and me, the man is a great mystery writer, but his attempt at a love scene was god-awful. Have a heart and help him."

Maxie looked out the window at Ian reading her book. She closed her eyes, but then heard herself promising Jan to give it her best shot. Pasting a perky smile on her face, she slid the door open. His back was to her, giving Maxie a moment to compose herself. She had just opened her mouth to address him when he tilted his head back and laughed.

Oh God, he was laughing at her writing! How humiliating. She pivoted, but must have made a sound of some sort because he twisted around in the lounge chair.

"Hey, what's wrong?"

Maxie realized she was scowling and tried to relax her facial muscles. "You were laughing," she accused, frown still in place.

"It's a comedy."

"Oh . . . so you think it's funny?"

"Contrary to popular belief, I do have a sense of humor."

He said it so seriously that Maxie had to smile. "So what about the . . . you know?"

"The sex?" He cocked a dark eyebrow and looked a little uncomfortable. "Fun to read, but a bit unbelievable."

Maxie took a step closer and tried not to be offended. "What do you mean?"

"Oh, come on, Maxie. Nobody has sex that good . . . for that *long*. Sex that good only happens in romance novels. A nice little fantasy. I guess that's why women read them."

Her anger must have shown on her face because he raised his hands and said, "Don't get me wrong. I'm finding the book surprisingly enjoyable."

"Surprisingly?" She drew out the word slowly.

"Oh, come on, Maxie. How many guys you know read romance?"

He had a point, but she wasn't about to let him know it. "Maybe if more guys would, the awesome sex wouldn't be so unrealistic."

"Get real. Maxie . . . uh, I mean *Marcie* had three mind-blowing orgasms in less than five pages."

"And your point?" She gave him a wide-eyed look that had him open his mouth, and then snap it shut.

He shook his head. "I like sex as much as the next guy, but all of that melting and shattering is a bunch of—" He stopped, knowing he was in trouble.

"Oh, no, do finish your thought." Maxie angled her head down at him, grateful that he was sitting and she was standing, giving her some advantage. It was almost amusing to see him with his foot in his mouth. When he remained silent, she decided to help him out. "Bullshit?"

"What?"

"I'd be willing to bet that was the word on the tip of your tongue. Am I right?"

He straightened up from his lounging position. "You really need to stop putting words in my mouth."

"Ah, so I *am* right."

"You think you can read my mind, too?"

"Pretty much. I write about arrogant, alpha males like you all the time. I know your type inside out." She gave him a little dismissive wave of her fingers.

His eyes narrowed, but his lips twitched at the corners. "Really? So, I'm just curious, do you think *I* could give you a mind-blowing, earth-shattering orgasm?"

Maxie felt her face grow warm at his unexpected question. *God yes. Without a shadow of a doubt.* Maxie gave him what she hoped was a haughty lift of her chin when the thought made her insides turn to jelly. "Not on your life. There is much more to sex than just mechanics, Ian, and there's not a romantic bone in your body." There. She told him.

His grin deepened. Good Lord, he had a dimple she hadn't noticed. Leaning forward in the chair, he rested his forearms on his knees and said, "Let's reenact the scene in chapter four and find out if your writing is fantasy or reality."

Her heart thudded wildly and you could have knocked her over with a feather. She couldn't quite figure out if he was serious or just trying to get a rise out of her. "You're insane. I'm not about to . . . to . . ."

"Prove yourself right?"

"I can't have sex with someone I barely know."

"Think of it as a hands-on workshop. Research, if you will. Taking care of business."

"I won't!"

"Marcie and Pete, in your book, *did*."

"It's not the same!"

His eyebrows shot up. "Because it's unrealistic, pure fantasy?"

"No!" How could she tell him that it was because Marcie and Pete lived happily ever after and at the end of the week Ian Parker would go back to Cincinnati, and she to Parkerville, Indiana.

She was looking for a fairy tale, and he was looking for a piece of ass. She wanted both.

"Your over-the-top scene would never work, anyway."

"It would!"

"Prove it."

"Okay!" Oh God. What had she just agreed to?

Chapter Five

Ian watched her retreat into the cabin and wondered what in the hell he had just gotten himself into . . . and why? He opened the book to Chapter Four and groaned. He'd never be able to perform like tongue-happy Pete. Damn, it had been so long since he had had sex, he'd be rusty as hell, much less able to give her multiple orgasms. "Fantasy, my ass." He hadn't expected her to agree and had made the statement just to get her riled.

Now he had to put his money where his mouth was. He thought about just where his mouth needed to be to make good on the bet . . . or was it a challenge? *Good God,* he thought, and chuckled weakly. *Now what?*

Study. He read and reread the five pages until he knew every lick, every nibble, and every stroke in the scene by heart. Finally, nature called, and he had to go into the cabin. Maxie was nowhere around, and he wondered if she was studying, too. This whole thing was a little weird, but titillating, and quite honestly, very out of character for him. But Maxine Mitchell had brought out several uncharacteristic qualities in the few hours he had spent in her company. Ian usually liked to keep to himself, not follow someone into the woods, but she somehow managed to bring out his protective nature. And he was never, *ever* spontaneous, yet he had spontaneously offered to play out a scene in her book. Ian ran a hand over his face and shook his head.

Not just any scene. Very energetic oral sex.

His stomach growled, and Ian wondered if low blood sugar was responsible for his strange behavior. He looked into the refrigerator for dinner ideas. Other than writing, cooking was his only creative outlet. After his mother had bailed on him and his dad, Ian had grown weary of canned stew and had taught himself to cook. By the age of twelve, he could create dinner from just about any three ingredients. "Aha!" He found two frozen chicken breasts, a jar of marinara sauce, and a hunk of mozzarella cheese. In the pantry, he found spaghetti and olive oil. "Chicken Parmesan. Cool." He rummaged around in the galley-style kitchen and was delighted to find a bread maker. Rubbing his hands together, he smiled. Food and seduction went hand in hand. At least his dinner would be orgasmic.

He turned on some music, tied on an orange "kiss the cook" apron, and went to work.

Maxie sniffed the air and frowned. She sniffed again. "Bread?" Did she really smell the aroma of baking bread? Maxie started to push back from the desk to investigate, but then stopped herself. She had come into the bedroom to escape, to keep her distance and regroup before facing Ian again. Glancing at her watch, she realized it had only been thirty minutes and she was already being sucked back in. But discovering the unexpected layers underneath Ian's cool exterior was fascinating. Could the man cook, too? Unable to contain her curiosity, she followed her nose to the door of the bedroom and opened it a crack.

"Ohmigod." Maxie had a clear view of the kitchen from the hallway. Ian, in an apron, no less, was puttering around, whisking, pounding. He paused to take a sip of red wine from a goblet and pounded some more. Maxie took another deep sniff. Ahh, basil, oregano, garlic. Italian cuisine was her favorite.

She watched a mesmerized moment longer, and two things hit her: One, she was starving, and two, Ian Parker looked incredibly sexy wearing an apron. Not wanting to be caught with her mouth watering, she quietly closed the door.

She had been reading Chapter Four for the gazillionth time, not that she was *seriously* going to take him up on his ridiculous challenge, but, well, it didn't hurt to be prepared. A soft knock at the door had her jumping a foot in the air. She clattered her fingers on the keyboard, pretending to be writing, and called out, "Yes?"

"Dinner will be ready in about forty-five minutes."

"Oh?" She tried to sound surprised. "I thought I smelled something good. I'll be finished editing in a little while."

"Great. I hope you're hungry."

"A little." She clattered on the keyboard again. When she heard his retreating footsteps, she sprang into action.

"What am I going to wear?" She looked into the mirror. "Oh God, look at my hair!"

After the near-butt-biting experience with the bear, she had showered, but let her hair air-dry, and now it was a riot of messy curls. "Damn!" With a sigh, she decided she would have to pile it on top of her head in a ponytail.

Digging around in her suitcase, she moaned. She had packed only jeans and sweaters, not anticipating the arrival of a man, much less *Ian Parker*. She finally decided on a pair of black jeans and a green angora sweater that had a deep V-neck that was a little revealing. Growing up flat-chested, she had never quite grown comfortable with her abundant cleavage, but tonight, doggone it, she was going to wear an underwire bra, and let those puppies shine.

She chose black silky underwear like Marcie wore in the scene in her book, but she was willing to bet that Ian didn't mention the sex scene. Maxie guessed that he had made the offer on the spur of the moment just to goad her, but on the off chance that she was wrong, she slipped on the black bra and panties. Not that she was going to see the whole challenge through. Really, she wasn't about to reenact a scene from her book. She just wanted to look her best to give herself a bit of confidence.

After tugging on the jeans and sweater, she piled her hair on top of her head, letting a few tendrils curl around her face and down her neck. Foundation to hide her freckles, mascara, smoky eye shadow, and peach-tinted lip gloss were the best she could do. She frowned into the mirror, wanting to be taller, thinner, with long, flowing hair. "Oh well."

She squared her shoulders, sprayed on a little perfume, and then pointed a warning finger at her reflection. "Don't chatter. It will drive him crazy. Just be silent and . . . pouty." She arched an eyebrow. "Sultry. Seductive." She giggled. "Yeah, right."

Taking a deep breath, Maxie headed down the hallway and into the kitchen. Things were bubbling, sizzling, but Ian wasn't in the room. The bread maker beeped. Maxie approached the big white appliance and looked into the little window and saw golden crust. It beeped again, making her jump. What should she do? Her idea of cooking was popping something into the microwave. She was impressed, but clueless.

"Is the bread ready?"

At the sound of his deep voice, Maxie jumped again and turned around. *Wow.* He wore a charcoal gray ribbed sweater that showed off his wide shoulders and set off his blue eyes. Freshly shaven and with dark, wet hair starting to curl over his ears, he smelled even better than dinner. He filled out his faded jeans to perfection, but was barefooted. Seeing the direction of her gaze, he grinned and said, "My shoes are still muddy."

Maxie looked down at his feet. Sexy. How in the hell he managed to have sexy feet was beyond her, but they were *sexy*.

"So is the bread ready?" he asked again.

Maxie shrugged. "The beeper thingie went off, so I guess so."

"I take it you don't own a bread maker?"

"I might."

He angled his head and asked, "You don't know?"

"My mother stocked my kitchen with all shapes and sizes of kitchen gadgets. She thinks my lack of culinary skill is why I'm still not married."

"So you don't cook?"

"I unwrap and nuke."

He chuckled.

"Hey, nuking takes considerable skill. I know just how many minutes it takes to thaw a bean burrito, and my microwave popcorn is to die for." She pointed to the stove. "Things are . . . bubbling."

"Whoa." He turned and began stirring, flipping, and turning knobs until he had everything under control.

Maxie simply watched, knowing that offering to help would mean ruining something otherwise delicious. Besides, it was fun to stand back and observe. She did manage to pour herself a glass of wine. She sipped while he cooked. "May I help?" she felt compelled to ask.

Ian turned from where he had just removed the golden brown loaf of bread from the bread maker. "You can slice the bread, but let it cool for a minute. There's an electric knife in the drawer."

"Okay." *An electric knife? Those things are scary, like having a chainsaw in your kitchen. Why did he have to ask me to do that?* "You can do this, Maxie," she said under her breath.

"What?"

"Nothing." She was about to confess her fear of kitchen appliances in general, and electric knives in particular, but he flipped the sizzling chicken breasts with the ease of Emeril Lagasse, and she decided she couldn't show how extremely inept she was in the kitchen. After all, her mother might be right. With a brave smile, she removed the lethal-looking serrated knives and attachment. She frowned, hoping she was hooking the knives correctly into the slots. Flying knives were not a good thing. With a silent prayer, Maxie plugged the contraption in and turned it on.

Buzzzzzzz. The silver knives moved rapidly back and forth. *God, a person could lose a finger!* Feeling like she should be wearing protective goggles, she approached the loaf, aimed the knife, and began unevenly slicing the bread. "There," she said proudly, and turned off the creepy, noisy knife.

Ian looked at the mangled bread and took a sip of wine to hide his smile. Maxie Mitchell was *lost* in the kitchen, and for some strange reason, he found that cute and very sexy, like he needed to take care of her . . . feed her.

Make love to her on the edge of the countertop.

She blinked up at him. "Can I do anything else?"

Oh yeah, come to Papa. "No, I'll load up the plates and bring them to the table. You can just have a seat."

"Okay."

She seemed relieved, and he had to hide another smile.

First, he dished up Waldorf salad and brought it to the table. "There weren't any greens for a tossed salad, but I found apples and, surprisingly, walnuts."

"I'm so impressed," Maxie said as she put her napkin on her lap. She took a bite. "Delicious."

Ian joined her, taking a seat across the small table. He expected endless chatter from her, but she ate in silence. Oddly, Ian found himself trying to draw her into conversation, but he was really bad at idle chitchat. He gave it a shot. "I didn't get a chance to read your private investigator questions, but I'll do my best to look them over tomorrow."

"Thank you." She licked a bit of dressing from her upper lip and then dabbed her mouth with her napkin.

He tried again. "So, when is your next book coming out?"

"December. It's a Christmas anthology."

"Have I done something to tick you off?"

Her green eyes opened wide, and she blushed a rosy shade of pink. "No."

"Then why aren't you talking to me?"

Her gaze lowered to the table. "I didn't want to annoy you. In case you didn't notice, we tend to . . . argue, so I thought I'd better keep my mouth shut."

Ian frowned. She was bringing out unexpected warm and fuzzy qualities again, making him feel like a jerk. "Well, your silence is more annoying." Oh damn, that didn't come out right. "No, what I meant was, your silence is—"

"Annoying? You've established that several times."

"You're putting words into my mouth again, Maxie!"

"I was quoting!"

Closing his eyes, he put his finger and thumb to the bridge of his nose. "I'm sorry. I suck at this."

"At what?"

He opened his eyes and looked across the table at her. "The whole dating ritual thing. All my parents ever did was argue. An only child, I would retreat to my room and read to shut them out, telling myself I would never put myself through what they did to each other. Finally, my mother left. And then there was silence."

"Ian, I'm sorry." Something inside of her melted. She understood. God, she wanted to leap across the table and love him, heal him . . . and she wondered with a hammering heart if she had found her real-life wounded hero. Her soul mate? Okay, she was taking it a little too far, but she was having a moment and wanted to milk it for all it was worth.

He grinned at her. "Don't look at me like that. Reading all of those Hardy Boys books made me into a mystery writer. When the books ran out, I made up my own stories." He sighed and his grin turned sheepish. "Look, I know I'd make a horrible husband, but I'd at least like to be pleasant company. So, Maxie, teach me how to chat, maybe crack a joke or two? Then, maybe, when I get back to Cincinnati, I can at least date with some success."

Date. *Right*. Other people. Maxie guessed her soul-mate epiphany was one-sided. She smiled, but his comment brought her romantic brain back to reality like a splash of cold water in her face. *Ah, well,* she thought sadly. At least she was getting more material for her books: *Perky heroine teaches brooding hero how to date.* Of course, in her book, they have lots of wonderful sex and fall in love.

"Maxie?" He was looking at her oddly.

Squelching her disappointment, she dug deep for her defense mechanism, her sense of humor. Surely there was humor in this situation? "I'll teach you how to flirt if you teach me some cooking skills so I can get married and make my mother happy." She thrust her hand across the table. "Deal?"

Chapter Six

For some reason Ian couldn't fathom, instead of shaking her hand, he brought her fingers to his lips and kissed her knuckles. Feeling rather goofy, he looked across the table at her, trying to gauge her reaction. When her green eyes widened a fraction, he let go of her hand. "Too smarmy, huh?"

"Wh-what?"

"The kissing-of-the-hand thing."

"Oh, not at all. I found the gesture charming."

"Really?" He was oddly pleased.

"Ian, I don't think you're nearly as hopeless as you think, especially—" She seemed to catch herself and remained silent.

"What?"

She gave him a small smile and shook her head. "Nothing. Hey, I'm hungry. Where's the main course?"

He thought about pushing her for an answer, but she was looking down at the table while toying with the stem of her wineglass. So instead, he pushed back from the table and headed into the kitchen for the chicken and pasta.

She was getting under his skin, and when she let her guard slip, he glimpsed vulnerability. And it surprised him that he wanted to know more, take away her mask of perky smiles and jokes and find the woman within.

But when he returned to the table with steaming plates of food, her smile was in place. She sliced through the chicken Parmesan and took a bite. "Mmm, heavenly. How about I just marry you and forget about learning to cook?"

He knew she was just kidding, but something about the statement made him feel . . . *weird,* and it seemed to hover in the air, like it could be grabbed and made true. Shaken by his runaway train of thought, Ian looked down at his wineglass, wondering if he had imbibed too much.

"Geez, Ian, don't look so wigged out. I was only playing."

Ian grinned. "Well then, let's play. Teach me the art of endless chatter."

She shook her head. "It is not endless chatter. It's called getting to know one another. That's what a man and a woman on a date do."

He raised one eyebrow. "Among other things."

She smiled. "Good. Very good."

He frowned and asked, "What do you mean?"

"Ian, you were flirting and didn't know it." She twirled a fork full of spaghetti. "Keep it up. Look over at me with those bedroom eyes and say something to make me melt."

"I never know when you're kidding or serious."

"Almost never serious."

"Damn, so I don't really have bedroom eyes?"

"Ian, you not only have bedroom eyes, but a bedroom body as well," she purred. "Surely you know that?"

He blinked at her.

"Are you kidding or serious?"

She sighed. "I'm flirting."

"Right." Ian reminded himself that this was all a game. She was probably spouting lines from a scene in her book.

His eyes widened. *The unending oral sex scene in her book.* He had almost forgotten—no, actually he had it memorized. He wondered if she was expecting . . .

"Ian, are you okay? Did something go down wrong?"

"Poor choice of words," he murmured.

"Excuse me?"

"I'm fine," he said shortly.

She pursed her lips and gave him a little head bob. "That's *not* a very flirty tone."

Ian had to laugh. "Maxie, you have me so off-kilter, I don't know if I'm coming or going."

She blinked at him and her lips twitched. "Do you seriously expect me not to touch that line?"

He laughed harder. "I . . . don't . . . know . . . what . . . to . . . expect."

"You're certainly not coming."

"Not yet, anyway." He tried to give her a wicked grin, but it dissolved into another fit of laughter.

"And I tried so hard in Maui."

"To make me come or go?" He laughed again.

"Oh, come on, Ian. I was pretty damn good at making you go. You hardly noticed me except to scowl and silently pray I would shut up."

He stopped laughing and looked at her. "What, then?"

"I wanted to make you laugh."

Something hard and cold inside him melted. "Why?" His voice was gruff, imploring.

She licked her bottom lip, and her green eyes were serious.

"Tell me, Maxie."

"No," she whispered. Getting serious made her feel open, exposed. She needed a flippant remark, a joke, but none would come. With a lift of her chin, she said softly, "You were so silent, so serious, always working. I wanted you to smile, to laugh. Doggone it, I just wanted to see you with a mai tai in your hand while you danced in a grass skirt and a coconut bra."

Ian chuckled. "I seem to recall that you offered me fifty bucks to dance the hula on stage that last night at the luau."

Swallowing the emotion in her throat, she smiled. "Those were my own mai tais talking. You gave me your patented scowl."

He cocked one eyebrow. "A grass skirt, huh?"

She wiggled her eyebrows. "And nothing underneath was part of my plan."

"Would you have slept with me in Maui?"

Maxie sucked in a surprised breath and felt her cheeks grow warm. *Without a doubt* was on the tip of her tongue, but she suddenly realized that wasn't true. "No."

"God, I'm sorry. I shouldn't have asked that question." He paused for a moment. "But since I did, could you tell me why not?"

She drained the last of her wine before answering, "Because I couldn't make you laugh. Ian, you made it quite clear that you didn't like being around me. I'm sure that if you could have switched tables, you would have." She gasped when he suddenly looked embarrassed. "Oh my God, you tried!" She pushed back from the table so swiftly that her chair almost tumbled backward.

Maxie headed for the back deck, suddenly in need of fresh air and distance from Ian, but he followed her.

"Maxie!"

She leaned her hands on the wooden railing. "Leave me alone, Ian."

"Listen!" He grabbed her arm and tugged her around to face him.

Maxie looked up at him in the soft glow of the setting sun. She waited, but he seemed at a loss for words. Instead, he lowered his head and kissed her. She would have resisted—really—but he had her pinned against the railing. . . .

And, God, the man could kiss. Warm, soft, but firm lips. *Mmmmm.* He cradled the back of her head and slanted his mouth at just the right angle to kiss her deeply with just enough pressure, just enough tongue, to have her opening her mouth for more. When his other hand slipped underneath her sweater, she moaned and wrapped her arms around his neck.

When his mouth moved from her lips to nibble on her neck, she managed to shakily ask, "Ian, what in the world are you doing?"

"Showing, not telling, remember? Maybe this time a bear won't interrupt."

"Showing . . . *oh* . . . showing . . . *what?*"

"What I wanted to do in Maui . . . and what I want to do even more now."

What he wanted to do in Maui? He cupped her breast, making it hard to think. "B-but what was all that scowling about? . . . Mmmm." When his thumb rubbed over her nipple, she hung on to his neck for support.

"Keeping my distance. You were a sexy distraction that I didn't need. But I couldn't keep you off my mind, no matter how hard I tried."

She frowned up at him and their eyes met. "I don't get it. I thought I annoyed you."

"You do," he growled into her ear and then nibbled on her earlobe. She pushed at his chest.

"No!" He held her tightly. "Listen. You annoy me because you're not the type of girl who is after a quick roll in the sack and will then go on her merry way."

"So *sorry!*" She pushed harder, but he held on, making her contemplate pounding on his chest.

He blew out a harsh sigh. "That came out wrong. What I mean is, you're smart, funny, sexy, and exactly the kind of girl I could never hold on to."

Maxie abruptly stopped struggling. "Come again?" She groaned. "Okay, poor choice of words. For a couple of writers, we suck at communicating. Now, please, explain!"

"Okay, I'll give it a shot, and for the life of me, I don't know how you're getting me to say all this stuff. I feel like we're in a scene from one of your romance novels."

"Then don't do it."

"What?"

"If this is a scene from a romance novel, then don't give me all the reasons why it couldn't work between us. That's the black moment, and we get to have lots of sex before that."

"You're joking, right?"

"Dead serious. Let's quit dancing around this thing that's been going on between us since we first met."

"Maxie—"

She put a finger to his lips. "This is the having sex part." What she failed to tell him was that after the black moment comes the happy ending.

And she hoped to get it. But for right now, the sex would do quite nicely. "Make love to me, Ian."

"Am I supposed to reenact the scene in Chapter Four? I have it memorized, but—"

Maxie shook her head. "This has nothing to do with the stupid challenge, Ian. This is your chapter. You call the shots."

He blinked at her for a moment, opened his mouth, and then snapped it shut.

"Oh, come on!" She snuggled against him and said, "Don't get writer's block now, for goodness' sake. Find your muse."

"My muse?"

"Never mind." She shook her head. "Look around. Think," she pleaded, nibbling on his neck.

"What's wrong with a bed?"

"Boring." *Like hell*, Maxie thought. Just the thought of being in bed with him made her heart race. But she wanted to do something daring . . . something memorable.

Something to make him want more.

With a long sigh, Maxie slid her hands underneath his sweater, up the smooth, warm skin of his back, and then raked her fingernails lightly back down. When he shivered and drew in a sharp breath, Maxie moved her hands around to his chest, enjoying the feel of silky hair, hard muscle, and more warm skin. She angled her head up at him. "Any ideas?"

Chapter Seven

an suddenly remembered his hot
fantasy about taking her on the counter in the kitchen. He opened his
mouth to tell her, but some of the reasons not to do this tugged at the
back of his brain.

"Tell me, Ian."

At the sound of her husky plea, the reasons vanished in a haze of
desire that curled like smoke, wrapping around his brain, smothering
any protests. "In the kitchen," he whispered in her ear.

"How?" She gazed up at him, her green eyes bright, hot.

The words started to unfold in his head.

"Tell me. Please."

Ian hesitated, but then he looked down at the forgotten linen napkin balled up in his hand and said softly, "Okay, but first I want you to
turn around."

"Why?"

"Just trust me, okay?"

Maxie looked up at him for a long, hot moment and then nodded and presented him with her back. Ian folded the napkin and proceeded to blindfold her.

"W-why the blindfold?"

"This is my chapter, remember?" he whispered into her ear. Actually he was just winging it, but having her unable to look at him gave him some courage to start telling his fantasy. "Now, just trust me and listen."

When she nodded, he wrapped his arms around her from behind and started talking softly into her ear. "First, I slowly strip you naked, until every inch of creamy skin is mine to see, to touch, and to taste. I lift you up onto the countertop, where the surface is cold against the heat of the desire pooled between your thighs."

"Go on." She bit her bottom lip between her teeth and let her head rest against his chest.

"And then, while you watch, I strip for you until I am standing in front of you, hot, hard, and ready." Ian paused, letting her see the scene behind her blindfold. He splayed his hands over her rib cage, just beneath her breasts. She arched her back just slightly, and Ian knew she wanted him to cup her breasts, but he refrained, not wanting anything to interrupt her visual.

"And . . . and then?"

Ian whispered hotly into her ear, "You reach for me, but I bend down, kneeling before you. I spread your legs, hook them over my shoulders, and scoot you forward to the very edge of the countertop. You have to cling to me or fall."

In between shorts breaths, she pleaded, "Enough telling, Ian. It's showtime."

With a growl, he picked her up. Still blindfolded, she wrapped her arms around his neck and her legs around his waist, bent her head, and kissed him while he somehow stumbled into the kitchen.

The cabin was dark except for one light over the kitchen sink. Ian set her down in the middle of the small room, and began removing her clothing with shaky fingers. First, he tugged her sweater over her head.

"God," he murmured when he saw the black lace bra that pushed her breasts up over the silk. Leaving the bra temporarily on, he kneeled down, unzipped her jeans, and tugged them down to the floor. While holding on to his shoulders, she helped by kicking off her shoes and stepping out of her jeans, revealing black silk panties, high-cut, dipping just below her navel.

"You are the sexiest thing I've ever laid eyes on," he said, and meant it. Her small stature only made her curves seem more lush, more feminine. She had the fair skin of a redhead, lightly freckled, making her appear fragile. With a groan, he slipped his fingers into the black silk and tugged her panties slowly downward, letting his hands enjoy the texture of her soft skin.

Still on his knees, he drank in the sight of her feminine mound lightly covered with dark red hair. He traced one finger over the smooth skin, realizing she must have just had a bikini wax. She shivered, clinging to his shoulders. "You're beautiful down there."

"Thank you," she said, and chuckled deep in her throat.

"I bet you get that all the time," he joked.

She chuckled again. "No, actually, you are the—Oh!" Her fingers dug into his shoulders when he buried his face there, giving her a brief but knee-weakening tease with his hot tongue and then leaving her wanting so much more.

Pushing the toaster out of the way, he then lifted her onto the countertop. She gasped, arching her back at the shock of the cold surface against the heat of her arousal, just like he had promised.

"Remove the blindfold, Maxie."

"Okay." She tugged it off and let it drop to the floor. "You were supposed to strip for *me*, remember?"

He looked at her for a moment and then began undressing. Swallowing, she watched as he tugged his sweater up over his head and tossed it carelessly to the floor. His shoulders seemed to fill the small room. He had a great chest, defined without bulk, lightly furred with dark hair that narrowed to an enticing line heading south. The bulge in his jeans made her inhale sharply, close her eyes, but then open them when she heard the rasp of his zipper slowly opening.

With his eyes riveted to hers, he continued to open the zipper, and then he pushed his jeans halfway down his lean hips, exposing white boxer briefs, the kind that were deliciously tight, leaving nothing to the imagination. The hard ridge of his erection strained against the soft cotton. Maxie reached forward to touch him, but Ian stepped back, just out of her reach, and slowly inched his jeans over his hips. Ian stood there for a moment and then let the denim slide to the floor. Stepping out of the legs, he carelessly kicked the jeans out of his way.

"Come here," Maxie pleaded, needing to run her hand over the hard length of his arousal.

With a wicked grin, Ian shook his head and took another step backward. Maxie's breath caught when he inched his boxers just far enough to expose the head of his penis.

"You've done this before," she accused, gripping the edge of the counter.

"Never," he said. "Only for you." He edged the boxers down a few more inches making his penis look like it was trapped and begging for release.

Maxie was just about ready to jump from the counter and yank the boxers to the floor when he did it for her. Until now, she had thought a penis was just, well, a penis. His, though, was . . . gorgeous. Tall, proud, jutting out of a nest of black curls, flanked by muscular thighs, his cock was big without being too huge, thick but long. "You have a perfect penis."

He laughed, making her blush.

"Hey, you said *I* was beautiful, you know, down *there*."

"You are," he said, kneeling down, obstructing her view of his perfect penis. Maxie leaned forward to get another look, but he parted her thighs, just like in his fantasy. She knew what was coming, which should have diminished the excitement, but instead, it only heightened the erotic anticipation. She *knew* he was going to lift her legs over his shoulders . . . and he did, scooting her forward like he had promised, to the edge of the counter.

"Oh!" With her legs draped over his shoulders, she had to reach up and grab the bottom of the cabinet above for support. She felt so exposed, but she couldn't close her thighs without squishing his head. Her heart pounded when he placed tiny kisses on her inner thighs, first one and then the other, while his hot breath caressed her sex.

"Ahh, Maxie." He leaned forward, spreading her legs even wider, and licked her labia lightly, a sweet caress that had her arching her back. "Mmmm," he murmured, licking a little harder, beginning a slow rhythm, and laving her up and down like he was enjoying an ice cream cone.

Her arms up, Maxie gripped the bottom of the cabinet above tightly, moving with his mouth. She teetered on the edge, supported by his hands on her bottom and her legs on his shoulders, totally at his mercy. . . .

But mercy wasn't on his mind. He was relentless, insatiable, devouring her slow and easy with languid licks of his tongue. Maxie craved more, more, *more*, arching her back, needing release. "Ian!" Her plea was throaty, desperate. Her heart pounded, her belly quivered while the pleasure increased. "Please."

He increased the pressure of his tongue just slightly, easing over her slick sensitive skin, but avoided her clitoris, making her wild with need. Maxie tried to angle her body, clinging to the cabinet while arching up, spreading shamelessly wider, needing his tongue to touch her *there* where she was swollen, throbbing.

She wanted to pound on his back, but couldn't let go of the cabinet. She wanted to scream for him to finish her off, but couldn't catch her breath. All she managed was a pathetic whimper. He must have sensed her desperation and gave her poor clitoris a little flick of his tongue. *Oh God. A hero in my novels would never be so mean. . . .*

He gave her another slight flick, and another, and *another.* Just when she thought he was going to end the sensual torture, he pulled away! "What?" she croaked. "You are so *not* a hero."

He chuckled wickedly and then stood up, still holding her up with his palms on her bottom. "Hang in there, baby. Wait for me." He turned around, bent down, and then came back sheathed in a condom.

"Ahh," and then he plunged his beautiful penis deep inside her. With her legs still over his shoulders, he had to angle up while he moved in and out with sure strokes. She banged her head on the cabinet, and he chuckled weakly and slid one arm around her back, allowing her to grab on to his neck.

"Hang on tight," he growled. And then he moved harder, faster. Maxie threw her head back while clinging to his neck, finding the right amount of friction until, with a sharp cry, he squeezed her ass and plunged deep. Maxie flew over the edge with a stunning climax that had her shaking, clinging to him.

Ian kept his arms wrapped tightly around her, nuzzling her neck, murmuring nonsense into her ear. "Maxie, you're beautiful, so sweet. So amazing. I want to stay inside you forever. Did I mention that you're amazing?"

Maxie smiled. She had the distinct feeling that Ian wasn't usually so vocal, so . . . cuddly, and this tender side of him made her absolutely melt. He continued to nuzzle, nibble, sending shivers down her spine even though she was still reeling from the explosive climax. "Take me to bed," she murmured into his ear. Wild was awesome, but now she wanted all night long.

He chuckled. "In bed isn't too boring?"

"Mmmm, no way. Now I want to explore every gorgeous inch of you. This scene, sweetheart, is all mine."

Ian pulled back from his nibbling. "I'll meet you in your bedroom in a few minutes," he promised, and eased her from his body.

"Okay," she murmured, leaning against him, "but don't be long."

He nodded as she left the kitchen, and then he headed to the bathroom to clean up. "Wow," he said, gazing at his reflection in the mirror. His fingers shook when he reached up and ran a hand through his mussed hair. He had been okay until she had called him *sweetheart*. It had been an unconscious endearment, he knew, but it shook him up, nonetheless.

It shook him up because he liked her calling him *sweetheart*. He wanted, needed, longed for intimacy, something that had been absent as a child and he had avoided as an adult. But intimacy meant feeling, caring . . . loving—all of the things missing in his life. All of the things he wanted. All of the things Maxine Mitchell could give him; he was sure of it. He had been sure of it in Maui and had successfully avoided her because feeling and caring meant exposing yourself to pain.

With a sigh, Ian turned on the faucet and splashed cold water on his face in an attempt to startle his befuddled brain into thinking straight. He reminded himself that he sucked at relationships and his few attempts had ended in disaster. Taking this any farther than extraordinary sex would be a waste of time and emotion. His dysfunctional childhood had left him craving but ill-equipped for love and with a jaded opinion of marriage.

Well, damn. He was going to have to warn her that if she expected anything more than sex, they needed to end this now. Tugging on his boxers, he opened the door to the bedroom connecting to the bathroom, prepared to tell her the terms.

Opening the door revealed a spacious master suite with a large, four-poster bed as the focal point of the room. It was piled high with pillows, the covers turned down, but Maxie was absent from the mattress. To the left of the bed was a nightstand laden with four fat candles flickering high in the cool breeze billowing through gauze curtains on the opposite side of the room. Cinnamon and vanilla scented the air, and the soft song of the night filtered in through the open window. Crickets? The ribbit-ribbit of a bullfrog, the hoot of an owl. It was earthy, sensual. . . .

Where the hell was Maxie?

Ian narrowed his gaze in the dim light, past the end of the bed to a corner fireplace where blue and yellow flames curled around a stack of logs. He wondered how she had started the blaze so quickly and then realized it was a gas fireplace. Two deep red leather wingback chairs flanked the fireplace, facing the flames.

"Maxie?" he softly called out, but before she could answer, he spotted her hand draped over the arm of one of the chairs. Pink-tipped fingers curled around a wine goblet.

"Over here."

Ian's heart picked up speed as he crossed the room. He looked down at her snuggled in the big chair. Wrapped in a dark green afghan, he realized with a rush of heat that she was naked except for the small, fringed coverlet. Her hair, a dark red jumble of curls in the dim light, picked up golden highlights from the flames. She took a long sip of wine and then looked up at him while letting the afghan slip from her shoulders to her waist.

Ian drew in his breath at the sight of her creamy skin bathed in the glow of the fire. Kneeling down, he cupped her breasts in his hands and drew one peaked nipple into his mouth, laving it with his tongue while rubbing his thumb over the other. When he heard her breath catch, he sucked, and then nibbled lightly.

He looked up to see her head lean against the back of the chair, her eyes closed, lips parted. He pulled his mouth from one breast and transferred it to the other while rubbing the wet nipple between his thumb and finger. She gasped, pushing her head back against the cushion, thrusting her breast deeper into his mouth while threading her fingers through his hair.

But then he pulled back, remembering that he was supposed to tell her—

"Carry me to bed, Ian."

He looked into her heavy-lidded eyes, and she gave him a sultry smile. Slipping his arms underneath her legs, he lifted her up and laid her gently onto the thick mattress. To hell with terms and conditions, fears and inhibitions. All that mattered was here and now. Tomorrow would come soon enough.

Chapter Eight

Maxie sensed his hesitation but wasn't about to let him back out. It wasn't about the sex; she could get sex any night of the week if she went looking for it. Her attraction to him went deeper and beyond that. She felt this man needed to be loved. *Loved.* She realized now that she hadn't been snubbed in Maui. He had been attracted to her as well, but afraid. Something was making him hold back, and Maxie was determined to make him let go. She knew she only had a few days to do it, and she was going to pull out all the stops.

"Come to me, Ian." Maxie raised her arms to him, letting the afghan slip off and fan out around her naked body. He lowered his big frame on top of hers, moving sensuously, skin against skin, while using the strength of his arms to hold most of his weight above her.

The steely hardness of his erection pressed against her sex, making her want to peel the skintight boxers off of him and feel the velvety texture of his penis before he slipped on a condom.

He dipped his head and licked her bottom lip, then kissed her long and deep until she could feel his arms begin to tremble. When the kiss ended, she whispered, "Roll over."

When he obeyed, Maxie rolled with him and straddled his waist. "I want to explore. Play." She trailed her fingertips over his chest, scratching lightly, making him shiver. She laughed low in her throat, leaned over, and licked a nipple, letting her hair trail over his chest.

"You know you're driving me nuts," he growled.

She answered with hot kisses on his abdomen, stopping at the waistband of his boxers.

"Maxie!"

She sat up and gazed down at him. His eyes were closed, his breathing harsh, and he was so beautiful, he took her breath away. Flickering light from the fireplace and candles cast a glow, turning his skin a rich golden color. High cheekbones, straight nose, square jaw—he was ruggedly handsome with a full sensual mouth made for pleasure. Unable to resist, she leaned down and kissed him softly, lingering with a slight nibble on his bottom lip.

He opened his eyes, and with a long shaky intake of breath, he skimmed his palms over her skin, making her back arch and nipples tighten almost painfully.

The chill night breeze made the curtains swirl and cooled her heated skin. Inhaling deeply, she savored the scent of cinnamon and sex, pine, and damp earth. She was hot, cold, dripping with desire. Up on her knees, she moved her sex over the boxers stretched to the limit by his straining erection, soaking the soft cotton with her wetness.

With a moan, he reached up and cupped her breasts, thumbing her nipples, causing her breath to catch in her throat. "Ride me, Maxie."

All she could do was moan as an answer. Shimmying downward, she tugged his boxers off and fumbled for a condom on the nightstand. When she couldn't even manage to open the packet, he took it from her, ripped it open with his teeth, and slipped it on.

"Now," he pleaded. With his hands on her waist, he guided her up and then down onto the hard length of his penis. Maxie shuddered as he filled her. Closing her eyes, she leaned forward and threaded her fingers with his, making love to him achingly slowly. At that moment nothing mattered but the night breeze on her skin, the heat of Ian's body beneath hers. She moved up to her knees and then slowly back down, savoring the length of him as he filled her to the core. He was raw power, male strength, arching up off of the bed to meet her thrusts, going deeper, harder, until her orgasm blossomed, opened like the petals on a rose, almost painfully exquisite, making her grasp his fingers tightly and then fall limply against him.

She felt Ian shudder, moan, and then he held her in a full-body embrace. With a long sigh, Maxie nestled her head just beneath his chin. She could feel the strong beat of his heart, the rise and fall of his chest. The sex with him had been absolutely amazing, but when he lifted his head slightly to give her a soft kiss on her head, that simple, tender gesture turned her inside out.

"Sleep in here with me tonight, Ian," she asked softly. His arms around her tensed slightly, and she held her breath.

"Okay," he finally answered, but she could sense his reluctance.

"I promise not to snore," she said, forcing lightness into her voice, "but I might steal the covers."

"Then I'll have to find another way to keep warm."

"Ooh, now I know I'm stealing the covers," she shot back. He chuckled, and she felt the tense muscles in his arms relax.

"I need a few minutes in the bathroom, and then I'll be right back."

Ian eased himself from her and headed for the bathroom. Once inside, he took care of business and then stared at his reflection in the large oval mirror. Damn, he looked . . . happy, relaxed. *This girl is good for you, Parker*, his reflection seemed to shout. Ian took a deep breath, telling himself to just let his damned guard down and go for this.

Maxie Mitchell had turned out to be everything he had dreamed about in Maui and so much more. *Which is why you had stayed the hell away from her.* Ian frowned at his reflection—or was it his reflection frowning at *him*? *You're no fucking good at the long-term thing, so back off. She doesn't deserve to be hurt by a jerk like you.*

With an oath, Ian pushed back from the sink. Promising to sleep in her bed had been a mistake. Easing the door open, he hoped she was asleep so he could sneak up to his own room. Gazing across the bedroom, he had to smile at her small form snuggled under the covers. Even breathing told him she was asleep. Ian felt relief quickly followed by a sense of disappointment. He was about to tiptoe from the room, when he decided to blow out the fat candles still flickering on the nightstand. Leaning over, he softly blew against the flames, sending up a thin curling cloud of cinnamon-scented smoke.

"So there you are," Maxie said sleepily. She drew back the covers and gave him a drowsy smile. "It's cold in here."

"I'll close the window."

"No, leave it. I love the smell of the night breeze. Just climb in next to me and warm me up with that hot body of yours."

He paused, but unable to resist, Ian slipped between the cool sheets and snuggled up close to her. God, she felt so good in his arms. "You're naked," he murmured into her ear.

"Don't get any ideas. I'm plumb worn out."

Ian kissed her bare shoulder. "Sleep tight," he whispered. Within a few minutes, Maxie was fast asleep. Ian, however, stayed awake a long time, savoring each minute he held her in his arms while time ticked toward morning. He buried his face in her silky, fragrant hair, memorizing the smell of her perfume, the feel of her smooth skin . . . because tomorrow, before the crack of dawn, he would be gone.

Chapter Nine

The smell of something burning curled into Ian's nose. With a groan, he snuggled deeper into the pillow. The smell got stronger until the danger of something burning registered and had him sitting up. Befuddled, it took him a moment to realize he was still in Maxie's bed instead of on the road to Cincinnati. He sniffed the air, suddenly afraid that the cabin was on fire. Had they left candles burning? Throwing back the covers, he slid from the bed, pausing only to slip on his boxers, hopping into them as he headed to the door.

Just as he swung the door open, the smoke alarm beeped a shrill warning. "Maxie?" he called, following his nose to the smoke. "Maxie!"

He found her in the kitchen fanning the thick gray cloud with a dish towel.

"Open some windows," she shouted, and then coughed.

Ian complied, throwing open the front door and then a window in the great room, allowing for a cross breeze. "What's burning?"

"Your breakfast," she said so glumly that he had to hide a smile.

Ian joined her in the kitchen and gazed into the skillet at the charred remains. "What was it?" he asked with a frown.

"Pancakes," she said, her bottom lip protruding. "I wanted to surprise you with breakfast in bed," she said over the beeping of the smoke alarm.

Ian looked at the huge mess she had created. Flour was everywhere, on the counter, in her hair. She swiped at a tear and he pulled her into his arms. She sniffed dramatically and he tightened his embrace, kissing her on top of her head.

"I'm sorry," she said, her apology muffled against his chest. "I suck. Suck, suck, *suck!*"

Ian chuckled.

"Don't laugh at me." She sniffed loudly and wrapped her arms around his waist. Tilting her head up, she said, "Teach me how to cook, Ian." She gave him a trembling smile. "I want to cook for you."

"Whatever happened to unwrapping and nuking?"

"There wasn't anything to unwrap and nuke. I looked. The pancake directions seemed simple enough."

Ian looked over her floured head at the thick, lumpy batter and winced. There was something so endearing about her dismal effort that he just had to kiss her. "Ah, Maxie." Tilting her chin up, he bent his head and covered her mouth with his. God, she was warm and sweet, and looked so sexy wearing his sweater. He would have eaten the damned charred pancake if it would've made her happy.

"What was that for?"

"Your Herculean effort." He picked up the pancake with a fork. "Blackened pancakes could be a new menu item at Perkins. You know, most recipes begin with mistakes." He took a bite. "Not bad. Needs a little tweaking."

Maxie fell in love with him right then and there. It burst upon her all warm and tingling. She had to bite her tongue from telling him because she knew it would scare the hell out of him. This was too sudden, too soon, making her head spin and her knees go weak.

But this was *it*. She knew it.

This giddy knowledge made her want to dance around the room, shout from the rooftops, and take on the world! She was in love. Oh God, she was going to cry. She tried to suppress her tears of he's-the-one joy, but her nose itched, her throat clogged, and a tear spilled out and ran down her cheek.

"Maxie, don't cry. We'll make another batch."

This made her cry harder.

He wrapped his arms around her. "Ah, baby, *please* don't cry."

He sounded desperate to make her stop blubbering, so she tried. Gulping, she sniffed loudly and pulled back to give him a smile. But as soon as she saw the concerned look on his handsome face, her resolve crumpled and she whimpered.

"Here, look, I'm eating it." He took a crunchy black bite and gave her a brave smile.

"Stop!" Maxie grabbed the charred pancake from him and tossed it into the sink. It landed with a thunk. "This isn't *Fear Factor*," she said with a watery giggle.

"I'll eat a cockroach if it will make you stop crying."

"Ewww." She wrinkled her nose, but then her chin trembled. "My God, that's so sweet."

Ian grinned. "Feel free to use it in your next book."

Maxie giggled. "Great title! *I'll Eat a Cockroach for You*. I'll pitch it to Jan."

He smiled, clearly relieved that she had stopped crying. "I'm getting this romance thing down pat, aren't I?"

Maxie's happy heart skittered to a halt. "Oh, you mean for when you get back to Cincinnati." She blinked up at him, hoping for a denial, reassurance. Something.

He hesitated.

Maxie held her breath, feeling pushy and pathetic. Forcing a smile, she didn't wait for him to answer. "That cockroach line will get the girl every time."

"Maxie . . ."

She turned away and began puttering around with the burnt pancakes. "Well, then, hold up your end of the bargain and teach me how to cook."

Ian hated the fake smile more than he had hated the tears. The mood in the room shifted, and he wanted the moment back. Totally disregarding the fact that he had planned on being on his way back to Cincinnati by now, he slipped his arms around her waist from behind and nuzzled her neck. To his surprise, she stiffened.

"What's wrong?"

"Do me a favor and have a seat at the table," Maxie said quietly.

Oh no, thought Ian. The black moment. "I'd rather stand," he said feeling his defenses rise to the occasion.

Maxie turned around and pointed at the small table. "It's hard for me to concentrate with you wearing that skintight underwear. Please sit down and hide your . . ."

Ian glanced down and felt a blush coming on. His defenses weren't the only thing rising. He plopped down in the chair and waited.

"Coffee?"

He nodded but then looked questioningly down at the big mug that she placed on the table along with a tiny cream pitcher and sugar bowl.

"It's okay. I have the coffeemaker mastered."

He took a sip of the strong brew and gave her a nod of appreciation. She nibbled on that damn full bottom lip of hers while frowning down at her toes. Engulfed in his gray sweater rolled up at the sleeves, with her mane of auburn hair tumbling around her face in a just-got-laid look, she looked both incredibly sexy and so fucking vulnerable that he wanted to gather her in his arms and kiss away the lines of worry etched on her forehead. When she took a deep, shaky breath, he had to grip the arms of the wooden chair to keep from doing just that.

"Okay," she finally said, raising her gaze to meet his, "I'm going to be perfectly honest with you."

Ian nodded.

She blinked her eyes and swallowed.

He gripped the chair harder.

"If you don't count the week of mooning over you in Maui, I've only known you for a couple of days, so what I'm about to say might seem a bit crazy, but I want to lay it all on the line before this thing goes any farther."

"Maxie—"

"Let me finish while I have the nerve. Last night with you was amazing, but my attraction to you goes deeper than just physical. That whole broody, cover-model mojo is enough to make a girl go into sexual overload, but to discover that you are a caring, intelligent guy with a hidden sense of humor is just too much. Add the fact that you can cook . . . Well, I'm a goner."

"Maxie, I'm far from perfect."

She raised one eyebrow. "About the only thing that could ruin you for me would be if you were, like, a serial killer, or have some unmentionable disease, or be a cross-dresser, and at this point the cross-dressing would be negotiable."

"So what are you telling me?" Ian wasn't sure if he should be amused or scared shitless.

She took a deep breath and blew it out. "I'm not telling—I'm asking. Is there a chance for a relationship beyond this? Because if not, I want to go back to the 'staying out of each other's way' plan."

"What happened to the 'lots of great sex before the black moment' thing that you suggested? Maxie, we've had this discussion. I tried to be honest with you from the start, and you chose to skip the reasons why we shouldn't be doing this. This was your doing, not mine."

"I know! But how was I to know that beneath that . . . that damned gorgeous body of yours was a great guy? How was I to know that I could fall so hard this quickly? Damm it, Ian, I'm half in love with you already. I don't want to go home at the end of the week depressed and needy." She turned away and gripped the sink.

This time the scared shitless won out. He was suddenly afraid of losing her, but even more afraid of hurting her. "You're right. Let's end this thing now."

She turned from the sink and looked at him with sad eyes. "That was quick."

Ian heated his cold hands with the warm coffee mug. "Well, then let me give you some reasons to make you feel better about staying the hell away from me. For one, I can be a real pain in the ass. Ask Jan. I work way too much; all the time, in fact. I'm a loner, and you're a people person. You laugh. I scowl. You like nature and I prefer concrete. You write about love and I write about murder. I could go on and on."

"I'm sure we could find some common ground, Ian."

He nodded slowly. "Probably, and I enjoy being with you. But, Maxie, *long-term* isn't in my vocabulary. If I didn't like you so much, we wouldn't be having this conversation. We'd be having sex."

Maxie gave him a wry grin. "Now, doesn't that just suck. We like each other too much to have more mind-blowing sex."

He gave her a small grin. "Mind-blowing?"

"Romance novel worthy." She angled her head at him. "For the record, why isn't *long-term* in your vocabulary?"

Ian inhaled sharply. "I saw my parents tear each other apart and vowed never to subject myself—or, God help me, a child—to that."

Maxie frowned. "That's crazy. You deserve a chance at happiness. For God's sake, Ian—"

He shook his head. "I should leave." He watched her wrestle with her emotions and knew he was making the right decision. He was hurting her already.

"No, I'll go. Jan said that you rarely take a break, and you seem to like it here in spite of yourself."

"You were here first," he argued. "I interrupted your peace and quiet."

"No, I'm leaving," she said firmly. "I'm going to pack right now."

Ian watched her walk out of the room with a heavy heart, hating the sadness etched on her face. Not trusting himself to watch her drive away without running after her like a lovesick puppy, he decided to take a walk in the woods, hoping a damned bear would gobble him up.

It's for the best, he thought as he trudged up the steep hillside. But when he heard the crunch of tires on gravel, he winced. Clenching his fists at his sides, he listened to the fading sound of Maxine Mitchell leaving the cabin . . . and his life.

"What do you mean, 'she's gone'?" Jan's voice shouted through Ian's phone, making him wonder how so much sound could travel through such a small contraption.

Wincing, he held the phone away from his ear. "It was either she or I."

"What do you mean? Did you two have a fight? Couldn't get along?"

Ian leaned against the deck railing and took a deep breath of pine-scented air. "No, we, ah . . ."

"Had sex."

"I don't think that's any of your—"

"I knew it! Oh, hot damn, this ole girl's good."

"What?" Ian gripped the phone tighter. "You mean you were setting us up? Matchmaking?"

"Damn straight. Now, *why* is she gone?"

"I sent her away," he said quietly.

"Why? The two of you are a perfect couple."

"Jan, we're opposites."

"And obviously attract."

Ian gazed out on the mountains, shaking his head. "That's not enough."

"Ian, Maxie is quite a catch."

"Granted, but I'm *not*, and you damned well know it."

"Sugar, you're easy on the eyes, successful, talented, and single. What more could a girl want?"

Ian laughed without humor. "I'm a moody, surly workaholic who is unable to commit to a relationship, mostly because I don't have a fucking clue how to love someone. I wouldn't wish me on my worst enemy. You should give Maxie a call and apologize."

For a long moment, Jan was uncharacteristically silent. "Were you a moody, surly workaholic this weekend?"

"I wrote a sex scene that'll curl your toes," he said defensively. "That was work."

"Before or after . . ."

"None of your damned—"

"After. Thought so. Tell me, how many times did Maxie have you talking, laughing, enjoying your sorry self?"

"That's not the point. I'm not the—"

"And the sex was fabulous, wasn't it? Maxie is an energetic, passionate woman. She's had a thing about you since Maui."

"She has?" he asked, but then wished he hadn't.

"And I bet you miss her already."

Ian was silent. He missed her so much it hurt. "It's better this way. I'm no good at relationships."

"That's a bunch of bull. Her cell phone number is in the paperwork I gave you. Call her."

*   *   *

An hour later Ian stared at the phone number and then stared at the phone. After fifteen minutes of staring, he dialed the number, but failed to hit the SEND button. This same scenario happened several times over the next two days. Writing became impossible since everything in the cabin reminded him of *her*. In frustration, he packed his things and left, thinking leaving Possum Creek would take his mind off of Maxie.

Wrong. On the drive home, every song on the radio reminded him of her. With an oath, he flicked the radio off and pushed harder on the gas pedal. Once he was home, things would get back to normal. With the dreaded sex scene out of the way, he could finish the novel and start outlining the next. Life would go on.

Then again, maybe not.

By the end of the week Ian was way beyond his grumpy, surly self. He couldn't bring himself to cook a decent meal. Showering became optional. And writing was a joke.

"Damn you, Maxine Mitchell," Ian growled, staring bleary-eyed at the monitor screen. He had typed two words in the past hour, and even they sucked. "To hell with it."

Shutting down his computer, he stood up and stared unseeing out the window. His stomach rumbled in protest of lack of food, and he realized it was well past lunch and he hadn't bothered with breakfast.

Running an impatient hand through his hair, making it stand on end, he headed down the stairs toward the kitchen. He opened the refrigerator and stared at the meager contents, hoping something would look appetizing. He was contemplating whether the leftover Chinese was still edible when the phone rang, startling him enough to make him bang his head on the top shelf.

"Ouch! Damn!" Picking up the receiver he barked, "Yeah?"

"Ian?"

The sound of Maxie's voice made his empty stomach do a stupid little flip-flop. "Yeah," he repeated, less rough, a little shaky.

"It's Maxie."

He cleared his throat. "Hey, what's going on?" There, that sounded normal enough.

"Oh, well, I was about to ask you that. Jan just called and said you wanted to get in touch with me. I've been in a writing cave, on a deadline. Sorry, if I've missed your calls."

She could write? That didn't seem quite fair. Ian frowned and wondered out loud. "Jan said I was trying to contact you?"

A brief silence and then, "Oh God. You weren't. Jan set me up, didn't she?"

She sounded as if she *really* wanted him to dispute her statement, so he gave it a shot, "Well, I—that is, I—"

"You weren't. Ian, I'm sorry," she said quietly. "Jan should mind her own business. Sorry to have bothered you."

She was hanging up! "No, wait—" he tried, but the line went dead. For a long moment he sat there with the dial tone buzzing in his ear. She had sounded ready to cry!

"Damn you, Jan," he growled, and punched her number into the phone.

"Hello," she said, innocently as you please.

"What the hell do you think you're doing?"

"Whatever do you mean?" Her soft, southern drawl was very pronounced, making Ian grind his teeth.

"You called Maxie and told her I wanted to reach her."

"You do. See, it wasn't a lie. If it is, deny it."

"I wasn't trying to call her!"

"Yes you were. You just didn't have the balls to follow through. Admit it."

Ian drew in a big gulp of air, sputtered a bit, and then admitted in a rush, "Okay, you're right, damn it. I'm ball-less."

"Then grow some."

Ian ran his fingers through his spiky hair. "Jan, it's not that simple. I don't know if I'm capable of giving Maxie the kind of relationship that she needs, that she deserves. I'm such a loner, and she's so full of life."

"Ian, she hides her loneliness behind smiles and jokes while you choose to wallow in it. Everybody has issues. Get over yourself."

He closed his eyes and sucked in a shaky breath. "I don't want to hurt her."

"That could happen. Life is full of chances, risks. Take this one, Ian. Yeah, you might be sorry, but you'll be even sorrier if you don't."

Ian chuckled. "Well, since you put it *that* way. Where does she live? In Indiana somewhere, right?"

"About two hours from you. She has a little A-frame house overlooking a lake on the far end of her parents' farm. I'll fax you the directions right now."

Ian took the steps two at a time up to his office and waited while the fax machine hummed and finally spit out the directions. After scanning the map, he stuffed the paper in the pocket of his jeans, hurried back downstairs, grabbed his keys, and headed out the door.

He was speeding along the interstate in his SUV, halfway there, when it dawned on him that he still hadn't showered, eaten, or bothered to call Maxie. Well, damn. He refused to stop for food, but was lucky enough to find a Snickers bar in the glove box. He bit into the candy with gusto, savoring the chocolate and peanuts.

Glancing into the rearview mirror, he grimaced at his day-old beard and spiky hair. A tentative sniff at his armpit had him wrinkling his nose. "Not too bad," he murmured hopefully, wishing he had taken the time to shower and change into something other than his frayed jeans and faded Black Sabbath T-shirt. He decided to call her and then realized he had left without his phone.

The woman was making him an insane person.

Thirty minutes later, he arched his butt up off the seat to dig inside his pocket for the directions to double-check the exit he needed to take. As he thought, it was the next one. His heartbeat sped up in anticipation. He was almost there.

Just minutes later, he pulled off the interstate and found Rabbit Road. A few miles on the two-lane road and he spotted her mailbox at the end of a gravel lane. Bingo. Kicking up dust, he quickly came upon an A-frame nestled in a wooded area overlooking a lovely lake. He didn't see her car, but there was a detached garage around the back of her property.

After a bracing deep breath, he parked his vehicle and looked in the mirror, trying to smash down his hair without any luck. "Oh well. I hope she likes the grunge look."

With his heart hammering in his chest, he walked up the short sidewalk, and mounted three steps to a wooden wraparound deck. After swallowing his fear, he knocked on the door. He waited a minute and then tried again. No answer. Finally, he tried opening the door. It was unlocked, so he took a step inside.

"Maxie?" He waited. No answer. He called her name again and finally let the fact that she wasn't home sink in.

"Okay, now what?" he wondered out loud, feeling a little like a wacko intruder. Spotting the phone hanging from the kitchen wall, he hurried over, picked up the receiver, and dialed Jan's number.

"Hello?"

"I'm here and Maxie's not. Now what do I do?"

"My God, you're there already? You must have broken the speed limit. Oh, that's so romantic."

He looked around, feeling stalkerish. "Maybe I should leave."

"Don't you dare! She must have run out to do an errand. Just sit tight and wait."

"I'll wait in my car. God, I wished I had showered," he said, itching his head.

"What?"

Ian wrinkled his nose. "I haven't showered in a day. Or maybe two."

"Good God, then do it!"

"In *her* shower?"

"No, the neighbor's. Yes, her shower. You can't stink! That's not romantic! Just do it quickly. You'll be done before she gets back, smelling sweet and doable."

"I don't know . . ." He looked around, feeling as if someone might suddenly jump out and handcuff him.

"Ian, you want to be doable, don't you?"

"Doable?"

"Screwable."

"Is there *anything* you won't say?"

"Go shower. Now."

"Okay!" He hung up the phone and sort of tiptoed down a short hallway until he located a bathroom. Feeling extremely strange, he turned on the water and then quickly shucked his clothes, entering the shower before the water had a chance to get hot. Shivering, he wondered if he had completely lost his mind as he lathered up with some feminine-smelling shower gel. Oh great. He was acting like a girl, and now he was going to smell like one.

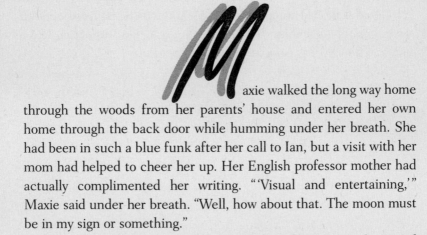

Chapter Eleven

Maxie walked the long way home through the woods from her parents' house and entered her own home through the back door while humming under her breath. She had been in such a blue funk after her call to Ian, but a visit with her mom had helped to cheer her up. Her English professor mother had actually complimented her writing. "'Visual and entertaining,'" Maxie said under her breath. "Well, how about that. The moon must be in my sign or something."

With a shake of her head, she opened the refrigerator and snagged a bottle of water, thirsty after the two-mile walk to her parents' house. After unscrewing the cap, she took a long guzzle and then froze. Cocking her head to the side, she whispered, "I hear water running. Oh God, did I leave the shower on?"

She hurried to the bathroom and swung open the door just as a big, very wet, very naked body emerged from the shower stall. A scream lodged in her throat as her gaze traveled from bare feet to muscled calves to a very nice tush, wide shoulders and . . . *What am I doing admiring the body of an intruder-rapist-very-bad-guy?*

The scream dislodged itself, and she looked for a weapon. Spotting the plunger in the corner, she reached for it and swung it over her head with malice intended, when he turned around and—ohmigod, it was *Ian*.

He raised his arms and caught the plunger inches before it whapped him over the head. "Whoa, Maxie! It's me!"

"Ian!" The plunger fell with a muted thud to the tile floor. "Wh-what are you doing?"

He grinned and grabbed for a towel. "I needed a shower."

She angled her head and asked, "So, you came all the way to Indiana for a shower?"

Ian tucked the towel around his waist and took a step toward her. He raked his hand through his wet hair, causing a delicious ripple of muscle that had her melting, drifting toward him. The wide wall of his chest, beaded with water, filled her vision. She watched as a droplet ran past his pecs and down his abdomen to where the towel hung low on his lean hips.

"I came all the way to Indiana for you," he replied, his voice whiskey-rough.

"I guess I should be impressed," she said, trying to sound flippant when her heart was banging in her chest like a bass drum.

"Well, I'm hoping . . ."

"Hoping for what?" Maxie tried to steel her heart against the sight of him standing there looking so unsure, so hopeful, so . . .

So damned sexy.

He closed his eyes and swallowed. "Hoping you'd give me another chance."

"Give me one good reason why I should." She tried to sound haughty, indifferent. "Well?" If possible, her heart thumped harder.

Ian opened his eyes and shrugged. "You probably shouldn't. I'm a jerk."

"Well, that reason sucked."

"Well then, how about I'm falling hopelessly in love with you?"

Maxie blinked at him for a moment while his words sank in. "Well, that reason is m-much better."

"Come here," he pleaded, holding out his arms to her.

Maxie closed the small gap between them in the steamy bathroom, needing to touch him, taste him. With a little moan, she wrapped her arms around his waist and licked a bead of water from his chest. He was so warm and tasted so good.

"Ahh, Maxie, I've missed you. I was a fool to let you leave."

Maxie looked up. "Now you're talking. See, if I had written that scene, your butt would have been chasing after me, and you would have been rewarded for your efforts with some really hot sex. Now, kiss me."

His mouth covered hers with a hungry kiss. She flattened her palms against his back, needing to get closer. His big hand cradled her head as he deepened the sweet invasion of her mouth. The touch of his tongue to hers sent a zing of white-hot desire that made her bold. She lowered her hands, dislodging the towel.

"Am I about to get rewarded?" he asked, nipping her on her earlobe.

"Is the black moment over with, Ian?" She raised serious eyes to his. "Because I'm really looking for happily-ever-after."

"I've been miserable without you. I can't eat. I can't sleep. I can't *write*."

A big, fat tear rolled down her face, and she sniffed loudly.

"My God, you're crying. See, I suck at this. *Suck*." He put the heel of his hand to his forehead and moaned.

Maxie tried to laugh, and it came out more like a gurgle. *Could he be more adorable?* Swallowing, and then clearing her throat, she looked up at him and said, "Don't you get what you just told me? You can't live without me. Oh, that is just the most romantic thing I've ever been told."

Ian lowered his hand from his forehead and blinked at her for a moment. Then, slowly, he smiled. "By God, I did."

The man had a smile that no woman could possibly resist. It softened his features and made his eyes crinkle at the corners. Maxie swayed against him and shook her head. "Don't do that very often."

"What?"

"Smile at me like that. I won't be able to resist you. Ever. It gives you an unfair advantage."

His smile deepened, and he tilted his head back with a deep rumble of laughter, which had her melting even more. Pretty soon she'd be a puddle at his feet. She gave him a little nudge. "That laugh will get me every time, too," she confessed, and then another fat tear ran down her face.

Wiping the tear away with his thumb, he told her, "Then we're even. I can't take your tears."

"But they're happy tears."

"Are they, Maxie?"

"Yep," she admitted and then moaned. "We sound like dialogue that would make my editor cringe. We're pathetic."

He wrapped his arms around her and grinned. "Well, maybe it's time for a little less talk . . ."

"And pages and pages of action?" With a giggle, she tugged on his hand, leading him from the bathroom to the bedroom, knowing in her heart that this wasn't the end of the story . . . but just the beginning.

LuAnn McLane lives in Florence, Kentucky. When she isn't writing, she enjoys long walks with her husband and watching chick flicks with her daughter, and tries to keep up with her three active sons. She loves to hear from her readers. You can reach her at www.luannmclane.com

What Happens
in Vegas

Patricia Ryan

For my dear friend and vacation buddy, Susan Uttal, who brings the homemade marshmallows and single-barrel bourbon, and who asked me the other day if I'd written any more erotic romances lately.

This one's for you, Suze.

"What happens here, stays here."

—Award-winning slogan of
the Las Vegas Convention and Visitors Authority

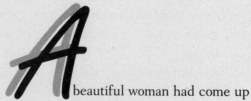 beautiful woman had come up behind Jay to check out the action at his blackjack table—to check out *his* action, he knew, because he'd been kicking the casino's ass for four days running, and people were starting to talk.

Also, he'd come to sense, over the past four days, when he was being watched—not just by the cameras in those little bug-eyed domes that pimpled the ceiling, but by someone lurking just outside his range of vision. Sometimes it was a casino flunky, sometimes just a curious tourist, but he could always feel it, like a fingernail lightly grazing the length of his spine. And right now, he was being watched.

Closely.

Jay knew it was a woman, even though she seemed to be standing pretty much directly behind him; she'd brought with her a whiff of something sweetly provocative, like the aroma of freshly baked sugar cookies wafting through a high-class brothel. He knew she was beautiful because the three other players at the table—a grizzled old Chivas-chugging bulldog named Archie, a sullen young Eminem-looking guy with a bandana around his head and the name *Daisy* tattooed on his neck, and even the dour, bespectacled Quiet Man—kept stealing glances at her over Jay's right shoulder, the kind of swift but rapt appraisals reserved for the foxiest of foxes.

The dealer, a white-blond android in a fringed vest and bolo tie, whose tin-star nameplate read "Helmut," gave her the once-over as he dealt Jay his second card.

Jay lifted the two cards and thumbed them apart: a jack and a two.

"Excuse me." It was her. She sounded youngish, thirty at the most, with a chenille-soft voice that made the incessant ding-ding-ding casino racket seem to recede into the background.

Archie and Daisy Do-rag swiveled their heads in her direction, expressions alert and accommodating. Helmut flipped his top card faceup before turning toward her with a smile—a first for this particular dealer.

"I'm a little confused," she said. Jay sensed her moving fractionally closer to him—a subtle shift in the air molecules between them, maybe, or a subliminal awareness of her breath teasing his hair, or more likely just his sex-starved imagination.

He mentally punched himself. *Keep your mind on the game, man. You can't afford distractions, not if you're gonna see this thing through.*

"I don't know much about blackjack," she said. "I've never played it, but I've seen it, you know, on TV, and—"

"The point is to get as close to twenty-one as you can without going over," Archie said in his scotch-slurred, nicotine-scoured voice. "You're playing against the dealer. Everybody bets, and then you get two cards, but you can only see the dealer's top card. Face cards are worth ten. When it's your turn, you can hit and take more cards, or you can stand. In a double-deck game, you hit by scraping the cards on the table, and you stand by tucking them under your chips.

There's some bells and whistles—doubling down, splitting—but that's the gist of it."

"But aren't the cards usually dealt faceup?" she asked. "Out of a . . . what do you call it, that thing that holds a bunch of decks?"

"A shoe." Ice clattered like dice as Archie drained his glass. "That's how they do it at most of the bigger casinos. But here at the Gold Dust they play a good, old-fashioned two-deck game, hand shuffled and hand dealt, facedown, like the Almighty intended." He wrestled a mangled pack of Salem Lights out of the back pocket of his Bermuda shorts, which he wore with a madras shirt and Elvis neck-tie, the latter secured with a big gold tie clip in the shape of a pair of dice. "Best damn game on the Strip."

"Mostly 'cause it's just the two decks," offered Daisy Do. "The fewer cards in play, the easier they are to keep track of."

"Keep track of?" She strolled into view, one hand cradling a glass of red wine while the other lightly stroked the backs of the two empty chairs that separated Jay from the other players at the tall, semicircular table. She was about five-eight or -nine, with a rust-stained mop of hair, a lissome build, and a remarkable face. At first glance, you'd think *corn-fed*, that's how wholesome she came off, but then you'd notice her eyes, how sharp they were, how oddly pretty, and you'd think, *hmm.* . . .

And then you'd realize you were staring, and you'd look away and scrape a hand over your jaw and wish you'd shaved that morning in-stead of heading down to the blackjack pit at the ass-crack of dawn, wearing yesterday's jeans and faded old Astro Boy T-shirt. Almost twelve hours had passed since then, and Jay had spent them all hunched over this table pushing cards back and forth. He was in peak physical condition—had to be, to do what he did for a living—but considering how stiff he was right now, he felt closer to eighty-two than thirty-two.

"You need to keep track of the cards?" she asked. "I thought you just, you know, hit on certain hands and stood on others."

"It helps to have an idea of how many tens and face cards are left in the deck," Daisy explained. With a sidelong glance at the dealer, he added, "I, uh, saw somethin' about it on the Travel Channel."

"It's called card counting." Archie lit his cigarette with an enameled lighter embossed with a pair of aces. "Gives an edge to the player, which is how come the casinos don't want you doing it. They'll back you off if they catch you."

"I didn't say *I* was doin' it." A livid stain was crawling up Daisy's throat.

"Neither did I, pal," Archie drawled through a pall of smoke.

"You implied it."

"I did?"

Jay swore disgustedly under his breath.

The girl slid Jay a look he couldn't quite get ahold of over the rim of her wineglass. Did she think he was a dick? Did she think he was the strong, quiet type? Did she think he'd woken up and come down here without bothering to comb his hair, which he had, or did she think he'd gone for a deliberate bed-head look, and if so, did she think he was gay, and if she did, did he care? *Should* he care?

Hell no.

Did he?

Jay sighed and rubbed his neck, which was knotted up tighter than a macramé plant hanger.

Archie asked, "Everything copasetic, Trump?" That's what they'd started calling him after he won the first million on Day One: Trump.

Jay was saved from having to respond to that—*copasetic?*—by the arrival of an aging but still pretty blonde carrying a tray of drinks, her ample curves shrink-wrapped in an ultra-abbreviated version of an Old West dance-hall getup.

"Cocktails?" she asked, of no one in particular.

Jay ordered a refill of his club soda, Archie another double Chivas.

As she sauntered away, Helmut regarded Archie with silent expectation; as the player to the dealer's immediate right, he went first. The big man rechecked his cards and scraped them toward him on the green felt tabletop. "Hit me."

Helmut flicked him another card. Archie looked at it, grimaced, and tossed down his cards, which totaled twenty-five. "Bust."

"Mind if I sit while I watch?" Red asked the dealer as she pulled out the chair next to Jay. She could have chosen the other empty chair and sat next to the Quiet Man instead. Which probably didn't mean anything, but God help him, he was getting a little hard just thinking about being that close to her.

"Fine by me," Helmut told her, "so long as you give up the chair if a player wants it."

"Thanks," she sighed, her bare arm brushing Jay's as she shimmied up onto the barstool-height chair, bracelets clinking. Her skin was sleek and warm and well perfumed. A shiver scuttled up Jay's arm and settled in his chest to mess with the rhythm of his heart. "I spent all afternoon shopping at Caesar's in brand-new heels," she said, "and now I've got brand-new blisters to go with them."

Jay took her in as discreetly as he could, from her black silk halter top, to a pair of mile-long legs in tan bell-bottoms, to her feet, which were strapped into black stiletto-heeled sandals. Maybe it was the sheer pink polish on her toenails, maybe the slight hesitation in her smile, but there was a hint of innocence underlying the sexual allure that only made that allure more potent.

Jay followed her line of sight to his right hand, which was when he realized he was shuffling two stacks of chips together one-handed, a manual dexterity exercise that had become a habitual tension reliever since he'd taken up blackjack. Helmut was watching him, too, which was not good; it would make him look too much like a cardsharp instead of just some vacationer on a lucky streak. He dropped the chips and flexed his fingers.

Helmut turned to Daisy, who laid his two cards, both kings, faceup and placed a second stack of four black hundred-dollar chips next to the stack already in his little betting circle. It was the biggest wager this kid had made all afternoon—and the biggest mistake.

"What's he doing?" asked Red.

"Splitting his pair." A cough rumbled out of Archie as he tapped the ash off his cigarette. "If you got two of a kind, you can play 'em as two separate hands if you want."

You could, but hardly anyone ever split tens or face cards. Why break up a beautiful twenty-point hand, when you might end up with two losing garbage hands? That is, unless you happened to be counting cards, as Daisy had been doing all too obviously all afternoon, and you knew that the remainder of the deck was rich in tens and face cards, in which case, you'd probably end up with not one winning hand, but two.

So, good idea to split those kings, right? Not if you really thought it through. Every casino in this town, even tired old joints like the Gold Dust, had security drones who kept watch over the table action via monitors fed by the Eye in the Sky—and they were especially attentive to whales like Jay who wagered thousands and won millions. They'd be scrutinizing the play at his table, which was why he took exceptional care to make it look as if his hot streak was purely a matter of luck. Never in a million years would he have split those kings; it was like waving a red flag. You get too greedy and you end up being barred from every casino on the Strip.

"Yes!" Daisy exclaimed as he was dealt a ten on one hand and a jack on the other. Now it was just a matter of waiting to see what Helmut had, but unless he came up with a blackjack—twenty-one on the nose—Daisy had just made himself a quick eight hundred bucks.

The Quiet Man went next. He busted, but was characteristically stoic about it.

"So, now it's your turn, right?" Red asked Jay as she leaned forward to rest her elbows on the rim of the table, causing a narrow strip of black mesh to peek out from above the waistband of her slacks. It was a thong, Jay realized. A sheer, silky, black mesh thong.

His cock twitched like a half-asleep puppy when you run your hand along its back.

"Earth to Trump." It was Archie, calling Jay's attention to the fact that everyone around the table was looking at him, waiting for him to stand or hit.

Rattled to have gotten so mentally waylaid from the game, Jay glanced at his cards, which added up to twelve, and scratched them across the felt in the "hit me" gesture, wincing as he belatedly took note of Helmut's upcard, which happened to be a four. Most of the time you'd hit a twelve, but never against the dealer's four; it was just basic strategy. And with the count at an astronomical plus-nine, it was suicide.

Sure enough, Helmut dealt him a queen. Twelve plus ten equals bust.

Too late to do anything about it now, Jay thought as the dealer reached out to collect his wager. *That's what you get for letting your mind wander from the game.* If only she wasn't a redhead. He'd always gotten stupid around redheads.

She counted the chips under her breath as Helmet scooped them up. "Eight purples and two blues," she said. "How much is that?"

Archie, answering for Jay, said, "The purples are worth five hundred, the blues a thousand. So that adds up to . . ."

"Six thousand." She turned to Jay with her mouth literally hanging open. "You just lost six thousand dollars."

"He'll win it back in the next hand, you mark my words," Archie said. "This fella's the luckiest SOB I've ever seen."

"Are you always this serious?" She was looking at Jay as if she thought she could read his mind if she just stared hard enough. "I don't think you've said a word since I've been here."

Neither had the Quiet Man, but she hadn't once looked in his direction.

"He's the type that likes to focus a hundred and ten percent on the game," Archie said. "Hey, he must be doing something right."

It was the dealer's turn to reveal his hand. Helmut flipped over his other card; it was a queen, which gave him a fourteen. He took a third card. Surprise, surprise, a ten.

"See, now, the dealer got over twenty-one, so he busted," Archie told the girl.

Daisy whooped in triumph as he gestured toward his cards: "Twenty-twenty, man. Pay up."

No sooner had Helmut forked over the eight hundred in chips than the pit boss, a Lucy Liu-alike in a form-fitting black pantsuit, came over and ordered Daisy out of the casino.

He gaped at her. "What the . . . You're kidding, right?"

"We don't want your action," she said with glacial stoicism. "Bring your chips to the cashier, take your winnings, and leave the premises."

"This is bullshit." Daisy looked from Lucy to Helmut to his fellow players, eyes wide with outrage. "Do you believe this?"

Jay, feeling a little sorry for the kid, screwup though he was, broke his silence. "Just do it, man. Cash out and split, and try to be a little smoother next time."

"But I didn't do nothin' wrong. They got no right to make me leave."

Two security goons in white-shirted pseudocop uniforms, right down to their clunky equipment belts, materialized on either side of Daisy. "Let's go, hotshot," said the meatier of the two, whose shaved head rose from his shoulders like a smooth pink salmon mold with two little black olive slices for eyes.

Daisy didn't budge. "I got a right to sit here and play."

"Card counting is against the law in the state of Nevada."

"Bullshit."

"You calling me a liar?"

"I'm saying I ain't done nothin' illegal, and nobody's got any right to make me—*Hey!*"

It had taken about a second for Salmon Head to get his handcuffs off his belt, yank Daisy's arms behind his back, and cuff them. *Snap, yank, click.*

"You shoulda left when you were told," the other guard said. "Now we get to take a little walk together."

The guards, each gripping one of Daisy's arms, hauled him off his chair and hustled him away, bitching and moaning.

The rotund, gray-suited floorman, whose job it was to oversee this particular table, came over and unwrapped the cellophane on two fresh decks. Normally the interval between deck replacements could be as much as several hours, but at Jay's table, the cards got switched every half hour, almost to the minute; he'd timed it. This meant a hiatus of several minutes while the dealer and the floorman performed the tedious ritual of examining and merging the new decks and introducing them into play, after which the old decks would be taken away and inspected for irregularities like marked or missing cards, which would indicate cheating. Irritating though it was to have the game interrupted so frequently, Jay had to admit it was his own fault for winning so much of the Gold Dust's money in a hot streak that had to be as baffling as it was frustrating to the suits upstairs. With no evidence that he was counting cards, what were they to think, except that he was either cheating or the luckiest guy they'd ever seen.

Helmut fanned a perfect crescent of cards across the table with one practiced glide of his hand. He checked them over, taking note of each and every card, as the floorman looked on and the security staff watched on a roomful of monitors somewhere upstairs.

"What's going to happen to that guy?" The girl cocked her head toward Daisy's empty chair.

"They'll probably just escort him to the cage to collect his winnings, then out the front door," Archie said. "That's what most places do. And they'll circulate his picture to all the other casinos, so he'll be barred from every blackjack game in town."

"So card counting is, like, cheating?" she asked as she raised her glass to her mouth.

Archie and Jay answered at the same time, Archie saying, "Sorta," and Jay, "No."

"Which is it?" she asked.

"It's kinda like cheating," Archie said, "'cause the ones that can do it have an unfair advantage over the ones that can't."

Loath as he was to debate the issue, Jay couldn't let that comment go unanswered. "In any game, the better player has the advantage," he said. "Fact is, the Nevada Supreme Court has ruled four times that card counting is perfectly legal, that it's just skilled play. But a business can exclude anyone they want, and the casinos don't like losing, so . . ." He shrugged.

The floorman glanced up briefly from the cards, which he was mixing up by sliding them around on the table, the way little kids do. Jay realized this conversation would get replayed for boys upstairs, but given that they couldn't peg him as a card counter, he knew nothing would come of it.

"Kid had it coming to him." Archie expelled a stream of smoke as he stubbed his cigarette out in the little amber-colored glass ashtray. "In the old days, that kind of punk-ass attitude would have gotten him a little visit to the back room."

"What do you mean?" the girl asked.

"They would have taught him a lesson, you know? Worked him over some, just to make sure he knew they meant business. That kind of thing don't happen so much anymore." He seemed almost wistful.

A knobby hand closed over Jay's shoulder and squeezed. "Still winnin', boy?"

Thelma Graham always made him smile, no matter what kind of mood he was in. "Yes, ma'am, Miss Thelma, but I confess I haven't been enjoying it till you showed up."

Snorting at his pathetic gallantry, Thelma hobbled around the table with the aid of a hickory cane. "Shoot, looks like first base is taken," she said in her gravelly Texas drawl.

"You like first base?" Archie rose from his chair, shoving his chips and ashtray to the next position. "Take it. I don't care where I sit."

"I like goin' first," Thelma said as she hooked her cane over the back of the chair Archie had just vacated. "Age before beauty."

Thelma was one of those women you know is old, but you'd be hard pressed to put her closer to seventy or ninety. She was stooped and wizened, but with a spark in her eye that was ageless. Among the photos in her wallet—she liked to pass them around during breaks in the action—was one of herself from the Second World War, when she'd been an army nurse; same spark, but with a lush head of auburn hair and a figure Barbie would have killed for. "Tell me I wasn't a hottie," she'd said, and Jay had had to admit she was.

"So you *can* smile." Red was looking at him with a frank fascination that made his skin feel oddly tight and prickly. "I wouldn't have believed it if I hadn't seen it with my own eyes."

"He bein' an asshole?" Thelma slid on the half-glasses hanging around her neck and set about digging through the canvas tote bag on her lap. "He gets that way sometimes. I keep tellin' him it's just a game. You *can* have fun while you're winnin'. In fact, that's kind of the point." She extracted her bulging pink wallet and pulled out a sheaf of hundred-dollar bills, which she proceeded to count out onto the table—a time-consuming procedure, given her arthritic fingers and the slickness of the crisp new bills.

"Club soda for you, right, handsome?" It was the cocktail waitress, back with their drinks.

"Thanks." Jay dug a dollar out of his pocket and stuffed it in her tip glass.

Miss Thelma, being Miss Thelma, eyeballed the waitress's name badge and greeted her like they were old friends. "How you doin' tonight, Missy?"

"Wish they'd let me wear flats," the waitress said as she emptied Archie's ashtray.

"I hear that." Thelma licked a blunt-nailed, red-lacquered fingertip and pried another bill off the stack. "My dogs haven't stopped barkin' since my thirty-fourth birthday."

"Isn't that a little young to be having problems like that?" Missy asked.

"Not if you're really forty-eight. I'll take a gin and tonic, sugar—and tell 'em to put some gin in it this time."

Looking from Thelma to Jay, Red asked, "So, you two know each other?"

"I've been here about a week," Thelma said. "One of those old-fart tours out of Fort Worth." Nodding toward Jay, she said, "The Grim Reaper showed up four days ago, planted his butt in this pit, and hasn't moved since. No side trip to Hoover Dam, no Cirque du Soleil, no Celine, no shark reef. Doesn't even want to check out the titty shows. Just wants to sit here and play blackjack."

"Can you blame him?" Archie asked. "Given how he's been winning? I noticed you like to sit at his table, Miss Thelma—probably for the same reason I do, and this fella here." He gestured toward the Quiet Man. "Hopin' some of his luck'll rub off on us."

Thelma said, "Honey, my luck peaked back in 'fifty-seven, when my husband got shot five times in the head and once in the pecker by the husband of the stripper he'd been bangin', and I found out he was worth a whole hell of a lot more dead than alive. God bless the genius that invented life insurance. Here, honey." She laid a stack of bills on the felt and said to Helmut, who was busy riffle-shuffling the new decks, "I'll take twenty-five hundred in chips when you've got a chance."

"How much do you need to get started in this game?" Red opened her big green straw shoulder bag and pulled out an envelope, the kind banks put withdrawals in. "Is a thousand enough?"

"Oh, sweetheart, you don't want to learn how to play at this table,"

Archie told her as he lit another cigarette. "This is a hundred-dollar table. That means you've got to bet a minimum of a C-note on every hand. I don't think there are any five-dollar tables open right now, but there's a ten on the other side of the pit there. That's a safer table to learn at."

"No, I want to play here," she said as she counted out twenty fifty-dollar bills. "I didn't come to Las Vegas for safety. I get plenty of that back in Buffalo. I came here to take a few risks, have a little fun, maybe even an adventure. Besides, there's always beginner's luck."

"If it's luck you want, you're sittin' next to the right fella." Pointing to Jay, Thelma said, "Get Trump to coach you, and you'll double your money in no time."

"Would you?" She turned toward Jay, hands clasped, eyes imploring. There's something about a gorgeous redhead in a posture of supplication. Still . . .

Jay shook his head. "I, uh, need to maintain my concentration if . . ."

"A nuclear explosion couldn't make you lose your concentration," Thelma said, "and you know it. Come on. Teach a pretty girl to play blackjack. Live a little."

Jay glared at Thelma. She cackled. That was the only way to describe her laugh: a classic wicked witch cackle, but with an unmistakable Lone Star twang to it.

"Please?" Red begged him. "I'll buy you dinner wherever you want." Glancing down at her feet, she added, "As long as I don't have to walk very far."

Jay kneaded his neck, rotated his shoulders, sighed heavily. "You know the basic rules, right?"

"Oh, thank you! Yes, I, uh, I think I'm pretty straight on the rules."

"In a two-deck game you can touch your cards," he said, "but only with one hand at a time. Before the cards are dealt, you place your bet in that little circle there. The higher denomination chips go on the bottom, the smaller on top."

"Be sure to keep your hands away from the chips once the cards are dealt," Archie added. "They don't want folks changing their bets once they realize what kind of hand they have."

"Is that all I need to know?" she asked.

"For now," Jay said.

"Stud Duck at six o'clock and closing fast." Thelma peered over her glasses into the distance beyond Jay. "The big guy himself. Three guesses who he's here to see."

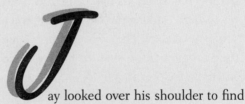

Chapter Two

Jay looked over his shoulder to find the Gold Dust's owner, a high-profile Vegas entrepreneur named Eddie Flynn, striding toward him in one of his signature Italian suits, gunmetal gray today worn with a black shirt, silver tie, and black-and-silver striped pocket square. Flynn was only about forty, and not a bad-looking guy in a tanning-bed kind of way, but with a glad-handing, hard-grinning, old-Vegas manner about him that made Jay's teeth feel like he was chewing on tinfoil.

Rarely seen without backup, Flynn was accompanied this afternoon by two older men, one of whom Jay recognized as his casino manager, William "Bull" Toomey. A holdover from the Vegas of yore, Bull was a Frigidaire in a silk suit, his snowy hair buzzed Marine-style, obsidian eyes framed by horn-rimmed glasses. Flynn needed

Toomey to run the place, because Toomey knew the gambling industry inside and out; Flynn was just playing at it.

The pit boss and floorman joined the group as Flynn approached the table, making for quite the entourage.

"Douglas." Flynn stuck a dildo-sized cigar between his teeth and gripped Jay's shoulder, diamond pinky ring flashing, as he shook Jay's hand. "Still stealing me blind, or has your luck turned yet?"

"Not yet," Jay said, confirming what Flynn already knew perfectly well. Not a penny was won or lost in this casino that he didn't hear about the second it happened.

"Won't rest till you've cleaned me out, huh?" Flynn asked, the glare off his teeth not dimming one watt. "Well, give it your best shot."

"I plan to."

Flynn let out a burst of laughter that struck an off note, since nothing that hilarious had been said. The forced mirth was echoed by his toadies, evoking the desperate sound of canned laughter on a not-so-funny sitcom. The only one not laughing was Bull Toomey, who fixed his glinty little eyes on Jay the way a hawk zeroes in on a rabbit scarfing up clover in a field.

"Got everything you need, Douglas?" Flynn directed the question at Jay even as his gaze crawled over the redhead, inciting an absurd crackle of . . . something—not jealousy, of course, but something close to it—that made the little hairs on the back of Jay's neck quiver on end.

"How's the VIP suite working out for you?" Flynn asked Jay.

"It's . . . unique," Jay said. He'd never realized how many things could be mirrored.

"I designed that suite myself," Flynn said, puffing proudly on the cigar. "Now, don't forget there's a limo and driver at your disposal. And if there's anything you want—show tickets, dinner reservations, accommodations of any kind"—he actually winked, the shameless bastard—"just call upstairs and you'll have it before you can hang up the phone."

"I'll be sure to keep that in mind."

"Good." Flynn cast another glance in the direction of the girl, who pointedly looked away. "Great. Well then." He thrust his hand out. "Ciao, baby. Enjoy your gaming, and don't hesitate to call, day or night."

"I won't."

"That's Eddie Flynn," Archie told Red as Flynn swaggered off, minions in tow. "You've prob'ly heard about him. He owns this place."

"Does he know you?" she asked Jay.

"We just met a couple of days ago," Jay said as he raised his glass of soda to his mouth.

"But he's being so nice to you, giving you all that stuff . . ."

"It's called comping," Thelma said, "and it's not about being nice."

"It's about keeping me here till I lose everything I've won so far," Jay explained.

"What makes him think you won't just keep winning?" she asked.

"All things being equal," Jay said, "if you play long enough, even with perfect strategy, no missteps, no playing your gut, you *will* eventually lose. Always. It's just a matter of time. That's how the casinos make their profit."

She nodded thoughtfully, but she wasn't making eye contact with Jay. She was looking at his right hand. Damn, he was shuffling chips again. He let them go, made a fist, stretched his fingers.

"So your name is Douglas," she said. "Do most people call you that, or do you prefer Doug?"

He reached reflexively for the chips again, pulled his hand back. "My, uh, first name is actually Jay."

"Jay Douglas . . ." She held out her hand. "I'm Libby Thatcher."

Jay hesitated, then realized what an ass he looked like, and shook it. It wasn't that he didn't like her. It was that he liked her a little too much—just enough to distract him from what he'd come here to do. For four days he'd been the little engine that could. He'd been single-minded, driven, kept his eyes firmly on the prize. But right now he had just one eye in that direction and the other on Libby Thatcher.

Not good. Not good at all.

Helmut had Thelma cut the double deck, and then he got back to the business of dealing blackjack. Libby was a quick study; over the course of the next hour and a half, she won more than she lost. Distracted though he was by having to coach her—hell, her mere presence in the next chair just about undid him—Jay did what he had to do, and managed to rack up another hundred grand.

When the floorman came over to switch out the cards at six thirty, Libby announced that she'd had enough for one day. "I'm up almost four hundred, and that's good enough for me. Quit before you lose, right? Plus, I shopped through lunch, and I'm starving. What do you say?" She smiled at Jay in a way that made it hard to breathe. "You gonna let me buy you dinner?"

"Hm? Oh. No, I, uh . . ."

"You do take a break every once in a while to eat," she said.

"Not that I've noticed," Thelma muttered.

"It's just not a good time," Jay said without looking at her. "Thanks for the offer, but . . ."

She said, "But I owe you a dinner, remember? For coaching me."

"You don't owe me anything."

"You're doing it again," she said.

"What?"

Libby nodded toward the two stacks of partially interlaced chips in his right hand. "What is it, a nervous habit?"

He dropped them as if they'd suddenly become radioactive.

She said, "Are you sure I can't talk you into—"

"No, really. I'm not even hungry. It would be a waste. And I'm on a roll right now, so if I went, I'd be distracted. I'd be lousy company."

Libby studied him for an agonizing interval, a blush staining her face the way it did with redheads. She was clearly confused and maybe a little stung by his lame excuses. As she rose from her chair, she said, "Okay. Well . . . maybe some other time."

"Yeah. Sure."

Jay got his first really good, head-to-toe look at her as she walked away. Her back, revealed by the halter top, tapered to an exquisitely narrow waist, and her butt . . .

Damn. Jay found himself shaking his head as he stared. There was nothing like a firm, round, womanly little butt.

Damn.

When she was out of earshot, Archie said, "Please tell me you're a homo."

"No such luck." Jay downed the rest of his club soda in one tilt, wishing it were vodka.

"Then you're insane."

Thelma said, "She's a keeper, Jay, and you pulled out the hook and tossed her back like she was some old shoe you'd reeled in."

"You know how many men would turn down a girl like that if she asked 'em out?" Archie let out a raspy cough as he ground out his cigarette. "I mean, besides you? None. Not one normal guy would let a girl like that walk away."

"I can't afford to get involved right now," Jay said.

"Who said anything about *involvement*?" Thelma asked.

Jay said, "Involvement's a given with a girl like that. You said it yourself—she's a keeper. She's the real thing, not a girl you just . . . you know."

Thelma rolled her eyes. "This is Vegas, for cryin' out loud. She's not lookin' for a diamond ring. She's lookin' for fun and adventure. She said so herself."

Archie said, "She's looking for a nice, hot little fling she can remember on those cold, snowy nights back in Buffalo."

"Easy for you to say," Jay said. "I'm the one who'll end up saddled with some big, complicated relationship at the worst possible time if you're wrong. Bottom line—I need to keep my mind on the game."

With a melancholy shake of his head, cigarette in one hand,

scotch in the other, Archie said, "You need professional help, that's what you need. I'm not even kidding. You need somebody to fix you, my friend, 'cause you just aren't right."

After Libby left the blackjack pit, she wove her way through the vast, cacophonous, *Gunsmoke*-inspired casino until she came to a door marked AUTHORIZED PERSONNEL ONLY. She climbed the stairs on the other side while rummaging in her bag for the badge that would provide her safe passage through the maze of well-guarded hallways that led to the inner sanctum of security operations at the Gold Dust Hotel and Casino.

As headquarters went, it wasn't much—a single windowless room about fifteen feet square—which made it all the more remarkable that it could accommodate not just a shirtsleeved staff of four, but scores of video monitors. Rows and rows of them lined the walls. They squatted on tables alongside computers, recording devices, and snarls of electrical cord. They perched on stands in the corners, dangled from brackets in the ceiling. About a dozen sat on the floor, trailing serpentine cables, which made it an Olympic event just crossing the room, especially given that the only illumination was the ambient glow of the video screens. The lights in the "Nerve Center," as Eddie Flynn liked to call it, were kept off so as to provide the best possible clarity from the monitors, which displayed mute bird's-eye views of the goings-on downstairs: doughy tourists plunking quarters into the Wheel of Fortune, rowdy young men whooping and hollering around a craps table, a thirty-something couple urging the roulette wheel to stop on their number . . .

And Jay Douglas sitting quietly at the hundred-dollar blackjack table, pushing a stack of about half a dozen blue chips into his betting circle. His image flickered across not one but five different monitors, from the five cameras they'd trained via remote control on his table.

He closed his eyes while the cards were being dealt, rubbed his neck, his face, ran his fingers through his thick brown hair. Jay Douglas was one of those men who can be scruffy as hell—unshaven, uncombed, probably unwashed—without losing one iota of sex appeal. He was lean and long-limbed, but with shoulders that stretched his threadbare T-shirt to the point where Libby half expected the sleeves to split along their seams any second.

His most compelling feature had to be his eyes, which were huge, dark, and far more expressive than he probably realized. It didn't matter how standoffish he acted, how cool he played it. It didn't matter that he'd barely spoken to her, that he'd had to be bullied into coaching her, or even that he'd rebuffed her awkward and unschooled advances. He might act disinterested, but he wasn't, not remotely. She saw it all in his eyes—the way his gaze lingered over her when he thought she didn't notice, the way it darted away the moment she looked in his direction.

Libby watched from five different angles as Jay smiled, probably at something said by the loquacious and oddly engaging Miss Thelma. She seemed to be the only person who could get a human reaction out of him. His smiled faded as he studied his hand. He looked tired, distracted.

When his turn came, he laid his cards faceup in front of the dealer, saying, "Blackjack"; Libby could read his lips. Yawning, he reached out again to spread his cards. The dealer counted his chips—there were actually seven altogether—and paid off the bet. Jay scooped the fourteen chips into the ever-growing pile in front of him.

"I thought I told you to dress hot."

Libby turned to find Eddie Flynn standing right next to her, squinting in the semidarkness at her outfit.

She thought she *had* dressed hot, hot for her, anyway, but she wasn't about to tell him that. Instead, she said, "You're not my boss, Eddie. I don't have to toe your line."

"That's what my ex-wife used to say. She got the heave-ho; you can, too. You want to end up out in the cold, like her, you just keep on back-talking me."

That was unusually surly, even for Eddie. The pressure—and humiliation—of getting cleaned out day after day by Jay Douglas must be getting to him.

Eddie scowled at her chest. "Where's the cleavage? Didn't I say cleavage?"

Braless under a silk halter wasn't good enough? "Do we have to have this conversation here?" she asked with a glance toward the other men in the room, who were making a big show of being studiously absorbed in their work.

With a roll of the eyes, Eddie gestured her toward a door across the room. "And *pants*? I said a miniskirt, preferably leather or vinyl. Do you remember anything from yesterday?"

If only I didn't, Libby thought as she followed him into a brightly lit, white-walled hallway. . . .

"Hello? Anybody here?"

She'd had an appointment to see Eddie yesterday afternoon in his office on the top floor of the hotel, but when she got there, she found his secretary's coolly modern anteroom empty. From behind the closed door to his office proper came music turned up so loud, it sounded as if it were playing inside her skull: Frank Sinatra singing "One for My Baby."

"Eddie?" No response; he wouldn't have heard her over Frank.

She knocked, but she couldn't hear her own fist striking the door.

She thought about just barging in there, but she didn't really know Eddie that well, having met him only the one time at her father's restaurant. He'd insisted on calling her Liz, proclaiming her nickname "square," made some wink-wink, nudge-nudge comment about her being a masseuse, then gone back to cruelly toying with her father under the guise of "negotiations."

Eddie was like a turkey buzzard trailing after some gravely wounded animal in anticipation of feasting on it, either premortem or post; it made little difference when you were a soulless, opportunistic scavenger of human carrion. Eddie knew Jimmy Thatcher's heart was acting up. He knew the widowed old restaurateur wanted nothing more than to sell the business and retire. He knew JT's Steakhouse was close to bankruptcy from all those years of illness. And he obviously knew that, as the only potential buyer, he could tender the lowest of lowball offers and probably eventually wear down his prey.

Eddie had been harassing her dad for almost a year—dangling offers, taking them back, demanding improvements that would "cinch the deal," then finding fault with them, pretending to change his mind, then reconsidering—all because he was too cheap to just pay what the place was really worth. Or maybe he just got off on jerking around sick old men.

In any event, Libby finally had had enough and convinced her dad to let her take over the negotiations. "We've got another buyer interested in the restaurant," she'd told Eddie by phone last week after she finally worked up the courage to make the call. It was a bald-faced lie, but she'd rehearsed it until it sounded credible. "As you know, three independent appraisers have valued JT's at half a million dollars. That's what I'm selling it for. If you want it, you have one week to go to contract for that amount, not a penny less. After that, I withdraw the offer altogether. Take it or leave it."

He'd asked for a few days to think about it, and scheduled this meeting to give her his answer. In the meantime, on the theory that one should know one's enemy, Libby had Googled Eddie Flynn, asked around town about him, and pored over articles about him in back issues of the *Las Vegas Sun* and the *Las Vegas Review-Journal*. In addition to corroborating what she already knew—that he was a smarmy, thrice-divorced, womanizing shark with a sentimental attachment to the Vegas of old—she learned that he owned, in addition to the Gold Dust, three restaurants, two topless clubs, a legal brothel out in the desert called the Kitty Farm, and half a dozen luxury car dealerships scattered across the Southwest. He had a well-deserved rep for doing as he pleased and grabbing anything and anyone that caught his eye, never mind the repercussions.

Because there never were any. Lack of accountability was Eddie Flynn's biggest character flaw, Libby had decided, the one that ultimately begat all the others.

The music cut off in midcroon.

"Bitch."

Libby cocked her head toward the door to the office, wondering if she'd really heard a man's voice—Eddie Flynn's voice—growling that word. There came a striking sound, followed by a woman crying out in pain.

Libby crossed to the door, drew in a steadying breath, opened it . . . and froze in shock.

Chapter Three

There were three people in the big, sunwashed corner office: Eddie Flynn, a pretty brunette, and a burly fellow wearing the uniform of a Gold Dust security guard—or rather, partially wearing it. The guard was lying back on a huge walnut burl desk with his steel-toed boots braced on the floor and his black trousers and tool belt down around his ankles, revealing a tattoo of a bald eagle gripping an American flag that covered his entire left calf. The young woman, her plaid skirt tucked up around her waist, white cotton panties on the desk next to her, gyrated atop him as he kneaded her breasts through her powder blue sweater set. Eddie, dapper as always in a pin-striped suit, stood to the side with a Ping-Pong paddle in his hand.

"Little bitch." He hauled back with the paddle, bringing it down hard on the reddened rump of the brunette, who yelped as the man beneath her groaned.

"Yes!" she gasped. "Give it to me. I've been such a bad girl. You know I need it."

Above a well-stocked wet bar on the opposite wall was the biggest plasma TV Libby had ever seen, on which a skin flick was playing with the sound off. Not just any skin flick, Libby realized, but a home movie in which Eddie, again fully dressed but for his unzipped fly, was hunched over a naked blonde on all fours, thrusting and spanking as she fellated this very same security guard.

Libby, her face warming, backed up and closed the door.

"Liz!" Eddie dropped the paddle and sprinted toward her.

She made a beeline for the door to the hall, but he was surprisingly quick and grabbed her before she could make her escape.

"Don't leave," he said. "I didn't mean to blow off our meeting. I just didn't realize it had gotten so late."

"That's . . . that's all right," she said. "We can do it some other—"

"No way. You're here. We'll do it now. That other can wait. Sorry about that," he added with a smirky grin. "You know how it is when you're, uh, in the middle of things. You lose track of time. It, uh, didn't embarrass you, did it?"

"Um . . ."

"I didn't think so, a sophisticated chick like you. I mean, you're a masseuse, right?" He grinned in a leering, I-got-your-number kind of way.

She thought she was gonna hurl.

"Um, look, Eddie . . ." she began as she edged toward the door.

"You want a drink?"

"No. I really think I should come back some other—"

"No, stay," he urged, his hand just a little too tight around her arm, his gin-and-Altoid breath making her nostrils flare. "In fact, I've got an idea. Some girls might dismiss it out of hand, but I've got this feeling about you. You're open-minded, am I right? And a smart cookie, too." Releasing her arm, he withdrew a colossal cigar and a silver cigar clipper from inside his suit coat.

No, I'm close-minded and a stupid cookie. What was she supposed to say? "Eddie . . ."

"How about you and me and, uh"—he nodded toward the partially closed door to his office as he circumcised the cigar—"Ashley and Steve have us a little party?"

She stared at him. "You have got to be kidding."

"And then maybe," he said, his voice dropping to an unctuous register, "afterward, the two of us can, uh, you know, come to terms about JT's."

"Come to terms."

"All right. Okay," he said with a much-put-upon but conciliatory grin. "Terms first. Business before pleasure, right?" He actually winked as he held a gold lighter to the tip of the cigar and suck-suck-sucked. "I *said* you were a smart cookie. Okay, here's my offer. Four-fifty for the restaurant, and he leaves the fixtures—tables, chairs, kitchen equipment . . ."

"Eddie, are you even remotely serious?" Was he actually offering to buy JT's in return for an afternoon of group sex?

"All right, half a million. Damn, you're a tough one. Maybe I can, uh, soften you up a little, huh?" he murmured as he fingered her hair. "Teach you a little lesson in compliance? You might even learn to like it. Ashley did."

From inside the office, a phone shrilled the refrain to "Luck Be a Lady."

"That's my cell, Ashley," Eddie yelled. "It's on the bar." Lowering his voice again and resuming the arm pawing, he said, "The, uh, fixtures, though . . . I *am* gonna need those to stay."

Ashley emerged from the office, tucking in her blouse while holding out Eddie's cell. "It's Mr. Toomey. That whale, the young guy at the hundred-dollar blackjack table? He just won his third million."

"*Shit.*" Eddie grabbed the cell, saying, "Ashley, bring me a

Beefeater martini, wet, two pepperoni-stuffed olives, and the same for Miss Thatcher. Bull," he barked into the phone, "can't this guy be stopped? What are we paying McGuffin for?" He frowned as he listened. "Yeah, but how can we prove he's cheating if he's too slick to catch?" His frown turned speculative. "You think?" He puffed thoughtfully on the cigar.

Libby reached for the doorknob.

"Hold on." Pressing the phone to his chest, Eddie said, "Liz, wait. I got a better idea. Another deal, but you're gonna like this one."

"Does it involve any personal contact with you or your Ping-Pong paddle?" she asked.

He hesitated. "Not unless you want it to."

She grabbed the doorknob.

"No! It's nothing like that." Raising the phone to his mouth, he said, "Ciao, Bull. Meet me in the Nerve Center in ten." He flipped the phone shut. "How much do you know about blackjack?"

"Um . . ."

"This guy, this high roller, is raping us down there at the hundred-dollar table. We need to find out how he's doing it, but so far, even McGuffin can't get a bead on him."

"Um . . ." What did this have to do with her?

"McGuffin Investigations," Eddie said. "A Vegas institution for over forty years, specializing in casino work. Been on the case for the past couple of days, watching this guy like a hawk down there in the pit, but nothing to report so far. Bull thinks we oughta keep McGuffin on the job, but put somebody else on it, too, somebody who can actually work on this cat—finesse him a little, not just watch him."

Ashley came out of the office with two martinis, followed by Security Guard Steve, now fully dressed, who said, "Will that be all, Mr. Flynn?"

"That's it for now, Steve, but keep your pager on."

Libby dumbly accepted the martini Ashley handed her. She took a sip and felt her throat spasm. Eddie guzzled his like tap water.

"Same payoff as before," Eddie said. "I buy your father's restaurant on your terms, but all I want you to do is a little undercover work. This guy, Jay Douglas, he plays it real close to the chest. Sit down at his table and play for a while. Pretend to be a tourist. Get to know him and get him talking. Get him to take you out somewhere. Find out how he keeps winning."

"This sounds pretty time intensive," she said. "I do have a business to run, you know. I've got clients, appointments . . ."

"Reschedule what you can," Eddie said, "and work around the rest. It shouldn't take you more than a couple of days or so. I damn well hope it doesn't, 'cause I can't afford to have him ripping me off much longer than that. Chances are he's cheating somehow, but we don't know for sure. If it's just dumb luck, I need to keep him around till he starts losing so I can make back some of the dough he's been winning off me. If he's cheating, well, we need to know that, too. We need somebody who can get him to lower his guard, somebody sweet but smart. And, uh, sexy as hell doesn't hurt."

She said, "Wait a minute. If you think I'm going to use sex to get to this guy . . ."

"I didn't say that. I mean, unless you're willing, 'cause it'd probably do the trick."

"Yeah, well, I'm not willing. Also, I'm not real sure I'd be able to pull it off, the tourist act and all that. I'm a lousy liar."

"Beautiful broads need to know how to lie. It'll be good practice for you. And I'll coach you on what to say. It won't be that hard."

Libby took another sip of the oddly greasy martini and gagged. She wasn't crazy about the idea of befriending some guy under false pretenses, but if he was more or less a criminal anyway, that made it a little more palatable. In a way, it was like undercover police work, only by private contract. And in return, her father—her loving, selfless father, who'd raised her on his own from the time she was six and worked his butt off twenty-four/seven his entire life—would get to live out the rest of his life in peace and comfort.

"Just cozy up to him," Eddie said. "Get to know him. Find out how's he doing it, and me and your old man go to contract for half a mill." He raised his right hand. "My word of honor."

Eddie Flynn's honor? Yeah, right. "Write it down and sign it," she said, "and you've got yourself a deal."

"Ashley!" he bellowed. "Get in here, and bring a blank service contract. Two copies." To Libby he said, "You'll have two days to find out how he's doing it."

"Two days? It's not enough," she said.

"Three, then, but that's all the time I can afford, at the rate he's winning. You've got seventy-two hours exactly. As of"—he checked his Rolex—"two twenty Friday afternoon, if you haven't hit pay dirt, the deal's off and your old man's out of luck. We'll make it official, and then I'll take you downstairs to meet Bull and go over the plan of attack. He'll give you a badge and some cash and a pager."

"A pager?" She thought about Security Guard Steve being summoned upstairs for stud duty.

"So we can keep you informed of this guy's comings and goings around the hotel. If the Eye catches him heading into the coffee shop, or the health club, or the pool, or whatever, you'll get a call. The better to 'accidentally' bump into him, *capice*?"

"Tell you what, I'll give you my cell phone number."

"You'll still need some cash for blackjack. And I want you to get yourself some new clothes, something hot. Check out the shops at Caesar's and the Aladdin, but forget the Venetian—way too *Town & Country*. What I got in mind is classic Vegas babe—miniskirts, fishnets, stilettos. I'm thinking animal prints, big jewelry, red lipstick. I'm thinking leather, I'm thinking vinyl. Plenty of jewelry, stuff with some flash, some class. A pretty doll needs a little bling. Oh, and cleavage. That goes without saying, right? Get yourself one of those, you know, Wonderbras or what have you. Hoist those babies up. . . ."

* * *

"And where's the bling?" Eddie demanded the next evening as he ushered Libby into the bright white hallway outside the Nerve Center. "I distinctly said bling. Two skinny little bangle bracelets don't cut it."

"I don't do bling, Eddie."

"You don't do bling? Jeez, if I was a broad, I'd be blinged out the wazoo."

"I'm all too sure you would."

In a classic Eddie Flynn speed-of-light gear shift, he said, "So McGuffin's given up trying to do a background check on this guy. They turned up some Jay Douglases, but none of them are our guy, so it's probably not his real name. We e-mailed his picture to every casino in town, plus Reno, Atlantic City, all the Indian places. . . . McGuffin pulled his prints off a glass and got a contact in the FBI to run them through their fingerprint database. Nada. Think you can get him to tell you who he really is?"

"I don't know, Eddie. He's pretty taciturn."

"Pretty what?"

"He doesn't talk."

"What do you mean, 'he doesn't talk'? Everybody talks."

How literal could you be? "He talks very little, Eddie. He's careful about what he says."

"Have you been doing like I said?" Eddie asked. "Playing dumb, asking a lot of questions about the game and whatnot to get him to open up?"

"Yeah, but he's . . ." Libby shook her head. "You've met him. You know what I'm talking about. He's . . ." *He's not like you,* she wanted to say. *He's the kind of man who thinks before he talks, who's comfortable keeping his own counsel, who has depths a worm like you could never dream of.*

"Here, I want you wearing this." Eddie pulled an elaborate beaded necklace from his inside coat pocket.

She took it from him. "I hope this doesn't mean we're going steady."

"It's a wireless camera. That's the lens, right there, and this part houses the transmitter." He pointed to the large pendant, from which trailed streams of beads, one of them dangling a nine-volt battery. "It's state of the art," Eddie said. "The antenna's hidden here, and this is the on-off switch. When it's on, it transmits video and sound to a laptop in there"—he indicated the Nerve Center—"which automatically records it on the hard drive and a DVD. We can play with it then, pause the action, slow it down, zoom in. . . . If there's something to see, we'll see it. Pretty sweet, huh?"

"Why do I need this?" she asked. "You've got cameras in every nook and cranny of this place."

"Just the casino and the guest floor hallways. And one each in the restaurants and health club. Oh, and one at the door leading out to the pool, but nothing in the pool complex itself."

"What about your office?" she asked, remembering his dirty home movie.

He grinned. "A guy's gotta have a hobby."

"You are some piece of work, Eddie."

"Wear this thing whenever you're sitting at the table with Douglas. Sit close and turn toward him so the Minicam's aimed right at him—ideally at his hands, so we can get a nice, close-up view. The Eye doesn't catch everything, and it's sure as hell not catching whatever it is he's doing."

"If he's doing anything." She shook her head as she studied the apparatus. "It's too risky, Eddie. He's not stupid. He'll figure out what it is."

"No, he won't."

"How am I supposed to hide this battery?"

"Under your clothes. Undo that top and I'll show you."

"Nice try." She stuffed the necklace in her shoulder bag.

"Where'd you tell him you're from?"

"Buffalo."

"Buffalo." He nodded, eyes narrowing in contemplation. "Buffalo. That's good. Cold, gray, far away . . . The anti-Vegas. Remember, you're here on vacation, but somehow you ended up without a place to—"

"I know, Eddie. We went all through this."

"Keep your eyes open," he said. "We're pretty sure he's not using any electronic devices. We have scanners that can detect those. So if he's cheating, he's doing it old-style. Watch to see if he's sneaking cards out of his hand and hiding them, or discarding more cards than he was dealt. Or adding chips to his bet when he's got a good hand, or taking them away when it's not so good."

"You've told me all this."

"Well, I'm telling you again," he snapped, reprising his earlier surliness. "I'm sick and tired of losing to this guy. It's like he drilled a hole in my vault, and now he's just sucking all the money out."

A door down the hall banged open, and two security men came out, the same two who'd escorted that kid with the *Daisy* tattoo away from the table. The guards were so enormous that it took Libby a second to notice the semilimp guy they were holding up between them. They had to virtually drag him out of the room.

"Oh, my God," she whispered when she realized it was the tattooed kid, only without the kerchief around his head, and with a split lip, a swollen nose, and two reddened, puffed-up eyes.

They were followed into the hall by Eddie's majordomo, the grim and thuggish Bull Toomey. Toomey noticed her staring, slammed the door shut, and hustled the others into an elevator.

"Liz!" Eddie called after her as she jogged down the hall. "It's nothing. Don't worry about it."

The elevator was the kind that you needed a key card to operate, so there was no way she could follow them downstairs. She spun on Eddie when he caught up to her. "Where are they taking him?"

"Nowhere. Outside. Into a cab, probably. We're done with him."

"I thought this kind of thing wasn't supposed to happen any-more," she said, "players getting worked over just for counting cards."

"He refused to cash out and leave." Eddie shrugged. "I'm a traditionalist—what can I tell you?"

She walked over to the door they'd exited from, which was marked PRIVATE, and opened it, revealing a small, dim room. There was a tinted window in the back wall that afforded a view into a second room, that one lit by a bank of overhead fluorescents. "What is that, mirrored glass?" she asked.

"Yep, with a one-way audio feed, just like the cops have. In fact, a cop friend helped me install it."

"Really." Libby had heard the casinos had the local police and most of Nevada's judges and government officials in their back pockets. She'd never believed it was quite that extensive, but you never knew.

There were cameras high up in all four corners of the stark back room, but they had cloths thrown over them. A straight-backed metal chair was set up dead center and facing left, a pair of handcuffs dangling from one of its rungs. On a table against the left-hand wall sat a Polaroid camera, and next to it, a snapshot of the poor guy they'd just taken downstairs, before they'd decorated his face.

The dark anteroom was furnished with a leather armchair facing the one-way mirror. Next to it sat a table bearing a big stone ashtray littered with cigar butts.

"You like to watch, huh?" she asked Eddie.

"It passes the time."

She went back out into the hall, shaking her head. "If this is how you treat card counters, what do you do to cheaters?"

"I call Metro."

"Metro?"

"The Las Vegas Metropolitan Police," he said. "Let the system deal with them."

"Right," she said as she thought about it, "because unlike card counting, cheating really *is* against the law."

"You got it."

"That's all you do?" she demanded. "Just hand them over to the police?"

"Trust me, the last thing I want is for the cops to show up here and find the perp they came after all beat up. That kind of trouble I don't need."

The elevator doors whooshed open and Bill Toomey emerged. His knuckles, Libby noticed, were scraped raw.

"What'd you do with the kid?" Eddie asked him.

"Threw him in a cab," Toomey said.

Eddie gave Libby his best told-you-so smile. "And what do we do with cheaters, Bull?"

"Call in Metro."

Another self-satisfied grin. Libby looked away, sighing. "I just don't want to be part of some . . ." She shook her head. "It's just . . . I needed to be sure. . . ."

"I know." Eddie patted your arm. "You're a broad. You're sensitive. I understand."

Libby looked at him for a long, weary moment. Then she turned and walked away.

Eddie clipped and lit a Galaxia as he watched Liz leave.

"Just so we're clear," he told Bull as he snapped the lighter shut, "I'm losing roughly a million bucks every day this Douglas bastard is sitting there at that table. That may be pocket change to the Bellagio, but it's pretty damn painful for me. He's not only bleeding me dry, he's making an ass out of me. If this chick finds out he isn't on the up and up in any way whatsoever—slick card counting, mucking, pinching and pressing, whatever—you make him good and sorry he picked Eddie Flynn to rip off. You got that?"

"Got it, boss," Bull said.

"Call in Metro?" Eddie said through a contemptuous gust of laughter. "Fuck Metro. This is personal. I don't want this bastard walking away laughing at me, *capice*?"

"*Capice*."

ell, hello there."

Jay opened his eyes and hauled his head up from the rim of the Gold Dust's outdoor spa, a round, sunken hot tub enclosed by dense foliage in a far corner of the pool complex. This being a fairly mild May night by Vegas standards, steam rose like smoke off the warm, churning water, obscuring the dark figure on the other side despite the underwater lighting.

He recognized her voice, though. It was the girl who'd sabotaged his game at the blackjack table this afternoon. Libby . . . something wholesome and Tom Sawyerish. Thatcher. Libby Thatcher.

Jay sat up a little straighter, scraped his damp hair off his face. He'd been half dozing up till now, but watching her walk toward him around the perimeter of the enormous spa provoked a spurt of adrenaline that made his heart race.

It was a classic fight or flight reaction. He could get up and head back to his room—"I was just leaving, see you around"—or he could stay and confront this threat to his equanimity. Conquer it. Subdue it.

Bring it to its knees.

That thought inspired a mental image so visceral—and physically evident—that getting up was suddenly no longer an option.

"You here all alone?" she asked with a smile as she stood over him at the edge of the spa, that green straw bag slung over one shoulder.

"Until now," he said.

She looked away, the smile vanquished. If it were daytime, he would probably see her blushing, as she had when he'd sent her off to have dinner all by herself.

"I didn't mean . . ." he began, then just shook his head. "I wasn't trying to be a jerk. It's just . . . It's been a long day for me, and I'm a little scorched."

She nodded thoughtfully. "And your back is sore from sitting at that table, so you thought a little hydrotherapy before bed would be just the ticket."

"Mostly my neck and shoulders, but yeah, that's the idea." That, and maybe it would relax him enough to get a good night's sleep before hitting the blackjack pit again in the morning.

"Don't you have a whirlpool tub in that fancy suite of yours?" she asked.

"Two, actually, one for each bedroom, but they don't have a view of the stars."

She raised her gaze to the night sky, searching . . .

"There's a lot of light haze from the Strip," he said, "but if you look, you can see—"

"Yeah, I see them," she said. "They're beautiful."

Libby's hair was caught up haphazardly, framing her face in stray tendrils. She had on a batik-printed pareo that fell almost to her ankles, and a white bikini top composed of two crocheted triangles tied together in front. Her body was toned but womanly: round breasts, round hips, flat but nicely unsculpted stomach. She untied the knot that secured her pareo at one hip, drawing Jay's attention to her arms and shoulders, which were sleekly muscled, more so than the rest of her. Interesting.

Jay raised his eyes to hers, and there was no doubt she'd caught him checking her out. She looked away, her tongue flicking out to lick her lips—a nervous gesture that made him groan inwardly.

When she returned her gaze to his, there was a look in her eyes—bashful but with a certain glint—that told him the heat might not be entirely one-sided. "So you, uh, don't mind if I join you?" she asked.

"Um, no. No, of course not."

She tossed the pareo and bag onto a chaise lounge, unveiling the bottom of her string bikini, which tied at the sides. Jay had seen more revealing swimsuits, but few as sexy. Its appeal wasn't in its brevity, but in the ease with which it could come undone.

"I came out here looking for a nice quiet evening swim," she said as she dipped an experimental toe in the water, "but there are all these smarmy singles over there, drinking frozen margaritas and hitting on each other." She nodded toward the pool on the other side of the spa's circular barricade of shrubbery, through which muffled conversation and laughter could be heard above the low, watery rumble of the spa's jets. "I thought I remembered something about a spa being out here, but it sure wasn't easy to find."

"Which is one of the reasons I like it."

Libby lowered herself into the water, moaning with pleasure as she settled next to Jay on the submerged bench that ringed the spa. She laid her head back and closed her eyes, emitting a kittenish little growl. "Oh, man, I've been needing this."

Jay swallowed hard and wrested his gaze from her. He should leave. He would.

As soon as he could stand up without making a spectacle of himself.

He closed his eyes and started reviewing basic double-deck black-jack strategy in his mind. *If you've got eight or less: Hit. Nine: Double down against dealer's six or less, hit against anything higher. Ten: Double down against dealer's—*

"I don't often ask guys out to dinner." She was looking at him. Her eyes, veiled by steam and lit by shimmering waves of underwater light, were the warm, iridescent green you might see at the edge of a forest pool.

"Um . . ."

"Actually, that was my first time ever. Pretty lame attempt, huh? Now I know why guys find it so hard."

"It wasn't lame," he said. "*I* was lame. I was . . ." He looked away, shook his head. "Preoccupied. It wasn't you."

"Really?"

"Trust me."

She smiled. "Thanks." The only part of her visible above the simmering water was her head, her shoulders, and the upper slopes of her breasts. Water roiled around her from jets in the backrest, some low, some high. The damp heat had corkscrewed those loose tendrils of hair, giving her a slightly untamed aura. "Normally I wouldn't have had the guts to ask someone out," she said, "but this is Vegas, you know? You're supposed to take chances in Vegas."

He nodded inanely, thinking this was the first time he'd ever tried to make small talk while he had a blue-steel hard-on. "So, uh, are you here alone, or . . . ?"

"Um, I'm here with a girlfriend. Jane." Libby bowed her head to slide out the chopsticks holding her hair in a twist at her nape. Setting the sticks on the concrete deck, she shook her head to loosen the unruly mane, which fell almost to the level of the water. "Problem is, yesterday morning, Jane met this guy and brought him back to our room, and he hasn't left since, so I've got no place to go."

"They kicked you out of your own room?"

"They said I should stay," Libby said as she stroked her fingers through her hair, fluffing it, "but they're, like, going at it nonstop, and they don't mind an audience, so it's a little . . . icky, you know?"

"Couldn't you just get a room of your own?"

"Um, I tried, but there are all these conventions in town right now. Every hotel is booked solid."

"So, where'd you sleep last night?" he asked.

"I hung out in the casino." She looked away from him, almost as if the subject embarrassed her. "Walked around. Played the nickel slots for a while. Walked around some more. Played some more slots."

"All night? You look pretty good for someone who hasn't had any sleep in the last day and a half. You must be exhausted."

"Not as exhausted as I'll be tomorrow morning." She closed her eyes and sank farther down in the water to let the jets hit her neck. "I'd give my right arm for a bed to sleep in tonight."

They fell silent as Jay contemplated the second bedroom going to waste in that big, tacky suite Eddie Flynn had moved him to his second day here. *Bad idea*, he thought as he pictured her stretched out on the bed, hair rippling like fire over the pillows, eyes gazing at him in gratitude as she untied the top of her bikini.

Eleven: Double down against all hands, he chanted to himself as his erection swelled inside his baggy swim trunks. *Twelve: Hit against two or three, stand against four through six, hit against seven and higher . . .*

"I was wondering about your shirt," she said.

He turned to find her looking at the Astro Boy T-shirt he'd dropped onto the deck nearby, along with his jeans and sneakers.

"That writing on it," she said, "what is it, Japanese?"

He nodded. "Astro Boy was the first Japanese animation introduced to the U.S. market, back in the sixties."

"Where'd you get that shirt?" she asked. "My nephew loves anime, and his birthday's coming up."

"Tokyo."

She blinked at him, nodded slowly. "Wow. You, uh, travel a lot?"

"Some." Quite an understatement for a man who'd been literally living out of a suitcase for the past decade.

The tension that had been seeping out of Jay as he soaked was reasserting itself, and not just in his groin. Part of him wanted to drag his deep-fried ass back to his room, fall asleep with playing cards dancing in his head, and wake up focused and charged and hungry for more of Eddie Flynn's millions. Another part, just as adamant, just as ravenous, wanted to grab this woman and hammer himself into her, right here—never mind that there were people milling around the pool right on the other side of those bushes.

Jay scrubbed his hands over his beard-roughened face, rubbed his neck, twisted it this way and that.

"Still aching?" she asked.

He sighed, thinking of his unrelenting boner. "You have no idea."

"Maybe I can do something about that."

He looked at her.

"I actually happen to be a masseuse."

It took him a moment to process that, given that very little blood was making it upstairs to his brain. "A masseuse."

She said, "Not that kind of masseuse."

"I wasn't thinking that," he said. "I mean, you're not exactly the type."

Her smile was disarmingly sweet. "Thank you."

"You're, like, a massage therapist, right?" he asked.

"Yep. I'm freelance. I've got my own studio, but I also come to people's offices, homes, hotel rooms. . . ."

"Is there much of a market for that in Buffalo?"

She stared at him for a second. "Um, yeah . . ." Looking away, she said, "Yeah, I do pretty well."

"I've never had a professional massage," he said. "They're, like, what? Sixty, eighty bucks an hour? Plus tip?"

She chuckled incredulously. "You play blackjack for thousands of dollars a hand, and you're telling me you can't afford a massage? My God, you've won how many millions in the past few days?"

"This time last week, I had less than a thousand dollars in the bank." Which would probably be about how much he'd have this time next week, once this little venture was wrapped up.

"Huh. Wow. You are one lucky guy."

"Yeah, guess so."

"Do you, like, use some special method?" she asked.

"Special method?"

"Like that card counting business?"

"Nah. I mean, I keep track of the cards. That's not hard to do, and it's just common sense to bear in mind whether there's lots of tens and paint left in the—"

"Paint?"

"Face cards—jacks, queens, and kings. But it's not that big a factor in . . . you know . . . how much I've been winning."

Her brow furrowed. "You count cards but it doesn't factor into your play?"

"It's . . . complicated," he said, wishing suddenly that he hadn't let the conversation ramble down this particular path. "And not really very interesting. Now, your job, that's interesting."

She gave him one of those I'm-on-to-you smiles. "You're changing the subject."

"I'm intrigued. Massage therapy, that's kind of a cool way to make a living. You any good at it?"

"Damn near brilliant, if I do say so myself." Her winsomely proud grin put him in mind of a little girl who'd just won the spelling bee. "But don't take my word for it."

Libby rose from the bench to stand facing him, waist high in the steaming water, which sluiced off her in a way that wreaked havoc with his composure. The muscles shaping her upper body must have been earned giving massages, he realized. She closed both hands over his shoulders.

"Wow, you *are* tense," she said with a soft little laugh when he involuntarily stiffened—not because he didn't like her touching him, but because he liked it way too much. "Relax," she murmured as she set about gently kneading his strung-out muscles. She was putting her whole body into it, smiling in a serene, Mona Lisa kind of way that told him she really loved doing this, it wasn't just a job to her.

"What's this?" she asked, lifting the cord strung with tiny beads, bones, and seeds that he wore around his neck under his shirt.

"It's a *rachamala*," he said. "A medicine necklace."

"Where'd you get it?"

"Nepal. A shaman made it for me."

She looked up at him.

He lifted his shoulders. "Like I said, I travel. There's this ancient religion in Tibet and Nepal called Bön-po that's even older than Buddhism. Its shamans serve as healers and guides to the afterlife, and they've got magic rituals they perform to help maintain the balance between people and nature. A very old, very wise Bön-po shaman gave me this charm and told me it would bring me blessings and good fortune whenever I wore it."

"So it's like a good-luck charm?" she asked as she went back to rubbing his shoulders. "Do you think it's responsible for your winning streak?"

Not wanting to go there, he said, "You ask a lot of questions for someone who's trying to get me to relax."

She bit her bottom lip. "Sorry. Bad habit. You do need to relax, too. You're holding a lot of stress here. And here," she said, gliding her hands from his shoulder to the back of his neck. "Loosen up, Jay. Let yourself unwind."

Jay closed his eyes, thinking she smelled, if anything, even better than before, in the casino. He breathed in, along with the remnants of her perfume, the scent of warm skin and a hint of something sweet and earthy on her breath. . . . Wine. Red wine.

Libby had an excellent touch, firm and confident, but finely tuned to the terrain on which she was working. She varied her technique, alternating strong, deep strokes with whisper-light ones. What would it feel like, Jay wondered, to be caressed with such deft enthusiasm on that part of him that needed it the most right now?

"I wish I had something to use as a lubricant," she said as she rubbed. "Some sort of lotion or oil to make my hands slicker so I could really get in there. God knows you need it."

Swallowing down a groan, Jay opened his eyes to find her breasts pretty much directly in front of his face. They weren't as large as some men liked them, but he'd always been more partial to shape and firmness over size, and in that department they were damn near perfect. Her nipples were hard as beads within the little crocheted triangles that cupped them, which were lined with something to make them opaque, worse luck.

Worse luck? Like this woman needed to be any hotter? *Get a grip, Jay. You need to stay focused. You need to remember why you're here.*

"What I really need to do," she said as she started on his scalp, "is get you lying down."

"Bad idea." The words came out a little gruff, as if he had a sore throat.

He looked up at her. She met his eyes; she got it.

She made no move to back away from him, though, as she might have, should have . . . would have if she didn't feel it, too. Damn, why did this have to be so hard?

Someone on the other side of the bushes shrieked with laughter.

"I, uh . . ." Jay lifted her hands from his shoulders. "I should probably turn in. Thanks for the massage. It was great, but it's . . . it's getting late, and—" He closed his hands around her waist to gently push her away.

"Yeah. Sure." Libby nodded, the color high in her cheeks, water beading on her goose-bumped skin, trickling between her breasts with every rise and fall of her chest. Her gaze shifted from his eyes to his mouth, then to his hands, still gripping her by the waist.

Let her go.

He pulled her toward him.

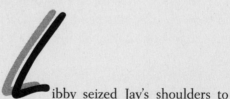

Chapter Five

ibby seized Jay's shoulders to steady herself as he hauled her astride his lap, water sloshing in a wave onto the deck. Gripping the back of her head, he lowered her mouth to his for a desperate, moaning kiss. He caressed her almost frantically—her breasts, her back, her hips . . .

He grasped her bottom, tucking her tight against the rock-solid ridge beneath his swim trunks. Libby shifted to maximize the intimate contact, shocked at her boldness. She'd just met Jay. She'd never done anything like this with a man she hardly knew, and then there was the fact that she was spying on him for Eddie Flynn. She should tear herself away from him, flee to safety.

She should, she thought as he pressed her to him, groaning into her mouth, his shoulders like iron beneath her hands. She rubbed against him shamelessly, hungrily, astounded that she was doing this, awed at how aroused she was, how close—

"Oh, God," she whispered against his lips, "this is insane. I never do this. Not with . . . I mean . . ."

"Me neither." He stilled, lungs pumping, hands trembling as he relaxed his hold on her. "We shouldn't be—" He swallowed. "We should . . . we should probably not . . ."

"Y-yeah," she managed, her hips shuddering as she fought the urge to thrust.

A moan rose in his throat as Jay surrendered to that urge, grinding against her just once, but so hard she almost came.

"Oh, my God," she rasped. "Jay. Listen. If . . . if we're gonna stop, we should . . . we should stop now."

"Yeah." His throat moved. "Yeah."

"So, uh . . ." She eased away from him reluctantly, thinking it was a good thing he was being strong, because she wanted this, needed this, too badly to stop on her own. If he were to waver even a little bit . . .

"You're incredible, Libby—amazing," he said, one hand lingering on her waist. "It's got nothing to do with you. It's just, you know, it's not good timing for me to get involved, and—"

"No, you're right." She stepped away from him, loving the feel of his rough hand lightly caressing her and half wishing he'd drag her back to him. "I should go. This is . . ." She shook her head, turned away.

He let go of her. She gripped the edge of the spa to climb out.

Jay growled something under his breath, stood, and grabbed her around the waist from behind. Libby closed her eyes, her right knee braced on the bench, her heart drumming in her ears.

He yanked at the strings securing her bikini bottom on both sides, letting the flimsy garment drift away. Libby didn't move, didn't breathe. The flesh between her legs felt swollen, electrified, painfully empty. Reaching around her, he slid a finger down her slick cleft, igniting a sexual jolt so powerful that she cried out.

"Shh," he whispered as he fumbled with the drawstring of his trunks. "They'll hear out there."

She turned toward him, but he spun her back around, replacing her hands on the rim of the spa and lifting her so that she was kneeling on the bench. One of the jets was aimed so that its stream surged directly at the juncture of her thighs, making her feel as if she were being licked there by a thousand tiny tongues.

"Here, just . . ." Jay tilted her hips slightly to provide him better access. He parted her from behind with urgent but nimble fingers, his breath harsh and fast on the back of her neck.

She sucked in a breath as he pressed into her, the broad glans rooting, stretching. He was slippery, too, even underwater, but so thick and hard, breathtakingly hard. Holding her still with both hands, he flexed his hips and pushed deep, deep inside her, a raw intrusion that had her biting her lip to keep quiet.

"You okay?" he asked hoarsely. "You're trembling."

"It's just . . . it's been awhile for me."

He wrapped her in his arms, nuzzled her damp hair, kissed her shoulder. "I'll keep still, let you get used to it."

Get used to kneeling in seething water with a veritable stranger cradling her in his arms while he stood buried inside her? Not likely. Still, there was something undeniably comforting about his strong embrace, the hot tickle of his breath in her hair, the cool weight of all those little amulets against her back.

He held her like that, motionless but intimately joined, while the jet shot a bubbling stream onto her ultrasensitized flesh. To be stimulated like that while being impaled from behind was heady stuff. Libby tried to keep still, to savor the escalating arousal that sizzled along her nerves like an electric charge, but it was too intense, almost painfully so, and within seconds she was teetering on the edge. . . .

She moaned in surrender, hips rocking as the pleasure crackled up her legs, her fingers digging into the concrete deck, or trying to.

"Shh . . . easy. Let it come. . . ." Tightening his hold on her as she writhed, Jay murmured, "You're so beautiful, so sexy."

"Oh . . . oh, God . . ." A guttural sob tore from her lungs as the pleasure detonated, shuddering through her with bone-jarring force.

"Shh . . ." One arm still banded around her, Jay closed a hand over her mouth to muffle her cries. "Shh . . ." There was something about being restrained that way that only intensified the force of an already shattering climax. She thrashed in sensual delirium as the pleasure crested and gradually subsided.

"Oh, wow," he murmured as she collapsed in his arms, trembling. "Here . . ." He drew himself out of her, turned her around, and sat her on the bench.

She slumped against the backrest, closed her eyes, and ran a quaking hand through her hair. Her nails felt jagged. She looked at them and saw that they were mostly broken off.

"You okay?" Jay asked.

Libby nodded, frowning in confusion as she watched him retie the drawstring of his swim trunks.

"I left my wallet in the safe in my suite," he said. "That's where I keep my condoms."

Appalled that she hadn't even thought of protection, Libby said, "I . . . I have some in my bag."

"It's not just that. It's . . ." He shook his head. "Don't get the wrong idea. You're . . . Wow. You're incredible, you really are. But it's probably for the best if we just . . . leave it as it is." He reached into the water and came up with her bikini bottom.

She took it from him and stood on quivering legs to put it back on.

"I wasn't thinking," he said. "It's been a long day, and I'm . . . I don't know what I'm doing, but I know I shouldn't be . . . you and I shouldn't . . ."

The hurt must have shown on her face, because he said, "The thing is, I've never been very good at dividing my attention—compartmentalizing, multitasking, whatever. It's not me. When I'm working toward something, I've got to focus all my efforts on that one thing, and right now, what I'm working toward is . . . well, it's pretty important to me."

"Winning at blackjack." It stung a little to be dismissed in favor of a game, even if he *was* on a hot streak.

Jay looked as if there were something he wanted to say, but he just looked away and shook his head. "Sorry."

"Yeah, me, too," Libby said, her throat tight. She was surprised, and appalled, to find herself perilously close to tears. She got out of the spa and stood with her back to Jay while she tied her pareo back on, thinking, *Don't cry, it's not worth it,* he's *not worth it. You screwed up. Deal with it.*

That's what she got for tossing back two glasses of merlot in quick succession after Eddie Flynn called to say the Eye caught Jay entering the pool complex and she ought to "get that awesome little butt down there pronto."

She heard Jay climb out of the water and zip up his jeans. "Libby?" He stroked her arm. "Are you, uh . . . ?"

She turned to face him, breaking the contact. "I'm fine. It's cool. You're right. This was a mistake."

He studied her for a long, grave moment. Finally he nodded, his jaw tight, turned, and walked away.

The air left Libby's lungs. Deflated, she dropped onto the chaise and sat staring at nothing while she reflected on what had just happened.

Nothing happened. Not in Jay's eyes, anyway. What had been a deeply passionate encounter for her was just an error in judgment to him, something to be brushed aside and forgotten lest it interfere with his blackjack game, for God's sake. Fine, then, she'd brush it aside. It wasn't important, not really. Her father was important. Her father was the reason she'd gotten acquainted with Jay in the first place. Her father was the reason she'd remain acquainted, or try to, until she'd found out what Eddie Flynn wanted to know.

"The hell with Jay Douglas," she whispered, thinking if she said it out loud, she might start to feel it inside. He was selfish, thoughtless. He'd led her on, made a fool of her. She owed him nothing.

She owed her father everything.

"Libby." Through the steam rising from the water, she saw Jay standing in the gap between the surrounding bushes that served as an entrance to the spa. He'd come back.

He was even taller than she'd realized, six-two or -three, with the broad-shouldered, lean-hipped build of an Olympic swimmer. His T-shirt clung damply to well-carved pecs and a true, classic six-pack.

Damn him. She sighed and rubbed her eyes.

So quietly she could hardly hear him over the churning of the spa, he said, "I really am sorry for . . . what happened. It was my fault entirely, and I don't blame you if you're mad at me."

She swallowed, shrugged. Striving to keep her voice even, she said, "Hey, it's Vegas. That's the kind of thing that happens here, right? People, they . . . do things they wouldn't normally. Then they go home, and it's business as usual. No harm done."

He nodded, frowning. "Yeah, well, I feel like I took advantage of you. And, um, I'd kind of like to make it up to you if you'll let me." He scraped a hand over his jaw. "I've got two bedrooms in my suite, and I can only use one. Why don't you take the other? I'll warn you, it couldn't be any tackier. It's got a round bed covered with purple fake fur, and one of Elvis's glitter jumpsuits in a glass case in the corner. But it's yours if you want it. I'll get you your own room key and everything."

She stared at him, thinking this was exactly what she—or rather, Eddie Flynn—had been counting on with that fairy tale about her having no place to stay. The closer she and Jay were physically, the easier it would be to finesse from him the secret of his success at blackjack. Of course, given what had just transpired between them, the prospect of sharing living space with Jay was daunting, at best. But maybe, like him, she should concentrate on one overriding goal—helping her father—and put the rest of it out of her mind.

"Just a friendly arrangement," Jay said. "No, uh, you know . . . expectations. You'll have your room, I'll have mine."

"What could be more civilized," she said.

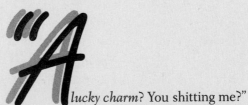

Chapter Six

"**A** lucky charm? You shitting me?" Eddie Flynn, sitting with Libby at a dark corner table in a bar at the Flamingo, took a puff on his cigar as he scooped up another handful of snack mix. "Please tell me you're shitting me."

"That's what he told me last night," Libby said wearily as she stirred milk into her third cup of coffee. Ten thirty in the morning, and Eddie Flynn was already half in the bag. He'd called her on her cell about an hour ago while she was in the blackjack pit at the Gold Dust, watching Jay rake in the chips, and asked her to meet him here for a progress report. Since then, he'd done nothing but gripe nonstop about how much Jay was "siphoning" from him, while sucking down whiskey sours, snack mix, and cigar smoke in the most extraordinary display of oral fixation Libby had ever seen.

"So, you and him got friendly last night, huh?" Eddie asked as he crunch-crunch-crunched. "The Eye caught him taking you up to the VIP suite at a quarter to eleven, and you didn't leave till nine this morning, when you went down to watch him play blackjack."

She shrugged with as much indifference as she could muster. "He offered me a place to stay, just like you wanted, so I can keep close to him."

"Pretty smooth answer, but you're blushing," Eddie said. "I thought you were too good to use sex to soften him up."

"It wasn't like that," she said, wincing inside when she realized what she'd just admitted. "It . . . it wasn't about softening him up. It was . . . it was . . ."

"Oh, jeez, kid, don't tell me you're falling for him. I thought you were smarter than that."

So did I.

"Lizzie, Lizzie, Lizzie." Shoving the massive cigar in his mouth, Eddie proceeded to poke through the assorted morsels in his palm, tossing all the minipretzels into the ashtray. "I hate these fuckin' things. Why do they put them in there? And there are never enough bagel chips." He yelled, "Sweetheart! Yeah, you," and motioned the cocktail waitress over to the table.

"Yes, Mr. Flynn?" Everybody in this town seemed to know Eddie by sight.

"Do me a favor, take this back"—Eddie thrust the bowl of snack mix at her—"and pick out all the pretzels, and those little sesame things that look like rat turds. Just leave the bagels chips and the peanuts and, uh, whatever those other things are, those little nuggety things."

"Soy nuts," she said.

"*Soy nuts?*" He looked as aghast as if she'd said *cyanide pellets.* "No, I don't eat that shit. Take those out, too, and bring me back the rest. ASAP, baby. That's my breakfast." He handed the waitress a fifty-dollar bill, leered at her ass as she walked away, then turned to inspect Libby through a plume of smoke. "You're not wearing the necklace," he said. "The one with the minicam."

"I told you, it's too obvious. He'll know what it is."

"It's custom-made, cost me some serious scratch, and you're wearing it or our deal's off. Tell your old man I said good luck with that bankruptcy petition."

Gritting her teeth, Libby dug the necklace out of her handbag and put it on, tucking the battery under her halter top—the same halter top she'd had on yesterday because she hadn't been back to her apartment yet to collect her things.

"Need any help with that?" Eddie asked with his trademark oily grin.

Libby gave him a baleful look.

"So Bull asked housekeeping if they'd seen anything interesting in this guy's suite," Eddie said, "and they told him there's this big-ass wooden trunk in the living room, real old, all scarred up, very mysterious looking."

"I know. I saw it," Libby said.

"Did you ask him what's in it?"

"Um, no, we didn't talk very much once we were back in the suite," she said.

"I'll bet."

She sighed and rubbed her eyes. "I was going to ask him about it this morning, but when I woke up, he was already gone, and I haven't been alone with him since then."

"If I were you," Eddie said, "I'd make a point of cracking it open and taking a look."

"It's got a padlock on it."

"Combination?"

She pictured it in her mind. "No, it's one of those old-fashioned iron padlocks with a keyhole."

"No problem, then. Just get ahold of the key."

"How am I supposed to do that?"

"You're a smart girl. You'll figure it out." Eddie raised his glass to his mouth, snorting with amusement as he swallowed. "Lucky charm . . . Jeez, you sound like my ex-wife. You even remind me of her. You're just a little too sweet and trusting for your own good. World-class knockers, though. Cassie, not you. Well, you, too, but Cassie was . . ." He cupped his hands about a foot from his chest. "The real thing, too, not that I turn my nose up at silicone, mind you, but Cassie didn't need none of that shit. She was all woman—one gorgeous babe."

"Why'd you divorce her, then," Libby asked, "if she was sweet and trusting and gorgeous?"

"That's just it: She was trusting to the point where you had to wonder about her. She was just one of those simple people, you know, unsophisticated, no real class. Very square views on marriage." He shook his head as he absently plucked a pretzel from the ashtray. "Never marry a showgirl. I married three of them. Trust me—it always ends bad."

"I'll take it under advisement."

Eddie popped the pretzel into his mouth, gave it a chew, then spat the remnants onto the table. "Jesus H. . . . Where the hell is that girl with my snack mix?"

"It's probably taking her a while to customize it."

Sitting back, Eddie gestured broadly with his cigar. "This was the first really big, fancy hotel in this town—I mean back when it was just a dirt road in the desert. You know who built this place?"

Everybody knew that. "Bugsy Siegel."

"Bugsy Siegel. The man was the ultimate visionary. The Flamingo back then, it was like this oasis of *cool* in the middle of nowhere. It's all been torn down and replaced, of course. Big mistake. They shoulda left it just the way it was. I'd give anything to go back in time and have a drink with Bugsy at the original Flamingo—anything."

Eddie puffed contemplatively on his cigar. "Yeah, Cassie, she was into that all that shit, lucky charms and that. She had her wish boxes, her mojo bags, her holy medals. . . ." Grinning, he leaned across the table and lowered his voice. "She had, I kid you not, the bone from a raccoon's dong, this, like, curved little spaghetti-looking thing. She used to put it under my pillow to try and keep me off the cocktail waitresses. Oh, and when she was pregnant, she swung her wedding ring by a thread over her palm to see if it was a boy or a girl."

"You have a child?" Libby asked.

Eddie's grin dissipated. The waitress set a bowl of picked-over snack mix in front of him, saying, "Here you go, Mr. Flynn," but he didn't seem to notice. He crushed out his cigar, drained his whiskey sour, and stood up, shooting his cuffs and adjusting his tie.

"So, it looks like McGuffin might have something for me," he said. "I should know more tomorrow—which also happens to be the third day of our three-day contract, you and me. If you don't find out how Jay Douglas is pulling this off by two twenty tomorrow afternoon— how he's really pulling it off, none of this lucky-charm shit—your old man can write off my half a mill and learn to eat cat food."

He turned to leave, then paused and said, "A word to the wise, Lizzie. This Jay Douglas? Don't make the mistake of falling for him. You don't want to complicate things, and anyway, trust me, he's not what he seems. Even the scummiest sicko creep can make a woman think he's a prince if he wants her bad enough."

"We're not all as gullible as your ex-wife," Libby deadpanned.

"You sure about that?"

Jay paused with his key card halfway into the slot above the door-knob. Should he knock? It was his own suite, so that would be kind of dorky. On the other hand, he'd been sharing it for the past twenty-four hours with a woman he barely knew.

Except, of course, in the biblical sense.

He slid the key out and rubbed his perennially sore neck. Last night hadn't exactly been one his proudest moments. After being a complete prick, yet again, to a woman whose only offense was being too terrific to ignore, he'd gone and ravished her in that hot tub like some kind of caveman. And then, lest she get too complacent, he'd put the brakes on right in the middle of things, leaving her reeling with rejection yet again, and him with the bluest blue balls he'd ever endured.

Served him right, of course, as had her coolness last night when he escorted her back to the suite and got her set up in the second bedroom. He'd been too distracted to sleep, at least not well, so at three a.m. he headed back down to the hundred-dollar table, where he spent most of the next seventeen hours. Libby first showed up around nine in the morning, and even if she wasn't quite her old self again—there was a hint of wariness toward him—it was close enough for him to feel like maybe he hadn't completely mucked things up.

She'd come by off and on all day and into the evening, playing a little, chatting up Miss Thelma, and just generally looking and smelling like a million bucks. Archie played for a couple of hours in the morning, the Quiet Man for another couple in the afternoon; otherwise, it was just him, Thelma, and Libby.

He'd found that he didn't really begrudge her being there, despite how it taxed his concentration. In fact, after she'd been gone for a while, he actually started anticipating her next visit—looking around for her, asking people if they'd seen her. Miss Thelma had cackled and reminded him that quickie weddings were a thriving industry in Vegas. "I'll spring for the reception if you let me walk you down the aisle." He'd had to listen to razzing like that all day, sometimes with Libby sitting right there at the table.

The upside was that Thelma had been right yesterday about his concentration being unshakable even in the face of a nuclear explosion—or a Libby Thatcher. His game hadn't suffered one iota from Libby's on-and-off presence at the table, proof of which was the check for almost $1.2 million, signed by Eddie Flynn, tucked snugly into the back pocket of his jeans.

So Libby wasn't the jinx he thought she'd be after all. If only he'd known that before his little coitus interruptus scene last night.

Jay slid the key card into the lock and knocked as the little light flashed green. "It's me."

A quick tour of the sprawling funkadelic love nest—seventies glitz furniture, heart-shaped whirlpools, naked faux Greek statuary, and mirrors, mirrors everywhere—revealed that she wasn't in the suite.

Jay figured she must be collecting her things from her former room; she'd said something about doing that this evening. He dumped his keys and change on a console table in the foyer, taking a moment to admire the view from the wall of windows in the living room: the Vegas Strip in all its amped-up majesty against a purplish desert sky.

Detouring to the safe to stow the check with the others, Jay headed for the master bathroom, where he shaved and took a long, scorching shower to pummel the aches and pains out of his blackjack-weary bod. He was drying himself off, with the door open to let out the steam, when he heard a rattling sound and realized he wasn't alone in the suite.

Pulling on only his jeans, he padded on bare, silent feet to the living room, where he found Libby, in a tank top and sweat shorts, standing over his apparatus trunk with her back to him. The trunk's lid was open, some of its contents—straightjackets, hoods, handcuffs, chains, rope—strewn around her on the orange shag carpeting.

"Libby."

She yelped and wheeled around, stumbling back against the trunk.

He shook his head, hands on hips. "Well, aren't you a bad little girl."

Chapter Seven

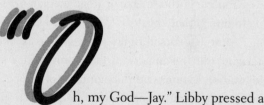

"Oh, my God—Jay." Libby pressed a hand to her heart as if that would keep it from ramming through her chest wall. "I—I didn't realize you were here."

"I guess not." His gaze lit on the kidney-shaped glass coffee table, where the trunk's big iron padlock lay next to his key ring.

Scalding heat flooded Libby's face, which she covered with her hands in sincere, excruciating shame. "God, I'm so sorry. You must think I'm . . . I'm . . ."

He chuckled. "I think you were curious. It's not a felony."

She uncovered her face to find him smiling as if at an absurd little child. He was bare-chested—except for the medicine necklace—and clean-shaven, his hair damp and towel-mussed. His jeans, zipped most of the way up but unbuttoned, rode low on his hips, showing off those corrugated abs and an intriguing little fringe of dark hair.

He stuck his thumbs in his pockets and shrugged. "Hey, it's Vegas. You said it yourself. In this town, you do things you normally wouldn't. And it's not like I've got anything to hide. No harm, no foul."

"Wow, that's . . . that's really understanding. I'd say you were the nicest guy in the world, but, to be honest," she said with a nod toward the unnerving array of restraint gear on the floor, "I *am* beginning to wonder."

"My tools of the trade," he said, crossing to the trunk—a very old, good-sized steamer trunk banded and hinged with iron. "I'm a . . . well, primarily an escape artist, but I do some sleight of hand, a little levitation, that sort of thing." Squatting down, he started collecting some of the smaller items—lock picks, keys, padlocks, hasps, hinges, and various other hardware—and returning them to the trunk.

"You mean you're, like, a stage magician?" she asked as she knelt to help him gather his stuff. "Like David Copperfield or somebody?"

"More like David Blaine," Jay said as he repacked the trunk, "with maybe a little Penn and Teller thrown in. I started as a street magician, like Blaine. Didn't have a lot of success here in the States, so long story short, I ended up overseas. The Far East, mostly—Japan, Hong Kong, Bangkok, Singapore. Eventually I started getting gigs in clubs, and then in bigger venues. I tend to be a little more conceptual than your run-of-the-mill rabbit-out-of-the-hat guy, a little less showbiz. They like me in Asia."

Jay seemed so relaxed and amiable this evening. It was almost as if last night hadn't even happened.

"So, what are you doing in Vegas?" she asked.

"Couple of months ago, I got a call from the Bellagio's vice president of entertainment. One of his scouts saw my act in Tokyo, and they want to give me a one-month trial run, starting in a couple of days. If it works out, I'll have a permanent gig there."

"Seriously?" She was gaping. "The Bellagio? That's *huge*."

"Yeah, I actually thought about turning it down, 'cause I was worried about them trying to mess with my act. You know—homogenize it, dumb it down. But they reassured me on that score, and I started thinking about how refreshing it might be to stop living out of a suitcase and have an actual home and a steady income, maybe save up enough to build a house outside the city somewhere. I've always loved the desert."

"Save up?" She let out a dubious little huff of laughter. "But you just won, like, how many millions at the blackjack table?"

He turned away with this odd look on his face. Instead of answering her, he picked up a small chrome gizmo and handed it to her. "You know what this is?"

She sat down cross-legged to look it over; it was heavy and sinister looking. "My grandfather used to have this nutcracker that scared the wee-wee out of me. You'd stick a nut in, screw the handle down, and it'd get crushed. This reminds me of it, but not quite. What is it?"

"Thumbscrews."

"Seriously."

"It's one of my escapes." He shoved his thumbs in the two little adjacent rings. "Here, tighten that winch."

She did. His thumbs appeared to be snugly captured.

"Is it, like, specially made to open with some trick?" she asked.

"No, it's the real deal." He yanked his hands in illustration; the device held tight. Sometimes I snap on one of those"—he nodded toward the padlock on the table—"but that's really just for show. It's almost impossible to do"—he slid his thumbs free and wriggled in triumph—"this."

"Wait a minute. How'd you . . ."

He grinned boyishly. "That one will go to the grave with me."

"Let me try."

He locked her thumbs into the device. She worked on freeing them for about ten minutes, but all she got for her efforts was two red, swollen thumbs.

"Where'd you learn to do this stuff?" she asked as he unscrewed the winch and set the nasty little thing aside.

"My father was a stage magician." Scooting close to Libby, Jay took her right hand and began massaging it, concentrating on the thumb and using just the right touch; his fingers were long, strong, and wonderfully dexterous. "He liked to teach us kids the tricks of the trade. This was his trunk, as a matter of fact. He gave it to me when he retired."

"How many of you were there? That feels great, by the way."

"Thanks. I'm not really sure, actually. Dad spent most of his time on the road, and he got around—four marriages, plus hot and cold running girlfriends. Between legitimate and illegitimate half siblings, my best guess is maybe eight or ten, but the only one who grew up with me was my big sister. Dad loved showing us the ropes, but he always used to remind us that it was just conjuring, not real magic."

"Did he actually believe in real magic?"

"Oh, yeah." Laying her right hand down gently, Jay lifted the left. "He spent a lot of time studying indigenous mysticism, and there were some forms of it he was convinced were for real."

"And you?" she asked, looking at his medicine necklace.

He frowned thoughtfully at her hand as he stroked and kneaded it. "I'm not sure what I believe, but I can tell you I saw some things in Nepal, things this shaman did, that I'll never be able to explain—and I know a thing or two about illusion and misdirection. Although, like I said, my specialty nowadays is escape."

"How do you get out of that?" she asked, nodding toward the straightjacket. "Is it, like, specially made for magicians?"

"No, it's regulation. Gimmicked straightjackets are pointless, 'cause the real ones are so easy to get out of. You just have to be flexible—and it helps if you can dislocate your shoulders."

She shuddered. "You can do that?"

"Yeah. Want to see?"

"*No.*"

Jay laughed as he reclined on his side, his head propped on a hand, his big body displaying a masculine grace that put Eddie Flynn's ersatz Greek statues to shame. He had a great laugh, deep and easy. It completely transformed him.

"Not to brag, but I've gotten to where I can pretty much outcontort the contortionists," he said. "I work out a lot—mostly yoga and jujitsu. And I do special manual dexterity exercises."

"What else do you escape from?" she asked. "Besides straightjackets and thumbscrews."

"That thing, for one." He nodded toward the trunk. "Steel boxes sometimes. Eighty-five-gallon drums."

"Yikes."

"Mailbags," he continued as he toyed with a pair of chained-together manacles. "Handcuffs, of course, all types. Leg irons, prisoner transport belts, belly chains, rope . . ."

"Rope? That doesn't seem so difficult, compared to those other things."

"It's a lot harder than it seems, if the rope is tied right. In Japan's feudal period, the samurai carried rope that they'd use to capture and incapacitate prisoners, and they studied different tying techniques as part of their martial arts training. It was called *hojojutsu*. The way a prisoner got tied up depended on his rank in society, what type of offense he'd committed, how strong he was, whether he was insane, violent . . ."

"Sounds pretty arcane," Libby said.

"It worked. Still does. There are Japanese cops today who are trained in *hojojutsu* and carry rope on their equipment belts. When I'm in Japan, I sometimes work with a friend, Tanaka-sensei, who's one of their top half-dozen or so master rope artists. He uses the ancient techniques to tie me up, and trust me, I've had moments where I wondered if I was going to get out of it."

"I don't know," she said. "I look at some of the other things you get out of—handcuffs, leg irons, chains—and I just can't imagine rope being that much of a challenge. I mean, it's a lot more pliant than steel and iron, and knots aren't like locks. When I was a kid, I had a fight with my loser cousin Bruce—who's in jail now for sticking up a liquor store, by the way—and he tied me to a tree in my grandmother's backyard with about sixty feet of clothesline. I got out of that."

"Some types of rope come undone more easily than others," Jay said. "And unless Bruce was a Boy Scout, and I'm guessing he wasn't, he probably didn't know how to tie a decent knot."

"They may not have been up to your standards, but there were a couple of dozen of them. I picked at them and wriggled, wriggled and picked. I was pretty flexible. Still am. I'll bet I could get out of anything this Tanaka could come up with."

"Be careful." Jay grinned, and for the first time she noticed a shallow dimple on one cheek that made her feel like she was fourteen and gazing at the most dreamy boy in the senior class. "In this town, when you say 'I'll bet,' people tend to take you seriously."

"I mean to be taken seriously," she said. "If this Tanaka guy was here, I'd let him tie me up just to prove I could get out of it." She'd seen the rope in Jay's box of tricks; it was pretty thin.

"What would you say if I told you Tanaka has been teaching me the art of *hojojutsu* for about the past six years, and that I've gotten pretty good at it, if I do say so myself, and that I'm tempted to tell you to put your money where your mouth is?"

"You want to bet me that I can't get out of your ropes?" she asked. "Are you serious?"

"Not for money. How about if you can escape within, say, half an hour, I have to grant you one wish. If you can't, then you have to grant one for me."

"Anything?" she asked coyly.

He held her gaze. "Anything."

She bit her lip as she considered it, then rose to her feet, and held her arms out. "Where do you want me?"

Jay stood up, rummaged around in the trunk, and came up with a length of twisted hemp rope wrapped into a neat, cylindrical bundle.

"This way." He turned and motioned her to follow him to his bedroom.

"Kneel on that." Jay pointed to his bed, a king-sized, black satin-draped four-poster made of brushed steel, the lofty posts joined by crosspieces as if to support a canopy, although there was none; it would have obstructed the view of the mirrored ceiling. "I need you at the foot of the bed, facing away from me."

Libby looked at the bed, which resembled a satin-lined cage in the dimly lit room, and then at him. She seemed a little uncertain, and he had the impression she wanted to say something, but instead, she crossed to the bed, slid out of her flip-flops, and knelt on the bottom edge. She wore her oversized sweat shorts rolled down to her hips, exposing the dramatically curved small of her back—one of his favorite places on a woman, next to the butt.

"Keep your feet close together and sit on your heels." Jay placed her hands on her thighs, straightened her back, and tilted her chin down so that she was sitting in correct *seiza* position. "I'm going to tie you exactly as I was tied the first time. It took me almost twenty minutes to free myself."

He looped the rope around her neck under her hair, secured it loosely so it wouldn't obstruct her breathing, then wrapped it around both upper arms, firmly but carefully; hemp against bare skin could chafe pretty badly.

Jay had tied people up before—other students of Tanaka-sensei's, mostly, for practice—but it felt different with Libby. She was so utterly soft, yet sharp in some ways that only enhanced her feminine allure. He loved how he could feel her warmth and suppleness, even through her tank top, as he passed the rope around her. He knotted it front and back in a classic diamond pattern, forming a web that framed her breasts while pulling her thin white tank top snugly across them, making it damnably hard to concentrate on proper *hojojutsu* technique.

Libby hadn't said a word, but he noticed she was breathing faster. It was normal to feel exposed and vulnerable when you were being tied up; Jay sweated every time. But he sensed, in addition to the normal apprehension, a hum of awareness that encompassed them both. Her nipples stiffened as he worked, pushing hard against the taut white cotton. A heaviness settled in Jay's groin, unfurling gradually but resolutely.

He cleared his throat, but still his voice came out low and rough. "Put your arms behind you and cross them at the small of your back."

Jay lashed her wrists securely and tied a final knot. "You've got to stand up now." He supported her with both arms around her bound torso, easing her into a standing position on the floor, but still facing the bed.

"Is . . . is that it?" she asked.

"Did I mention that the Japanese used *hojojutsu* for torture as well as for restraint?"

She turned to stare at him unblinkingly.

"Didn't mean to alarm you," Jay said with a devilish smile; he was enjoying this more than he'd thought he would. "Just wanted to put this next bit in historical context." He flung the rope over the high steel crosspiece above the foot of the bed, caught the free end, and pulled. "They'd break a stubborn prisoner by hanging him in a painful position. I understand it was pretty effective."

She gasped when she felt the upward tension in her wrists. "Y-you're not going to . . . to . . ."

"Lift you off the ground? No." Stepping up onto the bed so that he could reach the crosspiece, he wrapped the rope around it several times and tied it off securely. "I'm tethering you like this because it's how it's done with me, both to make the escape a little harder, and so the audience can get a good view of my efforts without me falling on my butt every two seconds. Rope suspension isn't practiced today—except in the bondage scene."

"You mean . . . as a sexual thing?" she asked.

He nodded as he stepped down off the bed. "In Japan, they like to use the old *hojojutsu* techniques for that sort of thing. When it's done for erotic effect, it's called *shibari*."

Jay stood back and inspected his handiwork, then heaped the black satin bed pillows against the headboard, reclined against them, and checked his watch. "Nine twenty-three. Give it your best shot, Libby."

She did. She wriggled and squirmed, as if that might loosen the rope, but of course it didn't. She yanked her arms, clawed at the ropes with her fingers, twisted this way and that, her hair falling across her face as she struggled. She braced her feet on the bed for purchase and writhed, bowing her back in a way that put her breasts on exquisite display. Her tank top was slightly sweat-dampened, and clung to her like skin; he could see the shadows of her nipples right through it.

"Had enough?" he asked, his voice breaking, one knee drawn up to hide his hard-on.

"How long?" she asked.

He checked his watch. "Twenty-eight minutes."

"I have two more minutes." She bucked and thrashed, grunting with one final, pull-out-all-the-stops effort.

"Time." He crawled across the bed to her. "That was some effort. I'm impressed."

"How do you do it?" she asked breathlessly.

"Same way the ninja did in the old days—by dislocating my joints."

She groaned, shook her head. "I should have known."

"I told you it's harder than it seems," he said gently as he smoothed her hair off her face. She was flushed and sweat-sheened and so wildly sexy that it made him throb just looking at her. "You okay?"

She nodded, smiled. "That's one new experience I'd never really thought about till tonight."

"New for me, too," he said.

"You never tied anyone up before?"

"Never a woman."

"Not into *shibari*, huh?"

He hesitated, rose to his feet on the bed, and started untying the complicated knot that secured the tether to the crosspiece. "A friend invited me to a private club in Tokyo once where they do that sort of thing, but it just didn't seem like my kind of scene."

After a moment's silence, she said, "You've thought about it, though." It wasn't a question.

Jay glanced down at her, then away. He'd thought about it fleetingly once or twice, but it had never struck him as really erotic—until now. Of course she knew how it had affected him, watching her writhe in her bonds. How could she not, with his desire so manifestly apparent?

Not knowing what to say to her, he went back to undoing the knot.

"You don't have to do that," she said quietly.

He stilled, looked down at her.

"I owe you a wish," she said.

ay stared at her for a long, breathless moment, as if wondering whether he'd heard her right.

And then he retied the knot he'd just untied.

It seemed to Libby that things started unfolding in slow motion. Kneeling on the bed, Jay brushed the last few stray strands of hair off her face. He ran his fingertip down her cheeks, across her lips.

She closed her eyes, kissed his fingers.

He took her face in his hands and closed his mouth over hers for a long, dizzying kiss. She wanted to take him in her arms and pull him close, but of course she couldn't, trussed up as she was. She whimpered in frustration and longing as she kissed him back.

If you'd told Libby yesterday that being tied up could be an erotic experience, she would have laughed—yet never had anything coaxed her, physically and mentally, to such an acute state of arousal. The friction of the ropes as Jay arranged them just so, the grazing of his hands as he knotted them, his utter absorption in the task, generated a feverish heat that intensified slowly but inexorably. The sensation of being bound like this, helpless and on display, excited something dark and reckless in her. She didn't just want Jay, she *needed* him, right now, like this.

So, maybe it was a little freaky. Good. It would help to remind her that what was happening between them was about physical passion, nothing more. There couldn't be more, because of the subterfuge that had brought them together. This was all they would ever have; it would have to be enough.

Still kneeling in front of her, Jay leaned down to kiss her throat, stroke her bottom. He lifted her legs and wrapped them around him. Libby gasped in alarm to be whisked off the floor with her arms pinioned behind her. "Shh, it's okay," he whispered as he banded one strong arm around her back, the other around her hips to cradle her against him, his erection like a steel rod through his jeans.

Jay bent to rub his cheek against her breasts, murmuring something she couldn't hear. He drew a nipple into his mouth through her tank top and suckled, hard and slow, as he ground against her. Arching her back in pleasure, she caught sight of their reflection in the mirror on the high ceiling. She was mesmerized by the powerful slope of his back as he hunched over her, the rhythmic flex and bulge of his shoulder muscles.

"I want you lying down." Standing on the bed again, he started tugging at the knot on the crosspiece, affording her an eyeball-to-zipper view of the erection straining against his jeans.

He grew still when he noticed the direction of her gaze. Looking up, she saw a raw hunger in his eyes that sucked the breath from her lungs. He looked at her mouth, started to say something, swallowed hard.

Leaning forward as far as her fetters would allow, Libby caught the pull tab of his zipper in her teeth and tugged, drawing it downward; he wore no underwear. Jay widened his stance and closed both fists over the crosspiece. He moaned at the first tentative stroke of her tongue.

"God, Libby. Oh, God," he rasped as she closed her mouth over him. "Take it deep." He pumped into her mouth as she sucked and licked and teased, slowly at first, then faster, his breath ragged, the bed's steel framework creaking with every thrust. "Back off a little. . . ." he panted. "Oh, God, stop. *Stop.*"

Jay swiftly untied the tether, shucked off his jeans, and stepped down. "Kneel like before," he said, supporting her around her middle as he guided her onto the bed. "Now lie facedown. That's right." Grabbing a pillow from the headboard, he tucked it under her hips, then slid a hand between her stomach and the pillow to untie her shorts. He rolled them down in an unhurried way, as if to savor the lingering striptease, then peeled down the white lace thong. With both garments bunched around her thighs, he caressed her upthrust bottom, saying, "I've been wanting to touch you here ever since I met you. God, you're beautiful."

Jay stripped off the garments, leaving her completely exposed from the waist down. The black satin felt cool and slick beneath her, enhancing, along with her bindings, her sense of nakedness, of vulnerability. He caressed her again, this time slipping one hand between her legs while the other massaged her lower back. So inflamed was she that she flinched in shock at his touch. "Easy, easy . . . Open up— that's right," he murmured as he positioned himself between her legs. "Wider."

Craning her neck to look at him over her shoulder, she said, "Um, we're gonna need a . . ."

Jay flicked his right hand; a little plastic packet appeared as if by magic between his fingers. He grinned as he rolled on the latex sheath.

His fingers were agile on her damp, inflamed flesh, his instincts about where to stroke her, and how, uncanny. *I do special manual dexterity exercises.* It showed. Before long she was moaning and thrusting against his hand like some mindless, armless creature. She was right at the brink when he drove into her, igniting a climax so explosive that she screamed with every spasm.

Still inside her, Jay lifted her hips so that she was on her knees, bottom raised, cheek resting on the satin spread. Grasping the ropes that crisscrossed her back, he rocked her against him in an even, measured rhythm. "You're so tight," he gasped as he plunged and withdrew. "So wet. God, you're amazing."

He uncoupled, turned her onto her back with the pillow still under her, and parted her legs. Faceup now, she could see herself in the mirrored ceiling, and it was a startling sight—a neatly tied package from waist to neck, legs widespread, hips offered up in carnal invitation. Leaning over her, Jay studied her closely, parting, exploring, probing.

"What are you doing?" she asked.

"Shh." It was as if he'd never really inspected this part of a woman before, and now he finally had his chance. He took his time about it, as quietly engrossed as if he were a scientist examining some rare species. His hot breath sent shivers coursing through her; his clever, curious touch soon had her squirming in an agony of renewed arousal. When he dipped his head, held her open, and glided his tongue lightly over her damp, engorged flesh, she cried out and bucked, throwing him off.

"Keep still," he said. "And hush."

"I can't."

"I can fix that." Jay picked up the length of rope trailing off her, pulled it down to her right ankle, bound it securely, and tethered it to the bedpost at that corner. He did the same to the left ankle, leaving her spread-eagled from the waist down. Only half-erect now, he rose off the bed and rummaged around in his dresser drawer. "Here we go."

There was so little light in the room that at first Libby wasn't sure what he was bringing back to the bed. When she saw that it was a rolled-up sock and a necktie, and realized what he had in mind, she said, "I'll be quiet. Really."

"I know," he said with a smile as he carefully wedged the sock in her mouth. Ignoring her barely audible, albeit halfhearted, protests, he tied the necktie over the gag to keep it in place and returned his attention to that part of her that seemed to enthrall him so. He pleasured her with his tongue and lips and those deft magician's fingers, bringing her right to the peak, then backing off again and again. Watching herself in the mirror, bound and gagged and utterly at his mercy, made her orgasm, when it came, all the more volcanic.

Kneeling over her as the aftershocks wound down, Jay stroked her face and told her how beautiful she was, how he loved it when she came, how excited it made him. "You good to keep going? Just for a little while? Your arms okay?"

She nodded, rubbing her cheek against his hand.

He crouched over her raised-up hips, dipped his fingertips into the dampness between her legs, and stroked it over his sheathed organ, now fully erect and then some. Crouching over her, his bent legs tucked under hers, arms braced on either side of her head, he took her with hard, steady strokes, every muscle in his upper body standing out in sharp relief.

Jay paused and closed his eyes for a moment as if striving for control, his face blood-flushed and slick with sweat. Sitting back, he untied her left leg and raised it over his shoulder, increasing his penetration so that she shook with every thrust.

He rolled her onto her side, reclining behind her with his head near her feet, and sank deeper still. Libby moaned through her gag at the sense of fullness, of utter and complete possession. He cupped her sex as he rammed into her, growling. They strained together like a single being as the pace quickened, grew erratic. She came first, her helpless cries muffled by the gag. A strangled groan rose from him. He stilled, then jerked against her, shouting with each sharp spasm.

"Oh, God, Libby," he whispered, shaking as the tremors slowly eased. "Oh, my God."

 ou awake?"

Libby opened her eyes to find Jay standing over her bed. He was in sweatpants and a Speed Racer T-shirt, his hair sleep-tousled, a tray of something in his hands.

"Good morning." She rubbed her face, pushed her hair back, squinted at the sun glowing through the sheer curtains. "What time is it?"

"Eight, maybe a little later."

"You slept in," she said through a yawn.

"You're a bad influence." Setting the tray down on one of the night tables flanking the big, ridiculous, round bed, he said, "I ordered coffee and croissants. A couple of bagels, too, and some granola. Some yogurt and fruit, scrambled eggs, bacon . . . I wasn't sure what you liked for breakfast."

"Just coffee, I'm afraid, but thanks anyway." She sat up against the quilted satin headboard, keeping the sheet tucked around her naked breasts—an absurd attempt at modesty, after what they'd done together last night.

Exciting though the ropes had been, it was a huge relief when Jay finally started untying them. She felt light-headed when they came off and she could breathe without feeling their snug embrace. Jay had rubbed her gently to get her circulation back, then pulled her tank top off over her head, turned out the light, and taken her in his arms. He'd kissed her softly, whispering endearments in the dark, and then he'd rolled on top of her and made love to her again, slowly and with aching tenderness.

She almost wished he hadn't.

She'd lain awake long after he drifted off, holding her tucked up snugly against him like something precious that he had to keep safe. What would he say if he knew that she'd contrived to meet him at Eddie Flynn's behest, that she'd been spying on him all this time? What would he think of her for deceiving him as she had, especially in light of what had happened between them?

Sometime during the night, she'd gently extracted herself from his embrace and returned to her room, where she soaked in the whirlpool tub until she was relaxed enough to sleep.

"Oh, honey, look at you." Jay stroked his fingertips over the livid marks braceleting her upper arms. "It didn't look this bad last night."

"I have sensitive skin," she said. "It marks easily."

"Your wrists, too." He pulled the sheet away from her upper body, paling when he saw the pattern of red lines and abrasions on her torso. "This is horrible. I had no idea. Does it hurt?"

She hesitated. "Only when, you know, something rubs up against—"

"I'll be right back." He bounded out of the room, returning half a minute later with a little jar that had Asian writing on it. Sitting next to her, he unscrewed it and scooped up a bit of pleasantly fragrant salve.

"What is that stuff?" she asked as he dabbed it gently on the rope burns encircling her arms.

"An herbal balm, great for this kind of thing. Tanaka-sensei turned me on to it." He shook his head as he glided the balm over the marks crisscrossing her chest; it was instantly soothing. "This happened because of how you struggled to get out of those ropes. That stupid bet of mine. I should have realized you'd end up like this."

"It's not your fault. Trust me, I wouldn't undo anything that happened last night."

He smiled a little sheepishly. "I, uh, hope just 'cause I, you know, got into things the way I did, you don't think all I'm ever gonna want to do is tie you up and use you like some kind of sex slave."

"Oh, darn."

He grinned and smeared a dollop of ointment onto the tip of her nose. "Let me see your back."

She moved down to lie on her side, facing away from him. "I never thought I'd get into anything quite that kinky. I guess it was just"— she shrugged—"Vegas."

"What are you like when you're not in Vegas?" He shifted behind her; she could tell he was reclining on his side also.

Libby didn't know how to answer that, having lived here all her life. "I don't know. Not much different."

"Do you have family back in Buffalo?" he asked as he stroked the balm onto her back.

She closed her eyes, thinking of her father, who'd sacrificed so much for her. Now it was time to return the favor. "Why all the questions?" she asked.

"Just curious, I guess. And maybe because this *is* Vegas, and we've gotten so heavy into . . . you know, the physical stuff without really getting to know each other."

"You don't want to know me," she said bleakly.

Levering himself up on an elbow so he could see her face, he said, "Why would you say that? Of course I want to know you. I want to know everything about you. I want to know what you looked like when you were a kid, how you did in school, whether you had braces, what your hobbies are, whether you dream in color or black and white, how you take your coffee, if you like to cook or not—although it's fine with me if you don't, 'cause I love to cook, and I'm not bad, if you don't mind a menu heavy on the raw fish and seaweed."

"You don't think . . . we might be moving a little fast?" she asked.

"Of course we're moving fast," he said, "but so what? I'm crazy about you, and unless I'm completely delusional, it's not one-sided."

If only it were. Libby shook her head, her stomach contracting into a smoldering little coal. "I just . . . I just think we should maybe keep things . . . you know. Friendly."

"I think we're a couple of steps beyond friendly at this point."

"You know what I'm saying."

"Yeah, but I'm not sure why you're saying it. Have I done something to—"

"*No.*" Rolling onto her back, Libby reached up to caress his prickly jaw. His eyes, filled with morning sunlight, looked incredibly huge and soulful this close up. "No, Jay, you've been nothing but wonderful. It's just that I . . ." *I won your trust and got you to let down your defenses, and now you're involved with a pretender who's just using you, and that pretender is me.*

"I'm falling for you," he said quietly, earnestly. "Hard. You know that, right?"

"Oh, God." She closed her eyes, covered her face with her hands. "You're . . . you're so great. I just wish you hadn't turned out to be so great. How am I gonna do this?"

"Go back to Buffalo, you mean?"

All she could do was shake her head.

"Stay here," he said quietly. "For a while, anyway, till we figure out what's happening between us, if it's . . . you know." He ran a balm-slicked finger down her throat, between her breasts, and over her belly to her navel, which he absently fingered. "If it's what I think it is. What I'm sure it is. It's not every day I get hung up on a woman virtually overnight. There's just something about you . . ."

"I'll bet you say that to all the easy girls."

He grinned wryly. "Even if you hadn't told me so, I'd know this isn't your MO, hooking up with a guy you just met. I'm the exception, which makes me feel like something special is happening here. You must feel it, too."

In a strained voice, because her throat felt as if it was closing up, she said, "I wish I could say yes."

The light dimmed in his eyes. "Oh." He sat up, screwed the lid back on the jar. "Okay."

"Jay." Libby sat up, too, tugging at the sheet to cover herself. "You don't know how much I wish I could tell you . . . what you want to hear, but—"

"No, that's okay," he said without looking at her. "I . . . misread things, I guess. I don't want to make you feel uncomfortable just 'cause . . ."

"Jay," she said, her eyes stinging.

"It's cool. Really." He looked at her, forced a smile. "Really. We'll, uh, we'll try it your way, keep things . . . friendly. Whatever." He rubbed his neck, shook his head. "If that's the only way I can . . . have you, I guess . . ."

"I hate this." The words came out in a choking sob as she curled up, burying her face in the sheet. "God, I *hate* this. How did it ever come to this?"

"Oh, honey, don't," he implored, gathering her in his arms and kissing her hair. "Shh, Libby, don't cry. I'm an ass. You know what? It really is okay. It is. I'm moving too fast for you, expecting you to feel things you haven't had time to feel." A humorless little gust of laughter tickled her hair. "It's just Vegas, right? I keep forgetting that. It's just Vegas."

"In case I forget to tell you later," she mumbled into his shoulder, "I'm really, really, really sorry."

"Shh. Don't be ridiculous."

Jay lowered her onto the bed, brushed the hair off her face, blotted her tearstained cheeks with the sheet. He kissed her damp eyelids, murmuring, "Mm, salty."

That drew a watery little laugh from her.

He smiled into her eyes. "You are one beautiful woman."

"Make love to me," she said, thinking they might not have many more chances, maybe none.

"You sure?" he asked. "You're not just feeling sorry for me."

She shook her head. "It's not about that. I just want you to be inside me, a part of me. I want it to take forever. I want it to never end."

"You know anything about Tantra?" he asked.

"Tantric sex, you mean? Isn't that where people make love for hours and hours?"

He smiled. "Best way I know of to spend a lazy day with a friend."

She chuckled. "I really . . ." *Love you. I really love you, Jay.* That was what she wished she could say. Instead she said, "I really think that's a great idea."

"I'm out of condoms," he said. "You have some in your bag, right?"

"Yeah, it's—" Libby cut herself off, remembering what else was in her handbag.

"It's right here." Leaning over the side of the bed, Jay lifted her green straw shoulder bag from the floor and opened it.

Libby sat up quickly, reaching for it. "Here, I'll find them."

Grinning, Jay turned his back to her as he dug around in the bag. "What, you're allowed to break into my trunk, but I don't get to snoop around in your purse?" There came a rattling sound that made her stomach squeeze tight. "What's . . . ? Oh, it's that necklace you had on yesterday. It's, uh, unique. . . ." He fell silent.

Libby heard the blood roaring in her ears.

He turned, holding up the necklace. "What's this?" he asked, frowning in bafflement at the nine-volt battery dangling from the pendant.

She opened her mouth, closed it.

He looked from her to the necklace and back again. Soberly he asked, "What is it, Libby?"

She couldn't answer him. What could she say? Her stricken expression must have said it all, because he scrutinized the necklace, swiftly homing in on the tiny camera lens housed in the pendant.

He looked at her with a kind of dead shock, as if he couldn't quite believe it.

"J-Jay . . ." she began.

"This can't be what it looks like," he said tightly. "Please tell me this isn't what it looks like."

Tears welled hotly in her eyes. "I'm . . . I'm so sor—"

"God. Libby. Oh, my God." He bolted to his feet, the necklace jangling in his fist, stalked away, spun back. "Who are you working for? Flynn?"

She nodded, her chin wobbling, tears spilling down her cheeks.

"God, I should have known," he growled as he searched through the strings of beads. "That bastard. I should have known he'd pull something like . . . *Shit.*" He found the antenna and yanked it into view. "*Fuck.*" He'd never used language like that in front of her.

"Jay, I—"

"There's a transmitter in here," he said, shaking the necklace. "Where does the video go? Some computer upstairs?"

She nodded miserably, clutching the sheet to her chest. "But—"

"So, he knows . . ."

"Knows what?"

"Or he will as soon as someone takes a look at the video. You were sitting right at the same table, usually pretty close. You must have picked up something."

Jay raked a hand through his hair as he crossed to the window and parted the sheers. "I've got to get out of this town—hell, out of the country. Shit, the Bellagio gig. *Shit.*"

"W-whatever you think he knows, he doesn't," Libby said in a quavering voice. "I just wore that thing because he made me. I never turned it on."

Jay mulled that over in silence, still staring out the window, then gave her a disgusted look over his shoulder. "You *would* say that, to pacify me so I'll stick around till Flynn can get his hands on me."

"You think I'd do that?"

He wheeled on her, roaring, "*Why wouldn't you?* Flynn's paying you to find out how I'm doing it, right? And you've pulled out all the stops to get the job done. You lied to me, fucked me . . . Where did Flynn find you? The Kitty Farm?"

"Please, Jay, what happened between us, you've got to believe that was—"

"I'm done believing you," he said with chilly calm. "I've got to pack and get out of here, but first there's someone I need to see. I shouldn't be more than about fifteen minutes." He flung the necklace back into the bag before turning away. "Be gone when I get back."

Thelma Graham, seated in the first-base spot at the hundred-dollar table, knew something was wrong just from the way Jay was walking through the casino toward the blackjack pit—a little too quickly, his hands curled into fists, jaw set.

When he was about ten yards away, two hulking security guards—the same two who eighty-sixed that hapless card-counting punk the other day—stepped in front of him, real casual like.

Jay grimaced like he'd been half-expecting it.

"Hold my spot," Thelma told the dealer as she grabbed her cane and hauled her rheumatic old ass off the chair. She was wearing her best, most broken-in orthopedic moccasins, the red suede ones with the rubber soles, but still, there was only so fast she could limp along with that damned cane.

The bigger of the two guards, the bald giant Jay liked to call Salmon Head for some reason, said, "Sir, we'd like you to come up-stairs to the office and speak to us."

"I don't think so." Jay strode ahead, muscling between the two guards, who blinked at each other.

"Attaboy, Jay," Thelma muttered as she shuffled toward them.

Salmon Head once again cut Jay off, halting him with a hand on his shoulder. "Sir, we need to see your ID."

"You've got it on file."

"Your real ID." Salmon Head seized Jay's arms while his pal snapped a pair of handcuffs on him from behind.

"You leave him alone, you apes!" Thelma hollered as she hobbled up to them. Raising her cane with both hands, she dealt Salmon Head a couple of good whacks on his broad back, but he seemed to barely notice; it was like hitting a concrete wall. A couple of slot players turned to look.

"Ma'am," Salmon Head said, "this is none of your concern."

"It's okay, Miss Thelma." Jay slipped off the cuffs like they were nothing, and handed them to the nonplussed guard. "You can tell Flynn my attorney will be in touch," he said as he turned away.

Salmon Head nodded to his cohort, who grabbed Jay's arms from behind. He slammed a massive fist into Jay's stomach, doubling him over, then hauled back again and punched him across the face. Jay's head whipped to the side; his legs buckled.

"You sons of bitches!" Thelma screamed, battering the guards with her cane. "I'm a witness! I won't rest till I see your sorry asses in jail!"

"Go back to your gaming, folks," Salmon Head announced as he and the other guard dragged Jay toward a door marked Authorized Personnel Only. "There's nothing to see here."

Chapter Ten

Jay roused to find himself sitting in a searingly bright, austere little room, his left cheek throbbing like a son of a bitch. His arms were drawn behind him over the back of the metal chair on which he sat, immobilized, as was the rest of his body right down to his feet, by what looked to be an entire roll of duct tape.

Duct tape . . . he mused blearily as he tested his bonds. *That'd be a good escape, if I can figure out how to do it. Let an audience member do the taping. . . .*

"He's awake," someone said; there came the click of a lighter, a whiff of mentholated smoke. Jay turned toward the familiar voice, hitching in his breath at a stab of pain in his lower chest. He'd cracked a rib or two.

Three men came to stand in front of him: Eddie Flynn, Bull Toomey, and . . .

"*Archie?*" Jay said.

"Jay Douglas," Flynn said, "meet Archibald McGuffin of McGuffin Investigations."

"Hey, Trump," said Archie, squinting through a haze of smoke. "How you feeling, pal?"

"Not bad, considering."

"Really? 'Cause you look like shit." Archie pointed to a big mirror on the wall to the left—a one-way mirror, no doubt—which confirmed his assessment. The left side of Jay's face from hairline to jaw was swollen and discolored, the cheekbone an open gash.

Archie shook his head. "Shame what they did to you. I keep tellin' Eddie he needs to hire Homo sapiens, but he doesn't listen to me."

"My boys only do what has to be done," Flynn said.

"Yeah, Eddie," Archie said, "but what are you gonna tell Metro when they come down here and find him like this?"

"Let me worry about that."

Jay glanced at the cameras in the corners, all of which were covered with cloths. "He's not planning to call the cops, Archie. He's gonna take care of me himself. Or he'll delegate the job so he doesn't ruin his manicure."

Archie cast a quizzical look toward Flynn, who pretended he didn't notice. "We've been on to you from the beginning, Douglas—or whatever your name is. We just didn't have proof till now." Flynn stepped aside to reveal an open laptop on a table behind him. "How do I do this, again?" he asked Bull Toomey.

"I got it." Archie pushed a couple of buttons, and a video started running. It was a close-up color image of a hand, Jay's hand, holding two cards; the sound track was a drone of voices and slot machine racket. From the angle of the shot, it was clear that it had been taken by one of his fellow players. Three guesses which one.

In the video, Jay tucked the cards under his stack of blue chips, indicating that he was standing. A moment later, he slid them out, took another look, and slid them back.

"That's it," Archie said as he punched a button to stop the video, cigarette ash raining onto the keyboard. "I must say, Douglas, I've never seen a slicker muck. You are one talented SOB, 'cause one-handed mucks aren't easy—and you've got a set on you, too, my friend, to brazen out a play like that. Gutsy but subtle. I musta pored over this video eight or ten times before I got suspicious about this particular move, and the only reason I did is 'cause it's so out of character for you to double-check your cards like that. That's something squares do, not experienced high rollers. So I had this techno geek on my staff start dicking around with the video—slowing it down, zooming in real tight, pausing it and analyzing every nanosecond. Finally we saw what you were doing."

"I'm still not seeing it," Flynn said.

Toomey said, "He's been dealt two cards, boss. One of 'em's bad, but he's got a ten he chopped out of play earlier tucked away under his shirt or in his pants. He switches the chopped card for the bad card, and suddenly he's got a twenty instead of whatever crap hand he had before."

"Sounds simple, but it takes real sleight of hand to pull it off." Archie diddled with the laptop's touch pad, and the video started again, in super slo-mo this time. Pointing with the hand that held the cigarette, he said, "Here he's tucking the cards under the chips, making sure the bad card is on top—right, Douglas?"

Jay said, "If you're trying to scam a confession out of me, you're gonna have a long wait."

Pointing, Archie said, "Okay, here he's reaching out to recheck his cards. You can't see it, but he's got the chopped ten tucked under his palm. He slides the ten under the two cards, palms the bad one from the top, and tucks it away. Bing, bang, boom, he's richer by six or eight grand."

"Eight on that hand," Jay said with a certain mean-spirited satis-faction.

Flynn was squinting at the screen. "How could you see what he was doing? The whole thing took what—five seconds?"

"Not quite four," Archie said. "It wasn't till the slo-mo and all that I saw it. Check it out." He paused the image and pointed. "If you look hard, you can see him sliding the chopped ten under the other two cards. See?"

"No."

Jay did. *Damn*.

"Only about an eighth of an inch of card is showing," Archie said, "right here—just for a fraction of a second, but it's enough to convict. God bless modern technology."

"Is that all you found?" Toomey asked. "Just the one muck?"

Archie shook his head as he stubbed out his cigarette. "Naw, once I knew what to look for, I came up with another one, plus a bet he pinched when he realized his hand was a loser. A couple other things. Oh, he used the old insurance play once to get his held-out cards back into the deck before it was taken away and inspected."

"The insurance play?" Toomey said. "He'd need a partner for that one."

Archie said, "Yeah, there were a couple of plays where he would have needed somebody to distract the dealer, hide what he was doing, that kind of thing."

Flynn turned to Jay. "Who are you working with?"

"Nobody. I fly solo."

"Tell us now, and Bull will go easy on you when the time comes," Flynn said. "Hold back, and, well, all I can say is there's a hell of a lot of desert out there, and Bull's a good man with a shovel."

"Must come in handy for cleaning up after your bullshit," Jay said.

Flynn nodded to Toomey, who calmly withdrew a set of brass knuckles from his coat pocket, shoved them on, and whipped them across Jay's face. Jay shook it off as best he could, but he'd have a hell of a shiner tomorrow to go with the rest of it.

"That's not a bad right cross," Jay told Toomey. "Why don't you take this duct tape off, and we'll see if you've got the balls to try it on a guy who can hit back."

Toomey answered with that sneer that every gutless bully from here to Katmandu seemed to know.

"Bull can do a lot worse to you than that," Flynn warned. "Tell us who you're working with."

"Why don't you ask your little redheaded Mata Hari?" Jay said. "If anyone can figure it out, she can. She'll do whatever it takes, and then some. Really fits in around here."

"You on to her?" Toomey looked dismayed.

"Who are you talking about?" Archie asked.

"Libby Thatcher," Jay said. "The woman who took that video."

"*I* took that video," Archie said. "You talking about that Libby chick that's been hanging around the blackjack pit? Flynn, what the hell? You hire some girl as a backup for me, and you don't even have the courtesy to tell me?"

"*You* took that video?" Jay asked.

Archie tapped his gold dice tie clip, then tugged at a cord running from the clip inside his shirt.

Flynn said, "Don't get your boxers in a twist, McGuffin. Toomey thought it'd be a good idea to put Liz on the job, but she was a complete waste of time. The boys in the Nerve Center waited all day yesterday for a feed from her Minicam. Nothing. Nada."

Jay stared at Flynn, thinking, *Oh, my God, she was telling the truth. She never even turned it on.*

Archie said, "You ever pull a stunt like that again, Eddie, hiring another private dick for one of my cases, I'll not only stop taking your jobs, I'll make sure no one else takes them, either."

"It wasn't like that," Flynn said. "She's not a pro, and I wasn't even paying her. Her old man's going bankrupt, and he's got a bum ticker. I was just gonna buy his business, that's all."

Her old man? Jay closed his eyes, remembering the things he'd said to Libby earlier. *You lied to me, fucked me . . . Where did Flynn find you? The Kitty Farm?* He sighed and shook his head, feeling like the Bastard's Bastard and wondering how this day could get any worse.

"*I've* got a deal for you," Archie told Jay. "Tell us who your partner is, and I'll see to it you go straight to Metro and bypass the ass-kicking Bull's fixing to give you. You'll still get sent up for cheating the casino, but you'll do it in one piece. I'll drive you down to the station house myself."

"The hell you will," Flynn said.

"How you gonna stop me?" Archie asked. "Sic Bull on me? Him and me go way back in this town, Eddie. I know stuff Bull probably wishes I didn't, and vice versa. Guys in our position don't go making trouble for each other. *Capice?*"

Flynn looked at Bull, who stood with his arms crossed, ruminating on the floor tiles.

"What is this," Jay asked, "the Vegas version of good cop, bad cop?"

"You've got my word I'll be your personal escort out of here if you talk," McGuffin told him. "Otherwise, I'm gonna have to just walk away and"—he glanced at Toomey—"let the brass knuckles fall where they may. It's a good offer. You should take it."

"Can't do it, Archie," Jay said. "Thanks, anyway."

"Your choice, my friend," Archie said with a heavy sigh. "But don't expect me to stick around and watch Bull go to work on you. I've seen what he can do to a fella when he's got a bug up his ass, and it's nothing I ever care to see again."

Libby was good and winded by the time she'd sprinted through the casino and upstairs to the back hallway in the Gold Dust's security area. She tried to open the door marked PRIVATE, but it was locked. She rammed a fist against it and was about to yell for someone to let her in when she realized that would draw the security guards patrolling the nearby hallways. Slumping against the wall, hands on knees, she replayed the last few minutes in her mind as she tried to figure out her best course of action.

After Jay left, she'd thrown on a T-shirt and jeans while still wiping away tears, and been halfway out the door of his suite when the phone started ringing. It rang five times while she stood there, wondering whether to answer it, then it stopped. She left the apartment and had just closed the door behind her when it started ringing again. Thinking it might be Jay himself wanting to hear her side of things, she dropped the suitcase, fumbled in her bag for the key card, and made it back inside just as the fifth ring began. "Hel—"

"Libby? Oh, praise the Lord. It's Thelma. They've got Jay."

"What?"

"They've got him," Thelma said, a frantic edge to her voice. "Those security goons grabbed him a couple of minutes ago. One of 'em punched his lights out, and then—"

"*What?*"

"—they dragged him upstairs, and they're gonna arrest him for cheating, and God knows what else they'll do to him, and I've got these damned useless legs. I didn't know who else to turn to. I know you've been stayin' with him."

"Maybe we should go ahead and call the police ourselves," Libby said. "I mean, if they're hurting him, that's a crime, no matter what he may have done. It's battery."

"Eddie Flynn has way too many cops on his payroll," Thelma said. "No way they'd come down here just 'cause he's roughin' up some blackjack cheat. That's why I was hopin' there was something you could do."

"I can get up there, where they took him." Cradling the phone in the crook of her neck, Libby slung her bag bandolier-style across her chest so it wouldn't fall off when she ran, and rooted around in it for her Gold Dust ID badge.

"Please hurry," Thelma implored in a damp, querulous voice that sounded very unlike her. "I'm so afraid for him, and he means so much to me."

Even preoccupied as she was, Libby couldn't help wondering, as she draped the badge around her neck, how Thelma and Jay could have managed to bond so tightly in less than a week.

"He's my grandson," Thelma said.

Libby stood stock-still, her jaw hanging open, while she contemplated this revelation, and how it fit in with all the rest of it. "So . . . so the two of you . . . you've been . . ."

"Taking the Gold Dust for everything we can get, which I'll explain, I promise. Right now I just need you to find him and do whatever you can to get him away from those bastards upstairs. That Toomey fella, he's only happy when he's got his fists bloody. I've known men like that—my husband was like that, and I've still got the scars to prove it. I'm beggin' you, *please* get Jay away from him."

"I will," Libby had promised.

But how? she wondered as she stood outside Eddie Flynn's little interrogation suite, wishing to God she knew what was going on in there. As if in response, the door swung open, slamming into her, and a man walked out. She grabbed the door before it could close, glancing at the man's back as he retreated down the hall. *Archie?*

Of course. *McGuffin Investigations . . . Been on the case for the past couple of days, watching this guy like a hawk down there in the pit. . . .*

Slipping inside the dark anteroom, Libby crossed to the one-way mirror. "Jay . . . oh, my God," she whispered when she saw him through the tinted glass, what they'd done to him. Toomey and Flynn were there, Toomey leaning against a table and toying idly with something that Libby recognized, with a clutch of nausea, as brass knuckles.

She tried the doorknob gently, just to see whether it was locked; it was.

"I shoulda known better than to trust that job to a broad," Flynn was saying, his voice rendered a little tinny by the audio feed. "They're not suited for work like that. Too sentimental, always getting emotionally involved. Got sweet on the guy she was supposed to be squeezing for info, and that was all she wrote. Women." He shook his head disgustedly. "If I never see that worthless bitch again, it'll be too soon."

Right back at ya, Eddie. There went the notion of talking herself into that room—as if it would even help, seeing as she had yet to come up with a plan for getting Jay out of there.

Eddie had told her he'd hand Jay over to the police if he nabbed him for cheating. He'd also told her Jay wouldn't be hurt. *Trust me, the last thing I want is for the cops to show up here and find the perp they came after all beat up.* Yet here was Jay, battered and duct-taped to a chair. Eddie clearly had no intention of "calling in Metro." God knew how this might end for Jay if Eddie Flynn had his way. Eddie didn't have the compunctions most people did, because he'd never had to answer for his misdeeds.

Accountability. Eddie didn't even know what that word meant.

Yes, but there are ways to make people accountable, Libby thought as she pulled Eddie's ugly Minicam necklace out of her shoulder bag, fastened it around her neck, and turned it on. She made sure her cell phone was accessible in case things turned ugly; surely, if she called 911 and told them someone's life was in danger, they'd respond.

Flynn was telling Jay he had "one last chance."

"Tell me who you've been partnered up with, and Bull just works you over a little and lets you go. But if you insist on being stubborn . . ." He shrugged in an I-can't-be-responsible way. "Bull, he has problems relating to stubborn people. Don't you, Bull?"

"I do."

"So I suggest you smarten up and talk," Flynn said.

"I'll be happy to talk," Jay said. "Just not about my partner, 'cause like I said, I work alone. How about I tell you why I went after the Gold Dust in the first place? Wouldn't you like to know that?"

"Greed—what else?"

"If it was just greed," Jay said, "I could have picked any casino—and it probably would have been smarter to move around, use disguises. . . . But being a family kind of guy, I figured why not give the business to my brother-in-law?"

Flynn froze. Toomey looked up from fiddling with the brass knuckles.

Libby sank into the leather armchair facing the window.

"Or should I say, ex-brother-in-law," Jay said. "I'm Cassandra's half brother."

"You're shitting me."

"As God is my witness."

Flynn snapped his fingers the way people do when they're trying to remember something. "Jacob . . . ? Jason . . . ?"

"Jason. Most people call me Jay, just like most people call Cassandra Cassie—but the two of us never used nicknames with each other for some reason. Douglas is actually my middle name. My last name's Graham, like Cassie's."

And Thelma's, Libby thought. "Jay Graham," she said softly, listening to the sound of it. "Jason Douglas Graham."

"Jason, yeah, the kid brother . . ." Flynn stared at Jay as if he'd never seen him before. "You're, like, what—some kinda hotshot sleight-of-hand artist out in the Orient somewhere."

"Among other things," Jay said.

"Sleight of hand?" Toomey said. "Figures."

"Jeez," Flynn said, "Cassie used to yammer on about you nonstop."

"We've always been close. So you can imagine how I felt when she called me and told me she'd just gotten hitched to some smooth-talking big shot at the Viva Las Vegas Wedding Chapel, with Elvis officiating."

"It was the Blue Hawaii package," Flynn said, "and for your information it was beautiful. They had smoke effects, hula girls . . . Cassie loved it."

"How'd she feel about the prenup that said she'd go away empty-handed if the marriage lasted less than five years?"

Libby sat forward in the chair, leather squeaking.

Flynn hitched his shoulders and looked away. "She signed it."

"'Cause she had no choice," Jay said, his eyes glinting, a vein rising on his forehead. "Funny how it was just two weeks before your fifth anniversary that you gave Cassandra her walking papers. So even though you chased everything in fishnets all through your marriage, and even though she was five months pregnant with twins, she got nothing."

Flynn held his hands up, as if warding off Jay's mounting wrath. "Hey, you got a problem with the terms of the divorce, blame the judge that came up with them."

"You mean Judge Willard Walsh, who actually believed you—or pretended to—when you claimed that Cassandra's twins weren't fathered by you? And who was somehow able, right after your divorce was finalized, to procure a brand-new silver Ferrari Spider? Wonder what a thing like that goes for. Oh, hey, you should know, Eddie. Don't you own a Ferrari dealership?"

Flynn, who'd grown increasingly subdued, just folded his arms and looked away with a smirk—but Libby could see his mind whirring. She stood and came up to the window, murmuring, "How does it feel to twist in the wind, Eddie?"

"Two hundred fifty thousand dollars," Jay said. "That's what the 360 Spider goes for. Strange that a judge who was making a hundred thirty grand a year should be able to afford a car like that. He must have had very favorable terms—like maybe free."

"I wouldn't know," Flynn said.

"Really?" Jay said. "'Cause that Spider came from a dealership you own in Scottsville, Arizona."

"You don't know that."

"I do." Jay smiled grimly. "And I can prove it."

Flynn rolled his eyes. "All right. Fine. You know what? That happens to be the way things are done in this town, okay? Vegas . . . it's not like Podunk, where everything's on the up-and-up or Grandpa has a heart attack. Here, things are a little looser, a little more . . . old school. You want something, you gotta give something. It's the way of the world."

"Eddie, you've just made my day." Libby pulled her cell phone out of her bag as she turned and left the room. But it wasn't 911 she dialed. It was 411.

Chapter Eleven

"The way of the world?" Jay said, a red-hot tide of anger washing over him. "Judge Walsh gets a quarter-million-dollar car, you've got your eight-million-dollar penthouse, plus about seventy million in other assets, and my sister—the mother of your children—gets food stamps." Every time Jay talked to Cassandra, she was a little more exhausted, a little more hopeless. It killed him inside to see her that way.

"You're laying it on pretty thick," Flynn snorted. "Food stamps?"

"You want to know how she lives? What you've reduced her to—her and your sons?" Jay described it for him: the trailer park, the hand-me-downs, the two roadside dumps Cassandra waitressed in. The joint she'd started stripping in, just to support those kids, before Jay came back from Japan and got her out of there.

Once or twice, he thought he was starting to get through to Flynn, but whenever that happened, Toomey would make some crack about Jay saying anything to get out of a beating, and he'd lose whatever ground he'd gained.

"So you figured you'd get revenge by stealing from me?" Flynn asked.

"You stole from Cassandra when you cheated her out of a divorce settlement. I figured if you wouldn't part with her fair share willingly, I'd part with it for you. I read a book on blackjack, and then I found an old retired card trick man who taught me a few things that weren't in the book. Then I came here and . . ." Jay shrugged as best he could, given the duct tape.

"And wasted a lot of time and effort," Flynn said, "'cause you're not getting a cent of that money now."

"What do you say, boss?" Toomey asked as he reached under the table for something on the floor. "How about I start with his fingers so he can't do that sleight-of-hand stuff no more?"

It was a baseball bat Toomey came up with. He slapped it against his palm, smiling malevolently.

Be cool, Jay told himself as he broke out in a cold sweat. *Don't show your fear. Don't give these bastards the satisfaction.*

"Showtime," Flynn said as he retrieved one of those jumbo-sized cigars from inside his suit coat. "I've got the best seat in the house on the other side of that mirror," he told Jay as he reached for the door-knob. "This is one performance I wouldn't miss for the world."

No sooner had he turned the knob than the door flew open, pushed by Libby, who barged into the room with a cell phone in her outstretched hand. Jay was too flummoxed by her sudden appearance to do anything but gape.

"It's for you, Eddie," she said.

"What . . . ?" he asked as he automatically took the phone. "Who . . . ?"

"It's Willard Walsh—the family court judge?" In a conspiratorial whisper, she added, "I think he's a little ticked off."

Flynn put the phone to his ear. "Hello?" he said, his dazed expression morphing into panic as he listened to Walsh's furious squawking. "What? No, Willard, of course I haven't . . . I won't. Why would I?"

Crouching next to Jay, Libby lightly stroked his left cheek, wincing at all the bruising and the open wound. Her concern, given what had transpired between them that morning, touched him deeply. "You okay?" she asked softly.

He nodded, glanced at Flynn. "What's going on?"

"Willard!" Flynn yelled into the phone. "Willard, listen to me. I'll take care of it, I swear. Don't do anything till I . . . Willard? Willard?" He shook the phone, listened again. "Shit."

Standing, Libby said, "I gather he said what he said to me—after I told him I can prove he took a Ferrari in exchange for favorable divorce terms. He said that he's in tight with the Nevada Gaming Commission, and if it gets out about the Ferrari, he'll make sure the Gold Dust gets shut down within the week—permanently—and that no one in this town ever does business with you again."

"Who's gonna talk about it?" Flynn asked. "You? Him?" He nodded toward Jay.

"They can't talk if there's six feet of desert on top of them," Toomey observed.

"We don't have to. This will do the talking for us." Libby withdrew a laser disc from her bag and loaded it into the laptop's DVD player. "Eddie, you remember telling me about that laptop in the Nerve Center, the one that records the transmission from this"—she indicated the minicam necklace she was wearing—"on the hard drive and a DVD? This is that DVD." She pressed PLAY.

The image that filled the screen was that of the spartan little interrogation room as viewed from the other side of the one-way mirror:

Jay duct-taped to the chair, his face ravaged, Flynn standing over him, Toomey fiddling with the brass knuckles. "I'll give you one last chance," Flynn was saying. "Tell me who you've been partnered up with, and Bull just works you over a little and lets you go. But if you insist on being stubborn . . ."

She fast-forwarded to Jay telling Flynn that he could prove Judge Walsh's silver Spider came from Flynn's Scottsville dealership, and Flynn rolling his eyes. "All right. Fine. You know what? That happens to be the way things are done in this town, okay? Vegas . . . it's not like Podunk, where everything's on the up-and-up. . . ."

"You filmed me," Flynn said with a kind of stunned rage, his gaze lighting on the necklace. "With my own Minicam. You sneaky, scheming little bitch."

"How does it feel to be on the other side of the lens?" she asked.

"Not to worry, boss." Toomey stopped the video, took out the DVD, dropped it onto the floor, and shattered it with a single whack of his baseball bat.

No! Jay thought.

"Way to go, Bull." Flynn whooped and shot a fist. "Got any more clever little surprises?" he asked Libby.

"Actually, yes. I took the laptop out of the Nerve Center—the laptop with that video on its hard drive?—and gave it to someone who, even as we speak, is burning a whole stack of DVDs. This person has been instructed to hand deliver one disk each to the news producers of all four Vegas TV network affiliates this afternoon if Jay and I don't show up for the noon fountain show at the Bellagio."

Now it was Jay's turn to crow. "Clever enough for you, Flynn?"

Flynn looked to Toomey, who swore under his breath and shook his head.

Libby said, "Here's the deal, Eddie. First, you buy my father's restaurant for half a million within one week. Second, you let Jay go—with his winnings—and never give him another second of trouble, whether he's living here in Vegas or halfway around the world."

Flynn said, "I, uh, I can live with that on the condition that he never sets foot in my casino again."

"This isn't a negotiation, Eddie," Libby said. "You can accept my terms, or you can make a bowl of popcorn and watch yourself on the six o'clock news. Your choice."

"The hell with them, boss," Toomey said. "Let's go on down to the Flamingo and get us a couple of stiff ones, pick us up a couple of broads."

Flynn turned away with a poleaxed expression. Pausing in the doorway, he looked over his shoulder at Libby and said, "Who knew you could be such a stone bitch?"

"What can I say, Eddie? I guess you bring out that side of me."

"Ciao, baby," Jay said as the two men left, slamming the door on their way out.

"Let's get you out of this." Libby set about unwinding the duct tape, starting with Jay's arms so he could help with the task.

"Who'd you give the laptop to?" he asked.

"Your grandmother."

"Ah, yes," he said as he peeled the tape from around his chest. "I should have known it was Miss Thelma who called in the cavalry. So, who's burning those DVDs? Thelma doesn't have a clue about computers."

"Nobody's burning any DVDs. I made that part up."

Jay laughed, clutching his middle to lessen the pain. "God, I love you, Libby."

She looked up from untaping his feet.

"I do," he said. "I don't expect you to feel the same way—"

"I do, though."

"You do?"

She smiled into his eyes. "And I've got a feeling it's not just Vegas."

"Come here." Jay took her face in his hands and kissed her—not deeply, because his jaw was bruised, but lingeringly, and with feeling.

When they'd gotten the last of the tape peeled away, Jay rose stiffly, gripping the chair for support like an old man. "Libby . . . honey. I'm really sorry about . . . before. What I said—the Kitty Farm and all that."

"*You're* apologizing to *me*? I completely deceived you."

"Trust me, saving me from Toomey and his baseball bat more than made up for it." With a grin, he said, "*I* never knew you could be such a stone bitch, either. It was kind of a turn-on."

"Yeah? Gee, maybe I should have left you taped up for a little while, huh? Had my bitchy way with you."

"That actually might not have been such a bad idea, if I was in a little better shape. Got a cracked rib in here somewhere."

"You broke a rib?" She touched his middle very tenderly, wincing. "Oh, my God. You poor thing." Her gaze lit on the bulge under his sweatpants. "Um . . ."

"It's 'cause of what you said about having your bitchy way with me. I'll never be able to walk past the duct tape aisle in the hardware store again without getting aroused."

"Same thing'll happen to me when I walk past the aisle with the rope," she said.

"Maybe we should think about doing our hardware shopping together from now on."

"No do-it-yourself projects for you till you're all better," she said. "At least, no major ones."

"I love having you fuss over me. I love"—Jay stroked her hair, her face—"everything about you. Except your taste in necklaces." Reaching around her neck, he unclasped the butt-ugly Minicam necklace and tossed it onto the table.

"Well, I love everything about you, *including* your taste in neck-laces." She pulled his medicine necklace out from under his T-shirt, rubbing her thumb over the auspicious little amulets. "For a while, I was actually thinking this might, you know, be responsible for your winning streak. That it could actually bring you—what was it, good blessings and . . . ?"

"Blessings and good fortune. Of course it does." He smiled as he gathered her into his arms, whispering against her lips, "It brought me you, didn't it?"

RITA award–winning novelist Patricia Ryan is the author of eighteen novels that have been critically acclaimed and published in more than twenty foreign countries. In addition to romances, she writes the Gilded Age historical mystery series as P. B. Ryan.

Brushstrokes

Toni Blake

To Michelle, for the inspiration,
to Lori, for the encouragement,
and to LuAnn, for a nudge
in the right direction

Chapter One

t was a bad day to be lounging in the bathtub.

It was an even worse day to be lusting over a man she didn't know.

It was Mia Drake's thirtieth birthday.

Lifting a bubble-covered foot from the water, she used her toes to twist the faucet off. She should be back in New York celebrating with her friends, she thought. She should be hitting her usual Lower East Side haunts, badgering the manager of her favorite Orchard Street gallery to look at her work. But instead she found herself in tiny Dawes, South Carolina, soaking in her great-aunt Clara's old claw-foot tub, pretending a few bubbles and the scent of an aromatherapy candle would make everything better. And if that wasn't bad enough, she was thinking dirty thoughts about Rick Rose, the brawny dark-haired bar owner she'd seen in town.

She lay her head back on the edge of the tub, indulging fully in the simple but effective fantasy.

The bathroom door opens and she looks up. It's him—all strong, sexy six feet three inches of him. Neither seems surprised to see the other; his eyes burn with a knowing, confident desire that makes her shiver despite the warm water. His gaze lands on her bare breasts, the nipples jutting through a thin film of suds, and she feels his look everywhere. Her breasts turn heavy, needy, beneath his scrutiny.

"Am I intruding?"

"No," she replies, her voice as smooth as melting butter. "In fact, I was just thinking about you, wanting you. Come into the tub."

He strips off his clothes with swift, sure movements, revealing a muscular chest, a great butt, and an incredible erection that makes her feel empty and achy between her thighs. She wants to wrap her hand around his length, caress him. No, more than that. She needs him to fill her.

Sadly, she'd never even met the man; she'd just seen him around—standing outside his bar chatting with locals, driving his Dodge Ram four-by-four up Main Street, eating in the local diner, and once shopping in the grocery store when she'd stopped to get some cherry tomatoes for a salad Aunt Clara was making. The mere sight of his face—serious gray eyes and commanding jawline—had delivered the same sensations she was experiencing now. She'd had a hell of a time selecting her tomatoes while imagining those strong arms closing around her, those big hands touching her. He struck her as a bit gruff—it was something in his eyes, something in his voice on the few occasions she'd heard him speak—but that didn't seem to lessen the effect he had on her. She'd lingered over the tomatoes until he'd collected a few ears of corn and an onion, then gone on his way.

After he eases into the water behind her, she leans back against his chest. His hands come around to cup her wet breasts as his hot arousal presses into the center of her bottom, making her rub against him. Turning her head, she draws him down into a delicious tongue kiss that adds to their indelible heat. As he caresses her sensitive breasts, squeezing her taut nipples ever so slightly between his fingers, his raspy voice comes as a whisper near her ear. "Ride me."

Of course, there were worse things than coddling herself with a little birthday fantasy, she decided as her face warmed with the impact of it. And certainly worse things than living with Aunt Clara for a while, until she got back on her feet. The truth was, if she'd stayed in New York, she didn't know where she'd be right now, but it probably wouldn't really have equated to that fun, buzzing-about-the-city birthday she'd just envisioned. Five out-of-work artists sharing a loft didn't add up to a rent payment, let alone a birthday party. She was just thankful Aunt Clara had always been so welcoming. It had been a huge comfort to have someplace to go where she wouldn't be a burden. When Aunt Clara's last letter had come, bearing the line, "I can't stand to think of you living in poverty, and I would love having some company around this old place," Mia had done the only practical thing. She'd packed her easels and canvases and brushes into the old family station wagon she'd never gotten rid of, and she'd headed south for the winter.

Now it was almost spring, though, and what had she done for herself? Painted a lot, yes. Found a way to make some money, no. And despite Aunt Clara's endless love and generosity, the guilt of freeloading weighed on Mia. She had to earn her keep and earn it soon. But . . . not right this minute, she consoled herself. It was her birthday, after all. And there was an imaginary man in her bathtub who needed to be ridden.

Turning, she straddles him in the water. His hands find her breasts again, and she glances down to see his fingers capturing the mounds of flesh, a few remnants of white bubbles peeking through. His slow, firm massage turns her breath thready as she looks into his eyes. They meet hers; they own her. Gripping the white porcelain with both fists, she leisurely slides herself up and down the column of stone between his legs. They both let out light moans of pleasure, but he's impatient, planting his hands on her hips, positioning her for entry, murmuring one demanding word: "Now." Then he pushes her down.

A knock came on the door and Mia flinched. For a fraction of a second, she actually expected Rick Rose to be on the other side. But then Aunt Clara's soprano tone echoed through the old wood. "Mia? Are you in there?"

Inside, she groaned. *Fantasy killer.*

"Yes," she said. "I'm taking a bath."

"Well, have a good, relaxing soak, dear. I simply wanted to let you know I'm home. When you're done, we'll have a nice birthday lunch on the back patio and I'll tell you what I found out in town today."

Mia looked toward the door. Her imaginary lover wasn't the only one in this tub who was impatient. Not that she suspected her aunt really had anything *big* to tell her, because what could Aunt Clara have discovered in town that would interest Mia, someone who didn't even belong here? "You can't tell me now?"

"You just take your time and enjoy your bath."

Sure, easy for Aunt Clara to say. She hadn't had a totally splendid tub fantasy doused with a huge splash of cold water just when things had gotten really hot. Besides, she could hear her aunt puttering around the house now, humming while she worked on lunch. There was no hope of sinking back into her sexy vision at this point.

With a sigh, she used her toes to flip the handle that opened the drain, then stood and reached for a towel. So long, imaginary birthday sex.

Drying off, Mia sighed. Sad when it came to this—thriving on fantasies. Clearly, it had been too long since she'd had a *real* man.

Ten minutes later, after changing into jeans and a T-shirt, she exited through the back door to find Aunt Clara waiting at a white wrought-iron patio table. She'd made dainty finger sandwiches of ham salad, as well as deviled eggs and baked beans, all served on old-fashioned plates and in bowls with roses circling the rims. Cups of tea had been poured, and a small birthday cake sat perched on an antique pedestal at the table's center. The bright sun of the early March day only added to the warmth that filled Mia. It had been a while since anyone had done anything this special for her birthday.

She smiled lovingly. "Aunt Clara, you're too good to me. This looks wonderful."

The old woman's face wrinkled around her grin, and eyes still as blue as the ocean shone beneath silvery hair, pulled back into a bun. "Now, you know I like having someone to do nice things for. It's been too long since I've had a proper tea party, and this seemed the perfect occasion."

As the two women sat and enjoyed the lovely lunch, Mia's thoughts still lingered over how much she appreciated Aunt Clara's presence in her life. She'd lost her parents in a car accident seven years ago, and since then, her mother's aunt had been her touchstone. They'd not known each other well while Mia was growing up— Aunt Clara and her now-departed husband, Frank, had lived down here in the Carolinas, "in a little town near the ocean," her mother used to say, and Mia's family had resided in upstate New York. Yet when the devastation of her parents' deaths had driven her to drop out of grad school and head to the city in reckless pursuit of her dream to be an artist, Aunt Clara had been there for her, with phone calls and letters and care packages, and plane tickets to South Carolina for a week every summer.

Sometimes Mia wondered if she'd been trying to hide by going to New York, by becoming one of the thousands of struggling artists who practically blended into the city landscape. Now she couldn't help but wonder if she was hiding *here*, in the proverbial middle of nowhere. She'd been in Dawes for over two months without earning a dollar, letting her aunt support her. Somehow Aunt Clara's unconditional love made Mia's lack of direction painfully apparent. As did turning thirty. For Mia, the age signaled full-fledged adulthood.

Even as she listened to Aunt Clara talk about the things she'd done and people she'd seen this morning in town, Mia found herself feeling as if she were at a fork in the road. Maybe it was time to grow up, time to be practical and take responsibility for her life. Maybe it was time to give up the dream.

"Where are you, dear?"

Mia lowered the deviled egg between her fingers to her plate. "Hmm?"

Aunt Clara's eyes turned pensive. "Your body might be sitting here with me, but your mind is someplace else."

True enough, yet Mia didn't want to admit her troubling thoughts. Aunt Clara would just pour on the sympathy, and that's not what she needed right now. What she needed was fortitude, the will to make herself do something it would be easier not to: quit feeling sorry for herself and make some practical life decisions. "Just thinking about my birthday," she replied. "Just thinking this is something my mom would have done for me. Thank you, Aunt Clara. For everything." She hoped her aunt understood the full measure of her gratitude. "Now, what were you going to tell me?"

"Oh me," her aunt laughed. "I'd nearly forgotten already. But I ran into someone who's looking for a painter."

"Looking for a painter?" Mia had the feeling Aunt Clara was barking up the wrong tree here.

The old woman nodded. "A sweet young man I've watched grow up over the years, along with his brothers. He needs someone to paint the interior of his tavern. You know, the one on Main? The place belongs to Rick Rose."

Mia couldn't have been more stunned to hear her bathtub lover's name on Aunt Clara's lips. Never mind that he wasn't a man who struck her as even slightly sweet, and that Dawes was apparently an even smaller world than she already thought—was her aunt actually suggesting she work for him?

"Generally, the Snapply family takes care of most folks' painting needs around here," Aunt Clara went on, "but Pete Snapply's down with a broken ankle and his boys are backlogged something fierce. I heard Rick say he's in awful need of a paint job, has been for months, but he doesn't have the time to do it himself. During the days, he helps at his parents' feed store out on Highway 45. So when he said he was looking for a painter, I told him my great-niece was a painter, and that I'd put you in touch with him."

Mia quietly digested the new information about Rick Rose. Up to now, he'd been only a name, a face, a body. Okay, one hell of a face and a body. But someone to think about in an almost abstract, this-isn't-real way.

Not that any of this mattered, Mia reminded herself. "Aunt Clara, I don't do that kind of painting."

The old woman shrugged. "Painting is painting, isn't it? Colors, brushes." She narrowed her brow and leaned forward slightly. "I worry about you, dear, being stuck inside this house all the time. I think it would be good for you to get out, start a new project."

And make some money, Mia thought. She knew that wasn't Aunt Clara's motive, but this *would* be a paying job, a way she could contribute to household expenses while she figured out what to do next. And painting some walls wouldn't require much concentration; the task would give her plenty of time to figure out her next steps in life.

Of course, other than having painted the occasional room, Mia didn't have the faintest idea how a painter—*that* kind of painter—worked. But how hard could it be? And it would also provide her with a first: she'd make money from painting.

The harder part would be approaching Rick Rose, fantasy bathtub stud, someone she'd never expected to have any dealings with outside her own mind.

Mia checked her watch as she traversed the sidewalk toward the Rose Tavern, its windows the only ones alight on Main Street. The dulled sounds of laughter and talk mixed with Bruce Springsteen's "Glory Days," growing louder as she approached.

It was ten thirty. Why had she waited so late to come? Probably because she'd spent the evening trying to talk herself out of it, trying to tell herself she'd go see him tomorrow, or maybe next week. But then she'd reminded herself that ambitious, determined people didn't put things off, and that she really wanted to repay Aunt Clara for her kindness, at least as much as she could.

Clearly, a lively Friday night crowd had gathered, and it probably wasn't the most conducive time to talk business with Rick Rose, but she would do it anyway. As she opened the heavy wooden door, the previously muffled noises blared out at her, and more than one eye turned her way. A few people appeared vaguely familiar from around town, but most were strangers. This was obviously a place where everybody knew your name—unless you were a temporary resident in Dawes, and one who stuck close to home while you were here, like Mia.

The men studied her approvingly, while the women only glared. She still wore blue jeans, but had traded in her tee for a casual yet fitted low-cut top that showed off a few curves. Not that she expected anything to come of it, but if she was going to have a one-on-one with Rick Rose, she wanted to look good.

She made her way to an empty bar stool, still aware of the curious glances, even as people went on with their conversations and laughter. She spotted Rick easily; he stood behind the bar, at the opposite end, flirting with two brunettes, one of them wildly overdressed—or was that underdressed?—in a stretchy skintight leopard-print dress, the fabric sprinkled with bits of metallic gold.

"Donna, what are you doing in here dressed like that?" Rick Rose asked, adding a rich, baritone chuckle. Despite the remonstrance, his tone said he didn't mind the view.

"Lookin' for love, sugar." Donna flashed suggestive eyes and leaned slightly over the bar to give him a glance down her cleavage, as if she wasn't revealing enough flesh already.

"In all the wrong places?" he asked.

She shrugged. "You know I'm not a stickler for right and wrong."

He laughed and gave her a wink. "And that's exactly what I like about you."

They were sleeping together, Mia just knew it.

"Hey, Rose, you got a customer down here."

Mia flinched as the middle-aged man two stools away hiked a thumb in her direction. "Uh . . . thanks," she murmured.

As Rick turned to look, Mia's body blossomed with the same awareness he'd brought out in her at the grocery store. Only this time she was forced to envision him naked, beneath her in an antique bathtub. A shiver snaked through her, especially when his dark eyes pinned her in place as if she were a butterfly in someone's collection case. Amazingly, his gaze left her with the same powerful sensations she'd experienced in the fantasy: possession, sexual ownership . . .

Crazy, she thought. She was taking the images in her mind too far, and had definitely gone too long without a lover.

Even so, one thing was clear: The man was a walking, talking chunk of raw sexuality. He hadn't noticed her in the vegetable section, but he was definitely noticing her now. Crazy or not, the mere knowledge made her nerve endings hum with a desire that felt almost dangerous.

He approached and leaned confidently against the bar, his predatory gaze never leaving her. "What's your pleasure, sweetheart?"

She considered being offended and telling him she wasn't his sweetheart, or maybe if she were smart she'd just take the cue and say, *You. Right here. On the bar. Closing time.* Instead, though, she swallowed nervously and replied, "I'll have a Bud Light."

Her fantasy man popped the top on a longneck and set it before her. "Glass?"

She shook her head. "Bottle's fine."

Still studying her in an unnerving way, he crossed strong arms over his snug navy blue T-shirt and tilted his head slightly. "Have we met?"

Kind of. I ogled you over fresh produce last week. She took a sip of her beer and set it back down. "No."

He leaned his head in the other direction, his gaze still intense. Never before had a man's mere look had such an effect on Mia. Her skin tingled and her breasts ached; she could almost feel her nipples puckering in her bra. The longer his eyes examined her, the more real the sensations from her fantasy became. "I could swear I've seen you around. Are you sure I don't know you?"

She took a deep breath, then followed an impulse. "Yes, I'm sure, but *I* know *you*. And I have a proposition for you."

A few chuckles and one low whistle from nearby reminded her that she was on a stage here, suddenly the main event of the evening in Dawes, South Carolina.

One corner of Rick Rose's mouth curved upward—not quite a smile, but enough to say she'd surprised him and he was enjoying the game. "I should warn you, this won't be the first time I've been propositioned by an attractive woman."

"I don't doubt it."

"So let's hear what you've got to offer."

"In private," she told him. "Do you have an office or something?"

A few more snickers filtered through the smoky air, but she kept her eyes on the man before her. His expression grew a little closer to a smile, the skin around his eyes crinkling slightly. "Sure, sweetheart. Follow me."

Chapter Two

The woman following Rick toward the back room was the freshest thing to hit Dawes in years. Despite her promise of a proposition, though, she didn't strike him as the kind of girl ready to lean him back against a wall and have her way with him, at least not this fast. She and Donna were in different leagues. But he was still damn intrigued.

Actually, he'd been intrigued from the moment he'd taken in those bright eyes and the smooth, sun-kissed complexion that told him she wasn't accustomed to spring on the South Carolina coast. Her hair hung in thin, messy, honey-colored spirals that made him instantly want to run his fingers through it, and her lips had that swollen just-been-kissed look. What the hell kind of proposition could this woman have for him?

Stepping into the room, he flipped a switch, illuminating the dim bulb overhead, then closed the door behind them, shutting out the crowd. Although he hadn't planned it, the move pinned her into a corner. He took advantage, placing one palm on the wall above her and peering down into pale blue eyes. She smelled of lavender.

Despite her denials, Rick knew he'd seen her somewhere around town. "So, who are you, sweetheart, and what brings you into the Rose Tavern?"

She met his gaze boldly and didn't seem to mind his nearness. "I'm Mia Drake and I want to paint your bar. My aunt Clara Winstead sent me."

Rick blinked. This was Clara's great-niece? Hell, he'd never in a million years expected someone so . . . sexy. Clara was a sweet little old lady, and for some reason he'd vaguely envisioned her niece as some younger version of her—short, stout, chatty. He couldn't have been farther off the mark.

And he couldn't have thought of a worse idea than hiring this woman to work for him.

For one thing, lust and labor made poor companions. And for another, the girl came with baggage. Clara hadn't told him much, but he knew her parents had died and Clara was the only family she kept in contact with. In fact, she was staying with Clara and, as far as he could tell from his conversation with the older woman, had no place else to go. "I can't help being concerned for the dear girl," Clara had told him today as they'd talked at Millie's Diner up the street.

Of course, if he'd thought the lovely, fresh-faced Mia was interested in a casual roll in the hay, he would be ready, willing, and able to oblige her. But already, just knowing what he knew, he had a feeling she wasn't that kind of woman—even if she *had* come into his bar sounding brassy and sassy. And if there was one thing important to Rick when it came to women and sex, it was keeping things light and casual. That's precisely why he got together with Donna from time to time, even if not as often as she came prowling for it.

At thirty-five, he'd had enough surprises in life, and he liked knowing what to expect. Despite their earlier banter, Donna wasn't really looking for love, and that suited him fine. Comparatively, Mia Drake was an unknown quantity; so even if he was drawn to her, exploring that attraction seemed like a lousy idea.

"Hate to tell you this, but you don't look a damn thing like a painter." He should take his hand down from the wall, he thought. And he should sure as hell quit staring at her like a thirsty man eyeing a tall, cool glass of water. But he didn't.

For the first time, she looked a bit ruffled. "Well, I *am* one." She pulled down nervously on the hem of her top, the gesture smoothing the fabric snug across ample breasts. A hint of nipples shone through the outline of her bra and made him thirstier still—or hungry was more like it, for a taste of what lay underneath.

"What have you painted?"

She let out a small disgusted sigh. "Rooms. Plenty of rooms."

"Do you have any references?"

Rick didn't think it an odd request, but maybe it was his tone that had her looking so disconcerted. "Look," she said, "I'm broke and I need a job. And it's my birthday. What do you say you cut me a break?"

He sighed. Already she was coming at him with a sob story. "All right," he heard himself say anyway. "You're hired."

She flinched, her eyebrows rising. "I am?"

He stood before her equally as surprised. Since when did he say the exact opposite of what he was thinking? He shook his head helplessly. "Yeah, sure."

The fact was, he decided, Clara was too sweet to disappoint. And it *was* the girl's birthday, after all; he wasn't a *complete* ogre. This just meant he had to institute an unspoken policy, right now, this minute—a hands-off policy.

It would have been a lot easier, though, if Mia's wide smile hadn't beamed right through him, bright as rays from the summer sun. "Thank you," she said. "Thank you so much." In her new enthusiasm, she lifted dainty hands lightly to his chest, then just as quickly removed them, her face flushing. "You won't be sorry, I promise."

Damn, he hoped not. That one little touch was currently ricocheting its way through his body like a bottle rocket. It would be so easy to drop his hand to the curve of her waist, so easy to press her back into the wall with a warm, slow kiss. He looked down into her eyes as need bubbled up inside him, nearing the boiling point. He didn't even know what the hell drew him to this woman so strongly. Then he thought again of her being an unknown quantity. It spelled danger, but also excitement. And she was sure as hell mooning up at him as if she wouldn't mind a physical connection herself.

But it was time to start putting that policy of his into effect, damn it. Maybe when the job was done, maybe when she was ready to leave town and go back to wherever she came from . . . maybe.

For now, though, no way.

"So when do you want me? To start?" she added softly.

Rick's stomach clenched with desire. If she hadn't added those last two words, he'd have been a goner. "Early Monday morning," he said, forcing his mind back to business. "And you'll need to work quick, because I'll have to close the bar until you're done. I want to reopen by next Friday night, at the latest. I can't afford to lose weekend business."

She nodded, and he realized how close to her he still stood.

Finally, he found the strength to back away, although his hard-on didn't thank him for it.

As if taking the cue, she moved toward the door, reaching for the worn brass knob. Yet as she opened it and the noise from the barroom came rushing in, she turned back to him. "Do you . . . have the proper equipment?"

He arched one eyebrow. *For what I want to do with you? Oh yeah, I've got the equipment.*

"I mean," she went on, sounding nervous, "scaffolding and drop cloths and that sort of thing."

Her words left him a little dumbfounded and shook him from his lust. "No, sweetheart. That stuff usually comes with the painter. Don't *you* have it?"

She swallowed visibly. "I'm on the road right now, couldn't bring it all with me."

"Well, you can rent whatever you need at Hamler's Hardware on the corner."

Her look was doubtful. "But I'm broke, remember? As in . . . seriously broke."

The words reminded him: sob story, baggage. *Distance. Keep your distance.* "Put it on my tab with Bob Hamler," he said, "and I'll deduct it from your pay."

"Speaking of which," she said, pausing to reach down into the front pocket of her faded blue jeans to pull out a crumpled five-dollar bill, "I owe you for the beer."

"It's on the house."

Late that night after the bar had closed, Rick lay in bed in his small frame house a few blocks off Main, trying to fall asleep. It would be easier if visions of Mia Drake weren't still dancing in his head.

He could have taken Donna up on her offer to get under that tight, shiny dress of hers—hell, he could have taken any of a number of women home tonight if he'd wanted to—but he wasn't in the habit of satisfying a lust for one girl by being with another. So here he lay, unable to drift off, despite the fact that it was after two a.m. and he was exhausted.

Clara's niece had stayed on his mind after she'd left, but only now, in the private silence of his home, did his thoughts have the chance to wander, did he have the chance to imagine what might have happened if he'd kissed her when he'd wanted to.

He could feel their bodies coming together, everything sturdy and hard about him meshing with everything soft and curvy about her. He could feel her warm skin beneath his hands, his fingertips skimming up her sides beneath her top, closing over her breasts—no bra. (It was a fantasy; she didn't have to have a bra.) He took possession of those two full globes of soft flesh, her firm nipples grazing the sensitive skin of his palms. Then her jeans were gone, fantasy-quick, and he was lifting her onto his old metal desk in the center of the room, parting her legs, entering her with one smooth, sure, solid stroke. *Yes.*

That's when the sound of Silas Carter's barking dog cut into his sleepy thoughts, shattering the imaginary ecstasy.

His eyes jolted open to stare at the blank ceiling. Why was he torturing himself like this?

To get her out of my system, that's why. One or two good fantasies and it would be almost the same as if it had really happened, and then he could forget the attraction and move on.

Okay, that was an exaggeration—a *wild* exaggeration—but he'd have to try to make it work that way. Having her around his bar for the next week would be much easier if he could look at her without seeing someone he wanted to get naked with.

However, as the dog quieted and Rick rolled over, another thought entered his brain. He *could* just follow his impulses and make a move on her. He could let himself enjoy her, forget his worries, forget tomorrow or the next day and just indulge. She wouldn't say no.

Or would she?

She'd looked just as ready as he'd felt, but was the sensuality he sensed in her real or only in his imagination? After all, she'd seemed to go from tigress to kitten with him in a heartbeat when he'd awarded her the job. Maybe it was just an act—get him hot, get the job.

And, he reminded himself, if they *did* have some fun between the sheets—or on his battered old desk—she might expect it to matter, to mean something. Rick had learned a long time ago that sex for fun, without any heavy emotions accompanying it, was the kind he preferred and the only kind he intended to have.

He knew better than most that needy women were trouble. The last needy woman in his life had taught him that the hard way. It had been years ago, but it had stuck with him, changed him, made him a little more untrusting of the world and of life in general. It was a mistake he wouldn't make twice.

So no indulging in Little Miss Sexy Painter, he reprimanded himself once more. Fantasies were a hell of a lot safer, and having decided that, he let his hand slide beneath the covers and fell back into his heated imagination right where he'd left off.

Mia tied the too-long bottom of her white T-shirt into a knot above her belly button, reached for the roller, then started painting, using the "W method" she'd seen on HGTV. *Paint a W, then go back over it and fill in the gaps.* She repeated the instructions to herself until she found the rhythm, and then the work became exactly what she'd feared—utterly boring.

But this wasn't about fun and excitement, nor was it about fulfillment—it was about money. And as she smoothed the eggshell-colored paint over walls that had yellowed with time, she at least felt she was doing something that obviously needed to be done.

The good news was that the work would be fairly easy. The tops of the walls curved right into the ceiling, which would also get painted, so the only pesky taping had been around the bar, a couple of doorways, and the dark wainscoting that circled the large room. The truth was, she thought, glancing around, it was a fabulous space full of potential. The antique cherrywood bar was probably older than Aunt Clara's bathtub, and a few nicks only added to its charm.

Sighing, she refocused on her work. *Paint a W and fill in the gaps.* Unfortunately, though, it just didn't take that much concentration, and studying the bar had reminded her of her only other visit here, three nights ago. She bit her lip at the memory of Rick Rose nearly pressing her to the wall with his broad, hard body.

"Big macho stud," she murmured, rolling her eyes, but the recollection filled her with an undeniable warmth. She'd been sure he would kiss her. Even with a roomful of loud people a few feet away, for a moment it had felt as if they were completely alone. She still didn't know him, but she wouldn't have stopped him.

No, that would have been one birthday present she'd have accepted wholeheartedly.

She'd gone home elated to think he was attracted to her, too; she hadn't expected that. But then again, he hadn't acted on it, so for all she knew, she was imagining the whole thing. Maybe all that heat had been one-sided, and staring into those intimidating eyes had only made her see what she wanted to.

Hell, for all she knew, the leopard-laden Donna was his girlfriend. Or maybe he even had a wife sitting at home while he was coming on to women in his bar. She hadn't asked her aunt any questions about him, not wanting to let her attraction leak out, but maybe she should have.

Either way, though, having sex with Rick Rose would be a bad move, much more complicated than her little bathtub daydream. Because even if she could play the sexy nymph for all she was worth, even if she could indulge her fantasies and succumb to her body's hungers, in the end, she'd get emotionally involved. And besides the fact that she'd soon be leaving South Carolina behind, one look into Rick Rose's gaze told a woman all she needed to know about him. He was everything hot and sexy a woman could want, but he was also the type to slap you on the ass when it was over, and send you on your way with a wink and a grin.

She'd shown up this morning to find a key and a note on the door, instructing her to let herself in and get started, so clearly he hadn't been bursting at the seams to see her again, and it was probably just as well. She'd gotten two guys from the hardware store to bring in a couple of ladders and an electric scaffold.

Which reminded her, back to work. *Paint a W and fill in the gaps.* But she let out a sigh at the very concept of having to cover this entire room with plain off-white paint. The fact was, it was a pure waste of architecture. High ceilings, original woodwork; she couldn't help thinking the curve where the ceiling met the wall should somehow be accentuated, not just blended in as if it were nothing. Looking up, she had the sensation that something should be spilling visually from the ceiling.

"What do you paint?" he'd asked her the other night. She could still hear his deep voice wrapping around the words, still feel his dark eyes penetrating her. Despite her answer, she'd been thinking, *Angels. I paint angels. Dramatic, passionate angels filled with desire.* She wondered now if she'd blushed, just thinking about her art while looking at a man who was certainly no angel, even if she *did* already have the urge to paint him naked.

In her private world on canvas, angels were perfect images of man and woman, all aching for a union angels simply couldn't have. They reached for each other without ever quite touching, their eyes replete with desperate yearning. They existed in a world of longing never fulfilled.

Sort of like my *life*, she thought glumly as she glided the roller over a new section of yellowed plaster. Maybe that's why she couldn't stop painting them. They yearned for a physical connection they could never achieve, and *she* yearned for a connection with others, through her art, that she was beginning to fear she'd never achieve, either. And as a result of letting that longing mean so much to her that she'd forsaken everything else, here she was now, painting a wall white, turning it into a blank canvas no one would ever fill.

Mia stopped then and glanced toward the ceiling once more, struck by the first hint of inspiration. What if . . . ?

The vision came to her almost instantly, clearly—within a few short seconds she understood what belonged on the walls and ceiling of this room, and a surge of creative energy shot through her.

If she was going to be paid for her painting, shouldn't it be *her* painting, her real work?

And if she didn't stop at normal quitting time and toiled around the clock, she could get it done without running *too* late—she knew it.

So that settled it. Lowering her roller of white paint back into the tray with a smile of anticipation, Mia grabbed her purse and headed back to the hardware store. Rick Rose would get much more than he was paying for, and she'd go away with a much greater feeling of satisfaction.

Rick pulled his truck to the curb in front of the Rose Tavern, spotted the doors and windows still open, and checked his watch. Five thirty. Hmm, maybe Little Miss Sexy Painter was a harder worker than he'd expected; he'd been sure the place would be locked up and empty again by now. Of course, this meant he would see her, which hadn't been part of his plan.

But he could sure as hell face an attractive woman without acting on his impulses, and he would prove that to himself right now.

The pungent scent of fresh paint met him at the door as he walked through. An initial glance around the quiet room revealed the requisite drop cloths and paint cans, as well as a fresh coat of white on some of the walls and, when he looked up, the largest part of the ceiling. That was when he realized something wasn't right.

A steel scaffold nearly reached the high ceiling, so he couldn't tell exactly what he was seeing, but bits of unexpected color—pale pink, black, a deep ivory—peeked out from above the platform stretched across the sturdy-looking lift. He felt his blood pressure begin to rise. What on earth did she think she was doing? She was supposed to be painting the place off-white. Simple, solid off-white. Instead . . . dear God, was that actually a person's bare leg on his ceiling?

"What the hell is going on here?" he boomed.

"Just a second," she called, her voice emanating from somewhere above—atop the scaffolding, he presumed.

"No, not just a second," he bit off gruffly. *"Now."*

The platform began to descend, lowering several feet, then Mia backed down the built-in ladder at the scaffold's end. Rick stood fuming, waiting to give her a piece of his mind. As soon as she reached the floor, he cut loose. "What the hell do you think—"

Shit. The sight of her stole his words. She wore blue jeans and a tight little T-shirt knotted at the waist, smudged with bits of paint that didn't prevent him from seeing the clear outline of a lacy bra. She had a silver belly-button ring. And her feet were bare.

"What the hell do I think about what?" she asked, looking surprisingly defiant and not in the least worried.

The anger tightening his chest now tightened his groin, too—and it wasn't anger anymore. Damn, he couldn't remember a time when he'd had it this bad for a woman this fast. Mere toes, a sexy belly button, and a snug, thin tee had turned him hard. He wanted her out of that shirt, out of everything.

With that one thought in his mind, he took a step toward her.

Chapter Three

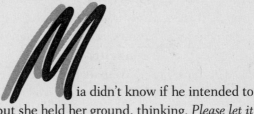ia didn't know if he intended to strangle her or kiss her, but she held her ground, thinking, *Please let it be the second one. Please just kiss me.* Like the other night, his intense gaze was laced with sensuality and a definite sense of power, and it was enough to send all her cautious thoughts from earlier flying out the window.

When the trill from his cell phone sliced through the air, they both flinched. He never took his eyes off her, but the interruption stilled him in place as he reached for the phone at his belt.

"I'm at the bar," he said into it a few seconds later. Then, "The paint job?" Leaning his head back, he cast a doubtful look at the ceiling. "Uh, the jury's still out on that one. Listen, I'm in the middle of something here. I'll call you later."

After pushing the button to disconnect, he spoke pointedly. "That was my brother Jake. He wanted to know how the paint job was coming along."

"So I gathered."

Rick looked toward the ceiling once more, then turned a steely gaze back on Mia. "I had no idea how to explain to him that there's a leg painted on my ceiling. So would you like to tell me why, exactly, you're painting *people* up there?"

For the first time, Mia felt a little worried about her decision. But that was okay, she assured herself. She'd just be completely honest, and she'd make him understand. Not that understanding seemed like Rick Rose's forte, but she had faith this would work out.

"I'm not painting people. I'm painting angels."

He blinked. Stared at her blankly. "Angels?" He said it in the same tone someone might say, *Martians?*

"Yes, angels. You see, that's what I do: I paint angels. This will be a mural that stretches across the ceiling. It'll give the place a lot of character and use the space much more effectively. And I'm not even charging you anything extra."

He spoke dryly. "Well, that's a relief."

She attempted to sell it with a smile. "Your ceiling will be the talk of the town."

Unfortunately, he wasn't buying. "What if I don't *want* my ceiling to be the talk of the town? This is a bar, sweetheart. People come here to drink and listen to music and bullshit with one another. Not look at angels."

"Well, that's the beauty of it. Since they're on the ceiling, they won't get in the way. No one *has* to look at them. In fact, you'll have to work pretty hard from down here—lean back awfully far—to see them." She demonstrated, exaggerating the motion. "They'll just be there, hovering up above, if anyone's interested. But they won't interrupt anyone's beer swilling or chitchatting. You're getting much more than you planned on when you hired me."

"You can say that again."

His derisive tone made her sigh, but she gathered enough courage to look him squarely in the face. And oh, what a handsome, sexy face it was—very easy to look at. Even though she barely knew him, she really wanted to make him believe. In her. In her vision. She spoke slowly, solemnly. "You'll like it. I promise."

She could have sworn a hint of regret shone in his eyes when he plainly said, "No."

Mia took a deep breath. She'd anticipated that he probably wouldn't be *wild* about the idea, that it might require a little convincing, but his bluntness left her incredulous. "No?" she repeated. "Just no?"

"Just no. It's a rotten idea."

She took the time for another calming, cleansing breath. "I think you're being narrow-minded."

"It doesn't matter what you think, sweetheart. This is *my* bar. I hired you to do a simple job—now do it."

So much for calming and cleansing. This time Mia let out an irate sigh. He was so . . . curt. Inflexible. Unreasonable. Grumpy.

And *hot*. She couldn't forget that one. In fact, as long as he remained in her line of sight, it would be impossible. Somehow, her attraction to him bolstered her, helping her to stay just as aggressive as she'd been when they'd met. "What if I won't take no for an answer?"

His eyes widened with a smug annoyance that pissed her off. "Then you'll be out of the job you claimed you needed so bad."

"Why not give this a chance?" she asked. *Reason with him. Make him get it.* "If you don't like it, I'll paint over it, no charge. Why not let me paint the ceiling and then decide?" The very thought of obliterating her work ripped a huge gash in her soul, but she'd felt she had to make the offer to make him take the risk.

"Because no one I know goes to a bar to be reminded of church."

"This isn't like that," she explained. "My angels don't make anyone think of church."

That concept clearly caught him off guard, keeping him quiet for a moment. After casting one more glance to the leg visible above, his voice went lower, more inquisitive. "Then tell me about these angels of yours. What are they like? Not the kinds you see on Christmas cards or—"

"Oh no," she interrupted, giving her head a quick shake. "Think Michelangelo, Botticelli. It's a bold comparison, I know, but I'm a bold woman."

His nod was short, acceptant, as if that last part went without saying.

"Think . . . romance among angels," she went on.

As his angry expression faded to something slightly more primal, his eyes began to simmer with a familiar heat that made her insides flutter.

The sensation drove her explanation haphazardly forward. "My angels . . . want something they can't have."

His voice came so soft it was barely audible. "What's that?"

"Each other. They want each other." She swallowed, her own words echoing fainter, her gaze connected to his by something invisible and magnetic. "But they can't . . . because they're angels, not humans. So their desires go unfulfilled."

Rick didn't reply, and the two of them stood staring at each other until the five feet separating them felt nonexistent. Mia's thoughts mirrored those of a few minutes ago. *Kiss me. Please. I can't stand it.* At the moment, she didn't care if it was meaningless sex, didn't care if he took her right here on the drop cloth, walked out afterward, and never mentioned it again. She simply wanted him so badly that she couldn't push it down. Nothing else mattered but having this man relieve the burning ache inside her.

"So," she finally said when the silent tension became unbearable, "do you trust me?" She glanced at the ceiling once more, perhaps to remind them both what they were talking about.

"I'm not sure," he said, then all tenderness fled his countenance. "But go ahead and paint your damn angels if that's what you want to do. Just remember they might not stay there, so don't get too attached to them."

It was like telling her lungs not to get too attached to air. And when Rick turned and stalked from the bar without another look in her direction, Mia couldn't breathe at all. Every ounce of blood seemed to drain from her body, and she reached for the bar to balance herself.

What the hell had just happened here? He'd told her she could paint the ceiling as she wished, yet the victory somehow felt sour since he'd also turned down what she'd been offering with her eyes, her voice. She knew he'd felt exactly the same as she did, knew this time, beyond doubt, that she wasn't imagining it. Rick Rose wanted her as much as she wanted him, but he'd walked away. Why?

"Damn," she murmured. In the midst of her pleas and her passion, she hadn't even thought to look for a wedding band. She'd have to ask Aunt Clara about that as soon as she got home.

But that would be late tonight, she thought, moving back toward the scaffolding. Very late. Because she had a ceiling to paint, tortured souls to create, and a short time to do it, all while her body suffered and throbbed for Rick Rose. She was beginning to think she had more in common with her angels than she'd ever realized before.

Rick felt like a blazing idiot for walking away from her, for not doing exactly what he'd wanted to do with her. And for the love of God, angels on his ceiling? What the hell was that about and why had he told her it was okay? He banged his hand on the steering wheel as he turned onto the two-lane highway that rimmed Dawes, heading to his brother's place outside town.

He knew who Michelangelo was, but he'd never seen any of the guy's paintings. Yet he'd given her permission to turn his bar into some kind of goddamn art gallery. Or church. Angels, for God's sake. On the ceiling of a bar? He rolled his eyes and let out a sigh.

When he'd found out what she was up to, he'd wanted to grab her and shake her. He'd also wanted to kiss her. Push her down on the drop cloth and bury himself inside her. Make her see a whole different kind of heaven than the one she was painting up above. But he'd ignored *all* the urges, at least as much as he could.

He felt absolutely adolescent. He was a big boy, and if there was something he wanted, especially something free for the taking, he usually helped himself. Yet with Mia Drake it was different. And insane. That initial danger he'd felt with her still lingered—enough to hold him back.

And as for telling her she could paint what she wanted . . . Just like when he'd given her the job in the first place, the words had simply left him, unplanned. He was a smart, decisive guy, not the kind who let a woman lead him around by the nose—until now, it seemed. He banged the steering wheel once more for good measure.

Rick pulled into the gravel driveway of his brother's house, his four-by-four small in the shadow of Jake's eighteen-wheeler. Two dogs circled the corner of the old farmhouse in full stride, barking a warning. His brother appeared on the railed porch, yelling at the German shepherd and collie. "Rhett! Scarlett! Settle down."

Jake had allowed their mom to name the dogs, much to all her sons' regret. But Jake's girlfriends always thought it was cute, and being a ladies' man, he'd refused to change them before the names stuck and it was too late.

"Come on in," Jake called as Rick slammed the truck door.

Inside, he found his other brother, Zack, still looking scruffy from a day at the construction site. For some reason, it irked him. "You couldn't clean up?"

"When did you turn into Mom?" Zack asked coolly, but Rick just rolled his eyes and didn't reply. He didn't even know what had prompted his remark, but as the oldest brother, he still felt entitled to make it.

When Jake wasn't on the road, the three brothers tried to get together for dinner once a week, and tonight Jake was grilling steaks on the back porch. The tempting aroma wafted through the kitchen window as they all sat down at the table, beer cans in hand, but it didn't make Rick feel any better.

"Well, for a man who's got a week full of nights all to himself," Jake said, "you seem like you're in a shitty mood."

"I've got a woman driving me crazy," he murmured, shaking his head, and the comment made both Jake and Zack look up. Rick seldom aired his woman problems.

Life just went a lot smoother, he'd learned, when you kept things to yourself. As for why he'd just walked in the door muttering about his current woes, he could only attribute it to the burn of arousal that still had him on edge and not thinking clearly.

"Is it the painter chick?" Jake asked.

Rick eyed his brother with curious annoyance. "How'd you know?"

"You sounded weird on the phone."

"Yeah, well, if you could see what's going onto the ceiling of my bar right now, you'd sound weird, too."

Jake cracked an accusing grin. "No. I mean you sounded weird, like . . . tense."

"Well, if you could see what's going onto the—"

"No, dude," Jake said with a laugh. "You sounded weird, like *horny*."

Clearly caught, Rick leaned his head back, letting out a small growl of irritation at being so transparent. "Here's the thing," he said, deciding it was no use to deny his feelings at this point. "She's totally hot, and each time I've seen her, I . . . almost can't control myself."

From there, he actually began to ramble a bit, about her being Clara's niece, about giving her the job without quite wanting to give her the job, about letting her paint freaking angels on his ceiling without quite wanting to let her paint them, about everything . . . until it finally occurred to him to shut the hell up and quit being so open. For one thing, his brothers sat staring at him like he'd grown horns. And for another, now they'd start giving him a bunch of unwanted advice.

"If you ask me," Jake began, pausing to tip his can to his mouth, "I say why fight it?"

"I didn't ask you."

Zack rubbed his stubbled chin. "It's not like you to turn down a willing woman."

"*Most* willing women," Rick pointed out. "But her parents died in a car accident and she has nobody in the world but Clara."

Jake leaned forward, eyebrows knit, clearly not getting the picture. "So?"

"So I don't want her thinking she has me, too. I don't want her glomming onto me, expecting me to take care of her or something. I'm not into charity cases."

Zack shrugged. "She doesn't sound like a charity case to me. In fact, she sounds pretty damn feisty."

Rick lowered his voice and shifted uncomfortably, already regretting what he was about to say, since it was something he didn't like talking about and seldom did. "Yeah, well, Gina didn't seem that way at first, either, and look how that turned out."

He caught his brothers exchanging glances before Zack said, "That was five years ago."

"Ancient history," Jake added.

Rick didn't like admitting this, but replied, "Not so ancient to me."

Jake tilted his head. "Don't tell me you're still hung up on her."

"No," he said, and that was the truth. "But . . . you know what happened." He wasn't sure he'd *ever* get over how things had ended. Nope, not so ancient at all.

"So this woman's painting *angels* on the *ceiling*?" Zack asked, squinting slightly as he changed the subject.

Rick shook his head in disgust. "I don't get it, either. But she'd already started when I got there, and she swore up and down that I'd love it, so . . ."

"So you said okay?" Levelheaded Zack still sounded disbelieving. "That it was okay to paint angels on the ceiling of your bar?"

Rick let out another sigh. "I know, I know. I have no idea why I told her it was all right."

"Uh, maybe because you wanted to get out of there before you jumped her bones?" Jake suggested.

Rick shrugged. "Hell. Maybe."

"Well, you can't let her do it," Zack insisted. "You're gonna have to put a stop to that paint job right now."

"Of course," Jake said, pushing his chair back and heading toward the door to check his steaks, "she sure as hell won't sleep with him after that."

Zack shrugged. "Doesn't sound like he's planning on it anyway, so he may as well save the bar from being completely ruined."

Mia's muscles ached as she eased quietly through the front door a few minutes past ten. The house was silent, but Aunt Clara had kindly left a lamp on. She slipped worn tennis shoes from her feet, thinking that her very *bones* felt weary. She'd painted for over twelve hours today. Of course, even as she stood there ready to melt into a deep, restful sleep, her veins still hummed with electricity. The passion her angels inspired. Or was it Rick Rose? The line was becoming bizarrely blurred.

She heard the creak of footsteps before Aunt Clara turned the corner, wrapped in a quilted robe and looking relieved to see her.

The guilt set in instantly. "Sorry I'm so late—you didn't have to get up."

Her aunt's usual loving expression stayed in place. "Oh, I don't mind. But I *was* beginning to worry."

Mia sighed. "I should have called, but as usual, I got absorbed in my work and lost track of time. Forgive me?"

The old woman smiled. "Nothing to forgive, dear. Now come in the kitchen and tell me about your day while I make you a nice turkey sandwich."

"Aunt Clara," she said, following her to the kitchen, "you don't need to make—"

"Of course I don't need to. I want to." Her aunt pointed toward the table. "Now sit. Relax. Unwind."

Rather than argue, Mia just obeyed. "It turns out," she began, "that the job got a lot bigger than I originally anticipated, and it needs to be completed before the weekend, so I suspect I'll be working these kinds of hours all week."

"My goodness," Aunt Clara said, spreading mayonnaise over a slice of bread. "That's a lot to ask. I'm surprised. Rick has never seemed like a slave driver."

"Oh, he's not. It's my fault. I just decided to . . . paint something special, more complicated."

Aunt Clara stopped constructing the sandwich and twisted to face the table, a small smile unfolding across her thin lips. "Your angels?"

Mia nodded, pleased that her aunt was one of the people who "got" her work, which was not surprising, she supposed, since she had inspired it—with a Christmas gift, a coffee-table book featuring the works of Botticelli. Sweet Aunt Clara seemed meek and innocent, yet she had no qualms about sending her niece pictures of naked people for Christmas. Mia chuckled inside recalling her initial surprise upon receiving it—but then the book had changed her art, her life.

"They're very evocative, Mia," her aunt said. "They'll be lovely, I'm sure."

"Thank you, Aunt Clara." As the old woman returned diligently to her task, Mia wondered briefly what Clara saw when she looked at the angels, suspecting there might be more passion to her aunt than met the eye.

"About Rick . . ." Mia said then.

"Yes?"

"Is he . . . married or anything?"

Her aunt's voice echoed from inside the refrigerator, where she bent loading sandwich supplies back in. "Rick? Heavens no." She withdrew, a carton of milk in hand. "Now, some years back he was engaged, and there was a nasty breakup. But I never thought much of that Gina he was with, no I didn't. Seemed to me she was a rather saucy girl. Other than her, though, Rick's always been a confirmed bachelor."

Part of Mia had almost hoped to hear he was married. A wedding vow would provide an excellent reason to keep her distance, and it would also explain why he continued keeping his. Now, though, she wanted him all the more. No obstacles stood between them. Well, none that she could identify anyway. After all, whatever kept him from making a move on her clearly *was* an obstacle. She found herself feeling stupidly jealous of "that Gina," and wondering just what had caused their "nasty breakup." Insane.

"Why do you ask?"

Mia looked up as Aunt Clara lowered a small plate and a glass of milk in front of her. "No reason. Just curious."

Settling in the next chair, Aunt Clara raised silvery eyebrows. "Have you taken a fancy to him, dear?"

Mia forced out a laugh, nearly choking on the first bite of her sandwich, then took a long swallow of milk to wash it down. "No, Aunt Clara, of course not. I barely know the man." For some reason, a vision of her bathtub fantasy filled her head just then, along with the imagined sensation of impaling herself on him, being filled by what lay between his legs. She felt herself flush and looked down, concentrating on her food.

"He's very attractive," her aunt prodded.

It would be stupid to even deny that. "Yes, he is," she said around a mouthful of bread and turkey. "But I probably won't be in Dawes for too much longer, and besides"—she stopped to swallow—"he and I haven't exactly gotten off on the right foot. He's not too crazy about the angels on his ceiling."

Aunt Clara looked thoughtful. "Well . . . he will be once he sees them in all their glory. You mark my words."

Satisfied that her sexual blush was gone by now, Mia raised her gaze and smiled appreciatively. "I hope so."

By the time he'd left Jake's house late Monday night, Rick had decided Zack was right—he'd have to tell Mia to nix the angels and get back to the simple off-white color he'd originally asked for. As he drove toward the Rose Tavern, he couldn't even believe he'd let her cockamamie idea go this far in the first place. Jake and Zack had gotten his head back on straight. Well, at least as far as the paint job went. As for Jake's suggestion that he quit fighting his desire for Mia, he was dismissing that altogether. In his book, temptation still equaled trouble where she was concerned.

When he arrived, she was gone, her beat-up station wagon nowhere in sight, the bar left dark and quiet. Not that he was surprised; it was nearly eleven. Even so, he shoved his key in the lock and went inside. Like earlier, the pungent scent of fresh paint filled his senses, and when he looked up . . . hell, he had to take a step back to get hold of himself.

The scaffold had been lowered, and the leg he'd spotted this afternoon was now part of a man . . . well, a male angel, he guessed. Who was naked. On his ceiling. Jesus H. Christ. He ran a hand back through his hair and let out a heavy sigh.

Of course, he couldn't deny her talent. The guy angel was life-size, as big as him, lounging on a small wisp of a cloud. Wings that looked as if they were constructed of real feathers spread behind him, and he appeared relaxed enough, with one knee casually bent and a smallish penis—on Rick's ceiling, for God's sake—at ease between his legs. Rick's gaze, however, was drawn mainly to the male angel's face, his eyes. Clearly, the guy was longing for what rested across the ceiling from him—only Mia hadn't painted that part yet, and Rick couldn't help being curious to see what the man angel wanted so fiercely.

But shit. There was a naked guy on his ceiling. With wings.

He walked behind the bar and yanked up a tattered phone book from underneath, flipping it open toward the back in search of *Winstead*. He knew it was too late to call, but he was going to do it anyway, going to put a stop to this ridiculousness. Naked angels on his ceiling? He couldn't have it. And he was going to explain that to Little Miss Sexy Painter right now.

Snatching up the receiver on the phone, he dialed Clara's number.

Then he pushed the button to disconnect before it had a chance to ring.

He couldn't say why.

Curiosity? To see what the angel yearned for? Or was it a bothersome tinge of compassion for his painter that stopped him?

He laid the phone gently back in its cradle, then peered at the angel once more—at the desperate passion burning in his eyes. They were blue. Like Mia's.

Tossing the phone book back under the bar, Rick walked out and went home.

*T*hree nights had passed. On each one of them he'd returned. Late, after her departure, so he could look at the ceiling.

The first male angel's expression of longing now rested on a woman angel, whose slender hand stretched toward him—but they didn't touch, *couldn't* touch; they lay just beyond one another's reach. A wispy, flowing swath of white fabric draped across her, but it only scarcely concealed her sex, and her breasts were left bare and beautiful. This angel, too, boasted wings of white, feathery enough that Rick swore if he climbed up and touched them, they'd be soft as down beneath his fingers.

Since the creation of those first angels, two more had taken shape. The second girl appeared more demure than the first, long blond hair falling over her breasts so that just the rosy tips peeked through. She didn't reach for her desired lover, but the look in her eyes said it all. It was a look Rick recognized, a look he'd seen in Mia. The new guy angel extended one hand in her direction, his eyes fraught with want, but his expression seemed to say he already knew he couldn't have her. His wings were darker than the other angels', the feathers accented with bits of cream and beige. Rick also couldn't help noticing that this angel possessed a considerably larger penis than the other male, which—God help him—actually gave him a laugh.

Jesus, naked angels on his ceiling. And he was laughing about it. How the hell had this happened?

The strange truth was that he'd enjoyed coming in each night, watching the picture, the passion, take shape before his eyes. And seeing the sensual vision of the angels longing for each other had only added to his desire for the painter.

Now it was Thursday night, and one look told him the bar wouldn't be ready for business tomorrow night. Could he even let people come in here and see the spectacle on his ceiling? The fact was, he hadn't thought that far ahead. For the last three nights, he'd simply been watching the mystery of her, the beauty of her, the sweet, hot passion of her, unfold. He'd been mesmerized.

He didn't like admitting that to himself. He'd only been this taken by one other woman, ever, and it sure as hell had required more than some paint slapped on a ceiling. Yet even now, as he glanced up at the expanding mural, his heartbeat kicked up, the blood raced through his veins faster than normal, and he felt himself begin to harden, thinking of her.

As he did a few nights ago, Rick walked behind the bar and looked up Clara's number. It wasn't as late tonight, only a little after nine. As he dialed, he wasn't even sure what he intended to say to Mia. *Get your ass in here and finish this mess so I can open my bar tomorrow night*, or *I haven't seen you in days and it's killing me.*

One ring. Two. "Hello?" answered a sweet, older voice he recognized.

"Hi, Clara, it's Rick Rose."

"Why, Rick, how are you?" She sounded as delighted as usual. "I hear the painting of the bar is coming right along, and I must say, I can't wait to see the finished product."

Did Clara know her niece was painting naked angels on his ceiling? He decided to sidestep that altogether. "Speaking of painting, I need to talk to Mia. Is she there?" Still, even as he said her name, he wasn't sure if he was going to tell her that she was fired or that he wanted to fuck her brains out. He was usually a decisive man who followed through on his intentions, but somehow Mia Drake changed all the rules in his life.

"Oh, Rick, I'm afraid she's already asleep. And she's been working such long hours that I'd hate to wake her, poor dear. Can it wait 'til morning?"

He took a deep breath, realized he felt disappointed. If she'd come to the phone, he wouldn't have fired her. "Sure," he said. "No problem."

Hanging up, he envisioned Mia sleeping and wondered what she wore to bed, and hoped it was something thin and skimpy, or maybe nothing at all, like her angels.

Mia lay on her back, brushing thick strokes onto the ceiling, adorning her newest angel with hair the color of midnight. Most of her angels were more fair, but she always followed her creative whims, and she'd had the urge to make this male angel darker than most.

Of course, she wasn't an idiot—she knew why she had the urge to paint a dark-haired man. Even without seeing Rick Rose in four days, he remained prominently on her mind. As absorbed in her work as she'd been, he'd lingered there in the periphery of her thoughts, sometimes in *more than* the periphery. At night she fell asleep imagining their bodies coming together, moving against one another, sometimes slow and hot, other times fast and hard. She imagined him kissing and suckling her breasts just before the warm weight of his body pressed into her, just before he filled the empty spot between her aching thighs.

God, she wanted him even now as she lay painting. Her breasts burned for his touch, and so did her crotch, held so tight and tingly within the confines of old blue jeans.

Rick's ceiling was the best work she'd ever done—she knew it without doubt. And she also thought she knew why. In her mind, she had somehow *become* the angels. She'd always connected with them, but never in such a starkly paralleled way. She'd known longing before—for success, for having her art loved and appreciated. And she'd certainly known longing for men. But something about her lust for Rick went beyond past desires, was new and complicated. Bigger than herself. It defied logic.

She barely knew him and had yet to have a truly civil conversation with him—but somehow, crazily, this felt like more than mere chemistry to her. And if it *was* only chemistry . . . well, then she'd never experienced such an all-powerful combination of elements between herself and any other man.

Aunt Clara had mentioned his phone call over a quick breakfast this morning, leaving her to wonder what he'd wanted. Her first thought? *I missed it. I missed hearing his voice. And I'm crazy for feeling this way about a man I've barely brushed elbows with, but I can't seem to stop.* Her second, more rational thought? That he hated her angels and was calling to tell her to paint over them. *Please, God, no.* If that was what he wanted, she didn't think she could do it, despite her promise. She'd rather get in her car and start driving to nowhere and never look back than to make them disappear by her own hand.

A thin ribbon of irritation had grown in Rick overnight. Thin, but it was getting thicker by the next morning when he climbed into his truck and started the engine.

What had begun as an image of her in his mind, lying in some big, lonely bed, needing a man to wrap around her and keep her warm while she slept, had somehow slowly transformed into a sense of contempt.

He'd been so absorbed in her painting that somewhere along the way, he'd almost forgotten his fears about her. Yet, suddenly, he was remembering.

It had hit him after his phone call with Clara. *Poor dear*, she'd called her great-niece, and it had brought to mind Mia's tragic past, and his original suspicion—that she was one of those needy types, and also a woman who played a part to get what she wanted, a tease. Her eyes always dripped with hot willingness, but Rick wondered again what would have happened if he'd taken her up on the unspoken invitation.

Part of his exasperation—hell, a *big* part of it—was at himself. For being so taken in. Even amid his doubts, he'd given her precisely what she'd asked for; he'd been unable to tell her no. Well, he'd given her everything but sex, and he had a feeling now that wouldn't have led anywhere anyway. She was probably real accustomed to pouring on the sexiness. That kind of charm could get you a lot in this world, and Mia Drake obviously knew it.

Despite the all-too-appealing vision of her in his head last night— he'd decided she wore something filmy to sleep in, sheer and gauzy, to go along with her teasing persona—he felt himself being slowly and surely manipulated. Gina had possessed the same skill, the ability to make him think exactly what she wanted him to think, make him do exactly what she wanted him to do, all without his realizing it before it was too late. Now, with Mia, he saw himself being drawn in the same way. Drawn in by her art, by lust, and by the intrigue of how the two somehow fit together.

She obviously wasn't the kind of painter she'd originally pretended to be. In fact, it was all making sense to him now, why she was here living with her aunt: She was some struggling, down-on-her-luck artist. Needy personified.

What really got to him was that he'd only met the woman twice.

His obsession with someone who'd barely crossed his path was . . . disturbing, to say the least. She and her damn angels had somehow taken over his thought process, but that was about to change.

The weekend was here and he obviously wasn't going to be tending bar, so maybe he'd call up Donna and take care of the hard-on that had been plaguing him all damn week. But first, he was going to pay a visit to Mia Drake and clear some things up. So instead of heading to the feed store like he did every morning, he drove toward the Rose Tavern.

For one thing, the angels had to go. They'd captured his interest and he couldn't dispute her talent, and there was even a small piece of him that cringed at the idea of painting over them, but it had to be done. They belonged on canvas, not in his bar.

And for another, she had three days to finish the job, three days to paint the place off-white like he'd hired her to. If she couldn't do it, all bets were off, no money would be exchanged, and he'd use the coming evenings to get the place painted himself.

Despite everything, though, Rick's biggest regret at the moment was that every inch of his body still prickled at knowing he would see her again within a few short minutes.

She hummed as she painted somewhere above him on the scaffolding—a light, breezy tune Rick couldn't quite make out, but the airy lilt in her voice crawled under his skin and made his nerve endings tingle. He envisioned her lying on the elevated platform, feathering tiny brushstrokes onto the ceiling. Michelangelo with curves—and the voice of . . . an angel.

Damn. His intentions were crumbling already.

He looked up, but couldn't see a single sign of her presence—only the humming gave her away. He kept right on staring, though, as if trying to see through the wood, trying to touch her with his eyes.

Emotion roiled inside him and his groin began to tighten. Because she was humming? No, it was more than that and he knew it. Instinct told him to leave, now. *Walk right back out that door and she'll never even know you were here*. Despite his resolve, though, his feet stayed rooted firmly in place.

And even as he approached the lift, then reached for the lever that would bring her a few feet closer to earth, he knew he wasn't going to yell at her. His chest ached.

Stop. Stop this now. He continued arguing with himself, but it did no good. He pulled the lever.

When the plywood began to descend, she gasped. "Hey!"

Locking the lift back in place, he slowly scaled the built-in ladder on the scaffolding's end. He was working on autopilot now, or maybe it was more like surrender. But his *new* intentions had just become extremely clear, filling his every move with purpose.

His first glimpse of her revealed the startled irritation in her pale blue eyes. She still reclined on the wood, a small paintbrush in one hand and an old margarine bowl of beige paint balanced on her stomach with the other, but she'd propped herself on one elbow to see what was happening.

Their eyes met and held, but he never stopped moving closer, climbing onto the scaffold on hands and knees, suddenly feeling like a cat on the prowl as he loomed over her. Finally, damn it, finally.

"What are you doing?" Her words came on a breathless sigh as he slowly pinned her to the platform, forcing her to lay back on it.

He reached for the bowl she held against her paint-smudged T-shirt, set it an arm's length away, then planted his palms on both sides of her head. "Something I should have done before this whole fiasco started."

Her glare didn't stop him from lowering his mouth possessively onto hers. The whimper of surprise quickly faded into silence as she went still beneath him, just before he felt the pressure of her warm lips against his. She tasted faintly of chocolate, which explained the candy bar wrapper visible just beyond where she lay. He deepened the kiss, easing his tongue into her mouth, as the scents of paint and chocolate and Mia curled about him, enveloped him.

Her arms closed around his neck, inviting him to slide his body against her lush curves in a way that, up to now, had been nothing but a fantasy. And as her kisses began to swallow him, he wondered who was seducing whom. He'd truly convinced himself she would push him back or tell him to get the hell off her. He'd thought his advances would offend her, make her quit, leave. But instead, her legs parted beneath his, making him groan as he pressed his hungry erection into the thick seam of her blue jeans.

Her quick sigh of pleasure shot through him, turning his kisses harder as he began moving against her to create sweet, hot friction. Damn, he wanted her. Even more than he'd known. All thoughts of driving her out of his bar and his life fled. This was completely about fulfillment now, the need to be inside her.

He reached for the hem of her loose T-shirt, just above their slow grind, and found soft skin underneath. His hands molded to her and slid slowly upward until they reached lace. Grazing his palms up over her bra, he closed his fingers gently, firmly, over the breasts he'd been dreaming about. The quivery sigh she issued against his lips echoed his own pleasure. Pleasure he wanted more of.

That's when she broke the kiss. "Wait."

It jolted him from his loss of control, and he gazed down on her wide eyes and slightly swollen lips.

Okay, he thought, *now* she would do what he'd expected. She'd tell him no, push him away. And despite the lush heaven in his hands, it was almost a relief, because as he'd lectured himself from the first time they'd met, making love to Mia would be a mistake. *It's better this way.*

Maybe they'd argue, maybe she'd quit and he could hire a *regular* painter. A *man* this time. And his life would get back to normal.

"What?" he said, working to sound gruff. "You want to stop?"

But beneath him, she gently shook her head. "No, I want to move to the bar."

Chapter Five

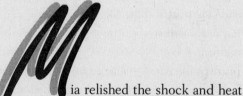

ia relished the shock and heat mingling in Rick's eyes. Oh God, right now she relished *everything*. Despite her request to move, she arched her back, pushing her breasts tighter into his grasp, and squirmed against his hard arousal below, frustrated that he'd gone still.

His voice was like a low-burning flame. "What's wrong with right here?"

"On the night we first met," she whispered, "I imagined us on the bar together. And besides, there are things I want to do to you that will be easier accomplished down there."

His stunned expression remained, even if he was trying to camouflage it. "Okay, that's good enough for me."

His gaze never left hers as he backed slowly off her body, even when he paused to lower a tiny kiss to the denim right between her thighs. She shuddered with all the heat she'd been storing up for him, then after he was gone, moved to the edge of the scaffolding herself. He waited below, his eyes gleaming like two dark embers, heating her up from the inside out.

The second her bare toes touched the drop cloth, Mia reached down to pull her T-shirt over her head, then tossed it in the corner. It seemed insane to wait, to waste time—she'd waited for this long enough. And she didn't know what it meant or why it was happening, but she wasn't going to question it. She wanted it too much. She'd never slept with a guy she barely knew before—but somehow, from the start, she'd known she was powerless to say no to Rick Rose. Nothing in her even wanted to try.

Rick's gaze dropped from her eyes to her breasts, straining against the lace that held them. Then he ripped off his own T-shirt, revealing a broad chest, hard nipples, and a muscular stomach, all covered by a thin matting of dark hair.

She was just about to run her hands over the expanse of his chest when he closed the distance between them in one short stride, using his hips to press her back against the cold steel rungs of the scaffold's ladder. She reached up to grip the rails at both sides of her head, thrusting her breasts forward. A silent offering.

His hands skimmed quickly up her sides before closing again over the cups of her bra, forcing a small, unplanned cry from her lips at the simple onslaught of pleasure. Then his rough fingers curled around the lacy edges and he gave a brisk tug that caused her breasts to spill out. At the sexy, shocking sensation, impulse took over and she heard herself murmur, "They ache for you."

The words made the hard column beneath his jeans throb against her, just once, before he reached around, grabbed her butt and lifted her onto a rung, then lowered his mouth hungrily to her chest. As he sucked at her nipple, she dropped her head back and cried out, in half pleasure, half pain. Opening her eyes revealed a glimpse of angels—lush and desperate.

Still gripping the side railings tight, she hooked her ankles around them as well, holding herself on and freeing Rick's hands. As he rubbed his erection where she wanted it most, he caressed and molded her breasts with a skilled touch, even as he continued to kiss them, suck them. Mia had never dreamed such pleasure could be found while pinned to a ladder, but the fact that her hands and feet were somewhat constrained, keeping her from falling off, only added to the sensation of being fully open to him, to anything he wanted to do to her. She'd given herself over to the moment, the man, completely.

When one hand dropped lower, stroking her through her jeans, she moaned and pushed herself against his fingers. She'd burned for his touch for so long—or at least it had felt like a long time—and it was more heavenly than she'd dreamed, even through denim.

As if reading her mind, though, he moved his fingers to the top button and flicked it open, then slowly lowered the zipper, a sensation which, in her present position—legs spread and hooked around the scaffold—gave her a thrill of unexpected measure. "Oh God, I want you," she whispered.

"Then let's get you out of these blue jeans." As he moved back, allowing her to step down onto the drop cloth, his gray eyes shone hot as ever.

She wasted no time in pushing her jeans to her ankles and kicking them off, ready to let him see her, all of her—but then she noticed her faded blue cotton underwear. In her world of scraping to get by, such worn and unexciting things were the norm, and for the first time since this had started, she suddenly wondered what Rick Rose expected from his women. Leopard print with gold sparkles? She felt surprisingly sheepish. "If I'd known this was going to happen, I'd have worn better panties."

He gave his head a short shake, his look focused on what she'd just revealed. "I don't give a damn about your panties," he murmured. "I'm just interested in what's underneath."

"Oh," she said, her voice becoming husky as her embarrassment disappeared. She concluded by following the next urge, pushing her undies down onto her thighs. *See me. I want you to see me.*

Without planning it, Rick dropped to his knees before her, like a worshipper at a shrine. The shrine of Mia, he thought. Every fiber of his body hummed with pleasure and anticipation, leaving him light-headed. Cupping the backs of her knees, he slid his palms swiftly up onto her ass, sweet and round in his hands, then sank his tongue into the thatch of pale brown curls at the crux of her thighs. Her cry speared him with raw passion as her wet folds parted, allowing him to taste the heat of her desire. Her legs parted, too, when she leaned back on the scaffold again, her arms extended behind her as she braced on a rung. They'd ended up back on the ladder when he'd had every intention of seeing exactly what she wanted to do to him on the bar, but that didn't matter—they'd get there eventually. The moment she'd lowered those panties, his mouth had been drawn here, like a fly to honey.

Her underwear was a hindrance now, though, so he drew both hands around to one of the side seams and yanked firmly, ripping them. They fell in a small heap at her opposite ankle and she let out a gasp, but quieted again when his palms returned to her ass, squeezing, massaging. He then resumed delivering those long, languid licks up her center, each one ending at the swollen bud at the top.

Above him, she moaned and whimpered and fueled his heat, and he forgot the rest of the world existed. The tips of his fingers played along the center of her ass, soon stroking the tiny fissure there, and what had begun as slow, grinding movements on her part now became hard, insistent thrusts. His tongue thrust back, and as her breath grew harder, heavier, tangled-sounding, he thought, *Come, baby. Come for me.*

He looked up in time for their gazes to meet just before her eyes fell shut and a low, guttural groan escaped her lips. She jerked against him and he never slowed his rhythm, letting her ride it out against his mouth. He only hoped she couldn't feel him shuddering with the pleasure of her climax, which had somehow seemed to echo from her body into his. Damn, *that* was new.

When she sank to her knees, collapsing against him, he hauled her into his arms. "Are you okay?" he whispered.

"Mmm." Her breath came warm on his neck. "My knees just gave way."

The warmth of satisfaction stole over him as he held her close, her delectable breasts brushing soft against his chest.

He wanted more, though, a lot more, so he didn't wait—he kissed her again, hot and demanding.

Her response was just as enthusiastic, and soon their tongues sparred and he wondered if she tasted herself on his. His hands roamed the smooth arcs and dips of her body until he was raking his thumb across one prominent nipple; his other hand grazed past the curve of her ass and into the moisture below. She was practically purring as he stroked her from behind, and when he slid one finger inside her, she let out a small cry.

Her breath grew heavy again, the way he liked it, and he thought she must be fully revived from her orgasm when her small hand snaked down between them to cup the rock-hard column still concealed in his jeans. He groaned at the welcome touch.

A moment later, she leaned away from him, wearing nothing but the white bra that now only outlined her full breasts. Damn, they were gorgeous—round, soft, their peaks dark and rosy. He wanted them in his mouth again and followed the urge to reach out, but to his surprise, she grabbed his hands, stopping him.

Biting her lip provocatively, she got to her feet and pulled him up as well. Then she drew him toward the bar.

He cast her a wicked grin of anticipation—and also of wonder, because he'd pegged her dead wrong every time he'd thought she might be a tease. He was perfectly willing to let her call the next shots, anxious to see what she had in mind.

Still half-dressed, Rick boosted himself onto the bar. When Mia positioned herself between his legs, he reached to help her up, but she only shook her head and stayed where she was, beginning to slowly caress his thighs through the denim.

He'd been hard since before their first kiss, but this new sensation—her splayed fingers raking their way up his blue jeans, along with the sight of her beautiful breasts hovering just inches above his aching erection—heightened his arousal. When she leaned forward to rain soft kisses over his chest, then his stomach, her breasts pressed into the hard bulge at his crotch. A moan broke free from somewhere deep inside him as he watched her ministrations, drinking in each sensual nuance—the way her hair brushed over his skin, the feel of her fingernails as they dug ever so slightly into his flesh, the sight of her body as she bent over him, her pretty ass thrust out behind her.

Just when Rick was beginning to wonder how much longer he could survive the tender torture, she lowered his zipper. His cock sprung from its confines, stretching his underwear to the limit, and he waited for her to free him completely, but she didn't. Instead, she ran her palm over his length through the cotton, gently testing the weight and feel of him in her hand—until he thought he'd go mad.

"Please," he rasped.

It was the first time she'd lifted her gaze to his in a long while. "Please what?"

His voice came out shaky. "Please touch me."

Rick berated himself even as the words left him. He couldn't recall a time when he'd ever begged a woman to do something to him. But he quit caring when she did it. Seconds after his request, she hooked slender fingers around the elastic band and lowered his underwear.

The way she studied his hard-on was almost enough to make him tremble, even before she ran one long fingernail from the head to the base. When she took him full in her grasp, he cried out softly, pushed his hands into her hair, and drew her into a rough kiss. Afterward, she cast a look of pure wantonness, and without ever taking her eyes from his, let her tongue dart out to lick the wetness from the tip.

"Jesus," he muttered as another tremor racked his body.

It only got worse when, apparently satisfied with her slow torture, Mia took him into her mouth. Sweet heaven. His breath came slow and heavy as he watched her lips slide up and down his length, each move pushing him further into sensual oblivion. She surpassed any fantasy he could ever invent. He tried not to thrust, but it was difficult and oh-so-tempting. Finally, he whispered, "Stop."

Releasing him, she looked up.

"I don't want to come yet."

Another wicked expression claimed her as she flicked her tongue across the head one last time—and it almost sent him toppling over the edge, but somehow he held on through sheer will.

When Mia climbed onto the bar next to him, Rick was more than ready to regain control of the encounter, but when he urged her to recline on the polished wood, she resisted. His first impulse was to wrestle with her, to recapture that sense of being in charge, yet when she pushed him to his back, he let her have her way—just like he *always* seemed to let her have her way. But dear God, she was straddling him, floating just above him, rotating her pelvis in hot, tantalizing little circles—so what difference did it make who was in control?

When she used her gyrations to dab her moisture onto the thick column between his thighs, he was more than ready to feel her lowering herself onto him, wrapping him in wet velvet, but instead she whispered, "Tell me you have something in your wallet."

Jesus, he'd *forgotten*? He *never* forgot. Until now.

"Yeah, I do." Lifting slightly, he wrenched the leather billfold from his back pocket and together they fumbled, suddenly maddened, rushing.

The instant he was sheathed, she sank onto him, taking his whole rigid length smoothly inside her. They both let out a gentle moan at the much-awaited connection, and no woman had ever looked at Rick the way she did just then. Her gaze brimmed with confidence and slow heat and sex, seemed to grab on to the moment and relish it, seemed to say: *Look at us, look at this incredible passion we're sharing, look at the way our bodies are joined.*

She moved on him with a soft, sensuous grind, in the same circles she'd teased him with moments earlier. But she wasn't teasing him now—she was riding him, hot and slow. He reached for her breasts, pushing them upward, squeezing her taut pink nipples between thumb and forefinger, until finally she leaned over and dipped them toward his mouth. He opened for her, took one rose peak between his lips, sliding his tongue around the hard pearl of her nipple even as he sucked, French-kissing her breast.

Her breath went ragged and he teetered near explosion. Even as he pumped up into her, he tried his damnedest to hold back. Just a little longer, a little longer. His entire body vibrated like a tightly strung instrument—an instrument she was playing agonizingly well. But soon those strings were going to break; he was going to come.

Her circles got tighter, rougher, as she sought another release. He drew firmly on her breast and she moved on him with rough urgency, and just when he was thinking, *Please, baby—hurry*, she cried out her pleasure, and the force of her thrusts drove him to ecstasy, too.

He released a growl as his body was lifted, transported, for a few long, perfect seconds of pure bliss. Then he was back on the bar, his arms closing around her as she settled onto him, kissing his neck, murmuring, "Oh, that was good. So, so good."

"Mmm," he said—all he could utter as the near-sleep stage struck.

But he was lying on a hard bar and it was the middle of the morning, and realizing that was enough to jolt him awake. "Jesus," he muttered when he glanced over and realized the door was standing wide open and the shade on the big front window hadn't been pulled. Anyone could have seen them—hell, maybe *had* seen them. Something about this woman totally shredded his common sense.

He leaned his head back in a gesture that felt strangely like concession, a concept he wasn't at all comfortable with, and looking up brought the angels above into focus. Shit. He couldn't deal with the issue of the ceiling right now.

He sat up, forcing Mia to do the same. She was naked and beautiful and sitting on his bar and they'd just had mind-blowing sex and he had no idea what to say.

So he kissed her, softly, just once, and murmured, "Thank you." Then he thought, *Thank you?*

Stepping down from the bar, Rick disposed of the rubber, then adjusted his underwear and zipped his pants, all the while aware of her climbing down behind him, and thought he should probably be helping her. But no, he should be doing more than helping her—he should be holding her and whispering things and sharing secret smiles.

Yet that's not how it was. He suddenly wanted to get the hell out of here and forget this had happened.

After fetching his T-shirt, he turned to see her pulling on her jeans—without underwear, because he'd torn them. The sight was so arousing he had to look away.

"Well," he said, "guess I'd better get to work. People are gonna wonder where I am."

When he peered at her again, the jeans were on and her bra was back in place. She looked as uncomfortable as he felt, combing slender fingers back through her hair. "Okay. I, uh, guess I should, too." Locating her tee in the corner, she bent to pick it up. "By the way, you probably figured out that today's Friday and the paint job isn't quite done."

He nodded. "I came here to yell at you about that." *And to tell you to paint over the angels.*

"I'm sorry. I'm really working as fast as I can."

Damn it, her tender, earnest look made him want her again, and he knew he had to go, now. At the same time, though, he was waiting for her to pour on the 'when will I see you again?' crap, the needy stuff he knew would come. It was written all over her face—all that remained were the words.

"I know you're working fast," he said, "but work faster. I'm losing money."

She simply nodded. No excuses, arguments, or needy pleas. Just acceptance. He was an asshole.

"I gotta go," he said, then stalked through the door and to his truck, taking in the light, midmorning bustle of Dawes and wondering cynically if anyone had happened past the show taking place in the Rose Tavern over the last half hour or so.

As his truck pulled away from the curb, he thought again of the damn angels he needed to get rid of—the ones he had just let her resume painting. Even so, there was no way he could tell her right now. He'd figure out what to do about that later.

For now, he had to go to work, get back to normal. He'd finally given in to his urges, and he'd come away much more satiated than he'd even imagined he could—far better than a quick encounter on the desk would have left him. But this was the end of it. No more.

Even if she hadn't acted all needy, he still knew she hadn't wanted him to go. And that seemed enough of a reason to get as far away as he could.

She needed to start painting, but she couldn't make herself get back to work yet. Her mind, her body, wouldn't let her focus on anything but what had just happened. She rested on her knees on the drop cloth just below the scaffold where he'd performed profound personal acts on her. Glancing toward the bar, she quaked anew just remembering his incredible erection. Incredible to look at, feel against her, kiss, taste, have inside her.

They'd done . . . *everything*. Even more than she'd imagined in her fantasies. It wasn't like Mia to get so intimate with a man she'd just met, nor was it like her to be quite that aggressive . . . teasing . . . commanding, but each and every physical connection they'd shared had felt as right and natural as it had shocking and thrilling. Her inner slut had taken over.

Yet just as she'd predicted all along, he'd simply gotten up and walked out.

Which she had decided would be perfectly okay with her, hadn't she? After all, you do it with a guy you don't know and what do you expect? His class ring?

She still felt sad, though. Because she *wanted* to know him. She'd been so drawn to him from the beginning, and even as physical as the attraction was, it went beyond that. She wanted to know his secrets, his hopes, his desires. She wanted to know if "that Gina" had broken his heart or if it was the other way around. She just wanted more. And she wanted the sex to matter. It was a curse, damn it, the curse of the softhearted female.

He'd seemed almost angry with her when he'd left. Not exactly a ceremonial ending to stupendous sex. But who knew—maybe it wasn't all that stupendous for him. As usual, the leopard-clad Donna came to mind.

Yet the fact remained that she had to finish painting his ceiling and she had to do it quickly. So, forcing herself up off the floor, she snatched up the old panties he'd torn off her and chucked them in the nearest garbage can in the back room. Then she took a deep breath, raised the scaffolding back to where it had been when he'd arrived, and climbed the ladder to resume her work. As she lay on her back, using her paintbrush to create the mere hint of a few black feathers in the wings of the dark angel, she couldn't stop thinking that even now, having had him, she still felt as desperate as the beings above her.

ick was leaving the feed store on Monday afternoon when Jake rolled into the gravel lot on his Harley. "What's wrong with *you?*" his brother asked as he removed his helmet. Damn, Rick knew he was easy to read, but this was getting ridiculous.

"Nothing," he groused as he headed toward his truck, realizing even as he spoke how stupid the reply sounded. Hell, he'd been biting people's heads off all day.

"You did it, didn't you?" Jake said with his usual, easy grin. "You partied with the painter chick."

Rick rolled his eyes, then looked around to make sure they were the only ones in the conversation. "Keep it down, would ya?"

But Jake just laughed. "Come on, dude. Spill. You got horizontal with your painter."

"And vertical, and perpendicular, and every other angle you can imagine," he admitted, sounding far less happy than such a statement deserved. He got in the truck and shut the door behind him.

"Aw, come on," Jake said in response to his tone as he approached Rick's open window. "Don't you feel better now?"

"My dick feels better. I don't."

"Ah. So that means she was all clingy at the end, wanted you to commit your life to her or something, just like you thought."

"No," he said shortly, "she wasn't. But I still have angels on my ceiling."

And lust in my heart, he thought as he put the truck in reverse and backed out of the lot. He'd lied—his dick didn't really feel all that much better. And he couldn't sleep, hadn't been able to all damn weekend. Visions of their sex had kept playing through his mind like a dirty movie. A really *good* dirty movie. He'd been the star, after all.

On Saturday night, he and Zack had gone to Mac's Bar on the corner of Beechnut and Summer Streets. The place was his only other competition in town, and it was *friendly* competition, but he'd taken some ribbing for not having the tavern open, and indeed, a lot of his weekend regulars had turned up there. Including Donna. She'd worn a tight purple micromini and rubbed up against him in all the right places. Except they'd felt like the *wrong* places, because her touches just didn't elicit the same response in him as Mia's had.

"Come home with me tonight, baby," Donna had purred in his ear. "You know you want to."

Only he *didn't* want to. "Not tonight, Donna," he'd said, and she'd moved on to Riley Hawkins and his big cowboy hat.

Now it was Monday afternoon and, God, he wanted Mia again. Wanted her so damn bad he could hardly breathe.

He shouldn't go back there with the intention of having sex with her again. Hell, he probably shouldn't go there at all, until she was done painting and out of his life. He should mail her the check and put in some extra dough, enough to get her back on the road and out of Dawes.

Because he still thought she was needy? Absolutely.

Okay, change that to maybe.

But the problem was bigger than that now, if he was honest with himself. She had more in common with Gina than just the tragic past and a potentially needy persona. She made him *feel* things. She turned him weak. He didn't want to be weak for another woman.

Although it was a few blocks out of his way, he drove past the tavern before heading home. As expected, her blue Chevy station wagon sat parked outside, late-day sun glinting off the old windshield—but he kept on driving. Taking the left turn toward home, he wondered if she was inside his bar humming. And what she was wearing. He wondered how late she would work, and if she stopped to eat while she toiled all those long hours. Any other guy would know at least that much, because any other guy would have had the common decency to make some normal conversation with the woman by now.

But he wasn't any other guy.

Mia worked and yearned, yearned and worked. The two seemed to go hand in hand these days. And maybe they always had, but the yearning seemed to become more torturous with each passing day. Even now, as she lay on the scaffold, brushing golden yellow swirls onto the ceiling, she ached for Rick between her thighs. He'd filled her so well.

The golden swirls flowed from the head of the woman angel desired by the dark angel she'd painted on Friday. Her hair was a riot of messy yellow curls—but much longer than Mia's, and different, she made sure, because she *wasn't* painting her and Rick. She wasn't.

"Hello," a voice called below her. Speak of the devil—or at least it *sounded* like Rick. But she couldn't imagine anything more out of character than him paying a *friendly* visit—well, unless he'd come to fire her or something.

"Hello," she said back. She couldn't sit up without sticking her head in wet paint, so she reached for the button that controlled the lift, lowering it a bit, then scooted to the edge of the platform and backed down the ladder upon which Rick had done such delicious things to her.

Peering through the rungs as she descended, she spotted him near the bar, setting down several small white bags. "Do you like chicken and dumplings?" he said in his usual detached tone without looking at her.

She smoothed her hands over the bottom of her white tank top. "Uh, yeah."

"Good. It was today's special at Millie's."

She still didn't quite know what to think; she cautiously approached the bar as he strode behind it.

"Coke?" he asked, grabbing a plastic cup from a stack.

"Sure," she said, remaining on guard.

He lifted his gaze only briefly before returning his attention to squirting soda in the cup. "I know you've been working long hours, and I figured you weren't stopping to eat."

"Not usually. How'd you know?"

He glanced toward the scaffold. "I saw the candy bar wrapper the other day."

"So you brought me dinner?" She tilted her head slightly, still not quite believing.

He gave her an unsmiling nod, handed her drink across the bar, and filled another cup—for himself, she guessed.

"Thanks," she said, then started nosing around in the bags.

She'd just started to realize it was dinner for two when Rick went to the back room and returned with a couple of the bar stools currently stacked there. "Mind if I eat with you?"

Her heartbeat kicked up another notch. "Uh, no."

They didn't talk much for most of the meal, just sat side by side at the bar, and it was somehow both awkward and pleasant; his knee pressed against hers as they ate. Every now and then, she glanced into the mirror behind the shelves lined with liquor bottles to catch him watching her, but each time, he looked away.

Finally, he peered into the nearly empty foam container he'd been eating from and said, "I'm sorry I walked out of here like that on Friday. I was a jerk."

She glanced down, too, feeling herself flush. She had no idea what to say. "It's okay. I mean . . . I don't really know you. I . . . shouldn't have let that happen."

For the first time since his arrival, he turned to look her in the eye. "Do you regret it?"

She swallowed nervously. "No." It came out too softly. "But I probably should."

"I was out of line even starting it." Again, his eyes sought the container below. "It's just . . . ever since we met, I've wanted you."

"In the grocery store," she blurted, her chest tight with nervous tension and excitement.

"What?" he asked, clearly confused and suddenly forgetting not to look at her.

"You thought we'd met before," she explained. "Well, we stood beside each other one day in the grocery store, in the produce section."

He tilted his head; then one side of his mouth slowly quirked into a half smile. "Cherry tomatoes?"

She laughed. "Yes."

"I remember. I remember wondering why you were concentrating so hard on them—they were all alike."

She lowered her chin, but still dared peer at him as she bit her lip. "I was concentrating on you."

He raised his eyebrows. "Even then?"

"Even then."

Rick's smile faded to an expression that was all too familiar to Mia by now. She couldn't begin to pull her gaze away. *Hungry.* The word stuck in her mind—it was how he looked and how she felt, and it couldn't be assuaged by chicken and dumplings. Their knees still touched, but suddenly the connection seemed to spark electricity.

"I can't promise you anything," he said, giving his head a quick shake, his voice deeper than before. "I mean, nothing. I mean, I'm not—"

She cut him off, couldn't bear to hear any more. "I understand that. But the truth is, I'm still dying to . . ." Oh God, what was she saying?

"What?" It was the merest of whispers. "Tell me."

She took a deep breath and let her gaze meet his. Why lie? Why not just spit it out? "I'm dying to feel you inside me again."

His look alone turned Mia weak, ratcheting up the burn of desire spreading low and deep inside her. Lifting one hand to cup her cheek, he leaned in to kiss her in a long, languid meeting of tongues and lips. By the time it was done, her hand kneaded his warm, sturdy thigh. Her whole body tingled with the knowledge that it was happening again—this magic, this mystery of sex with Rick Rose.

Sliding her hand a little higher up the denim, she leaned in for another kiss, but he pulled back slightly. "Wait."

Recalling her identical protest three days ago, she teased him. "You want to stop?"

His grin was soft and warm. "Not possible." But he lifted a finger, silently asking for a minute, then left his stool to pull down the large window shade, before turning the lock on the door until Mia heard a pronounced click. "Just don't want to take any chances this time."

She offered a short nod, her voice sounding too husky when she replied, "Yeah, I thought about that afterward."

Gently taking her hands, Rick urged her to her feet, where he drew her into another kiss. Like the first, this one was slower, sweeter, more lingering than those of their previous encounter. His touches this time were less insistent, more leisurely, exploring. His large hands roamed her shoulders, the arch of her back, before slipping briefly down onto her bottom. His fingertips rose to play over the sensitive skin of her arms.

Slowly, their bodies came together until his oh-so-powerful erection pressed into her, escalating her need to something rough, demanding. Once again, Mia spared a thought for her angels and all she had in common with them. *But at least I'm getting what I want, what I need. My lover's hands are on me, mine on him.* Not forever, she knew, and perhaps that provided the reason for her feelings of desperation, but she got to have him at least one more time, and she planned to savor every second, every touch, every whisper of his lips across her skin.

As his kisses trailed over her cheek and down onto her neck, she sighed at the sweet, intense pleasure such a simple act could bring, and let the heat of delight flow through her body like a spill of thick, warm paint.

"I want to lay you down," he whispered just below her ear as he drew her onto the drop cloth. They sank to their knees amid kisses, and he gently eased her back to the floor. She caught a glimpse of her angels above, but was drawn back to the joys of earth as he slowly began raising her top, swirling his tongue around her belly-button ring, then kissing his way up her stomach. Pushing the white ribbed fabric over her breasts, he sprinkled a thin line of kisses across the ridge of flesh above her bra, turning her breath audible, weighted. His fingers peeled back the top of one lace cup, and he had just dragged his tongue slowly across her sensitive nipple—making her moan—when someone banged on the door.

Mia's stomach jolted. She looked to Rick, and he looked toward the noise. "We're closed!"

"Come on, man, I want a beer," a guy's voice called.

"Jesus, Zack," he muttered quietly, then yelled, "Try Mac's."

"What the hell are you doing in there with the lights on and the place all locked up?"

Looking annoyed as hell, Rick rolled his eyes. "Think about it!"

The man outside paused, then spoke a bit less loudly. "Oh. Damn. Sorry." Then finally, blessed silence.

"My brother Zack," he told her, still balanced on one elbow above her, his face mere inches from hers. His thumb gently stroked her beaded nipple.

"How many Rose brothers are there?" Her voice came out sounding breathy.

"Three. Jake lives on a small farm outside town and drives a semitruck. And Zack has his own construction business. I'm the oldest."

She nodded. "Why am I not surprised?"

Rick arched one brow, looking half amused and half as if he were daring her to explain herself.

"You have a . . . very commanding edge about you," she said, offering a suggestive smile.

A slow, sexy grin stole over his face in response just before he dropped a soft kiss on the tip of her breast. Pleasure fluttered downward.

"So, do you do this often?" she asked. "Have sex with women in here?" Not deriding, just an honest question.

The shake of his head came with a light chuckle. "No."

"Then how did he know? I mean, you could have been doing anything."

He ran the tip of one finger along the same curve of her breast he'd just kissed. "I . . . might have mentioned being attracted to my sexy new painter."

She tipped her head back on the drop cloth. "Ah."

"Lift your arms," he instructed, his playful demeanor shifting into his more authoritative tone. She complied, not minding, and let Rick relieve her of the tank top. When he lowered a kiss to the valley where her breasts met, it was like a star bursting in her chest; then he pulled back for another steamy, I'm-so-ready-for-this look. Or maybe that was just how *she* felt.

He brushed his thumb over a spot on the cup of her bra that still covered her. "What's this?"

She glanced down to see a smudge of dark turquoise and thought the answer obvious. "Paint."

"You paint in your bra?"

"I used to live in New York City and didn't have air-conditioning. If it was over ninety, yeah, I painted in my underwear."

"Now that's something I'd have liked to see." His expression brimmed with sensuality. "Brings . . . erotic visions to mind."

She flashed a curious smile. "Like what?"

He hesitated, then let a slow grin spread across his handsome face. "That's for me to know. . . ."

Reluctantly, Mia let it drop, although she yearned to learn his fantasies and would have told him hers—about the bathtub—if he'd asked. She couldn't imagine anything more sensual right now than sharing that with each other. But Rick Rose was obviously not a man to be pushed.

He suddenly seemed insistent on getting their clothes off, working at the zipper of her jeans and pulling them down along with her white bikini panties when she lifted for him. After he shucked his shirt, he hooked one thumb beneath the strap of her bra and skimmed it from her shoulder. "Take this off," he said, and she complied. She didn't mind being bossed by Rick when his demands came with the promise of having him inside her, making her feel as whole and complete as she had the first time.

She lay back and watched, hands behind her head, as he shed his jeans and underwear. Dear God, he was a beautiful man, all hard muscle and sinew. The muscle jutting up from between his legs appeared particularly hard and turned the crux of Mia's thighs warm and weepy.

"Now," he said, kneeling next to her, "close your eyes."

Despite her thoughts of a moment ago, this time she hesitated. She was open-minded and could scarcely think of anything she wouldn't do with Rick right now, but she liked to see what was coming.

He must have read her uncertainty. "Trust me."

That was a leap, but she let her eyes fall shut anyway, wanting to please him.

She waited for something to happen, but merely heard him shifting around her—rustling noises, things being moved. What was he doing? The tension of wondering heightened her awareness, and having her eyes closed made her feel extraordinarily on display. Was he watching her right now? Studying her expression? Her body? Her nerve endings prickled and her sense of excitement grew; her breasts felt as needy and swollen as she did below.

Then the oddest sensation trailed over one breast, making her gasp. Soft, soft, soft, and very wet. She opened her eyes and what she saw stole her breath.

Pale pink color arced across her flesh as Rick used one of her artist's brushes to paint her. The vibrations the brush sent pulsing through her were undeniably exquisite, and she understood—this was his erotic vision.

Her voice trembled. "What . . . is it?"

"A heart," he said, and she could see it now as he reached the point at the bottom, then came back up to start the other half. He raised his gaze to her with a sexy grin. "What do you think? Do I show any promise?"

A heated smile escaped her, and her words came out in a purr. "Oh yes, Mr. Rose, your work appears *quite* promising. I look forward to seeing what else you can do."

His voice dropped an octave. "Does it feel good?"

Growing quivery inside, this time she could only nod. Then watch. Somehow the completion of the heart made her feel as if he'd placed his mark on her, as if she belonged to him. As if she wanted to.

Next, he reached for a new brush—this one he dipped in the shade of blue she'd been using for her angels' sky—then lifted it to her other breast. When he painted a slow, thin circle just beyond her nipple, a thready sigh echoed from deep within her. His brush then looped around the edges of her rounded flesh until she realized he was creating a flower.

"They're beautiful, by the way," he said.

"What?"

"Your breasts."

Immersing the brush back in the can of blue, he painted a wide squiggly line down the center of her belly that sent an incredibly sexy tickle skittering through her. She pulsed between her thighs, aware the wiggling stroke was heading in that direction. Considerately, he skipped the brush over her belly ring, then ended the line just above her pubic hair, finishing by turning it into an arrow that pointed south. She laughed lightly, but when he parted her legs and began painting tiny pink hearts on her inner thighs, the sensation nearly undid her.

She rose up on her elbows to watch him work, and he looked as deep in concentration as any artist she'd ever known. Each little heart was like a fingertip climbing oh-so-slowly toward the core of her need. By the time his brush had worked its way to within an inch of where she throbbed, she'd turned whimpery with lust. "You're driving me crazy," she whispered.

He seemed unsurprised, didn't even look up from his work. "I know."

Somehow his cool, confident nonchalance made her thighs flinch—as if her body were saying, *Pay attention to what I want*. "I don't think I can take much more," she pleaded, moaning lightly as a particularly gratifying heart came into being. "You've got me so hot."

"Mmm, I know that, too," he said in the same unhurried tone, and this time it was worse because his warm breath washed over where she was moist and ready for him. He used one finger to painstakingly trace the outer edge of her arousal, the slow touch making her even wetter. "You're so open, swollen, pink," he murmured. As she shuddered in reply, he added, "Don't worry, sweetheart. I'll take care of that . . . eventually."

As Rick painted another heart a fraction closer to the juncture of her thighs, she decided it would be his last.

Rising up, she snatched the paint brush from his hand, slapped it down on the drop cloth next to them, and said, "On your back," more forcefully than she knew she could.

He appeared surprised, but not bothered. Moreover, he looked positively impassioned. She pushed his shoulders toward the floor, aware that he went easily, then straddled his hips, ready to have her way with him.

"Careful—you're not dry yet," he said with a teasing grin that shattered her sense of dominance.

She quickly regained it, though, along with the will to torture them both a little longer—but mainly him.

Moving gingerly, so as not to scrape her wet thighs against him, she bent down, letting her breasts hover above his face. "Kiss them," she said. He started to reach for them as well, but she reminded him, "Ah ah ah—wet." She used the opportunity to grab his wrists and trap them above his head while he took careful turns circling each distended nipple with the tip of his tongue, avoiding the painted edges.

It was almost enough to bury her resolve about making him suffer, but she found the strength to pull back, before instructing him, "Roll onto your stomach."

"Why?"

She grinned, since he obviously didn't like relinquishing control quite *that* completely. "Because I said so."

His look challenged her at first, then grew warmer, as if to say, *Okay, I can do this—I can go along with the game.*

Once Rick lay prone, Mia reached for one of the brushes, dipped it back in the sky blue paint, and began creating what she hoped would be especially tantalizing little swirls on his firm, round butt. She heard him sigh after the very first.

She started at the roundest part of his ass and worked inward, slowly, slowly, listening as his breath grew pleasingly heavier. After one curling stroke in particular, he moaned, "Jesus." As her swirls extended toward the center, she swept them downward, as well, until she was painting the little marks nearly behind his balls.

That's when he finally said, "Stop."

Ignoring the command, she painted another, and he responded by rolling roughly over to his back, away from her. When their eyes met, his appeared harried, frantic. "No more. I'm already too close." His voice softened then. "Time to get back to *you*."

Despite her earlier frustration, Mia didn't argue now. Concentrating on tormenting her lover had somehow soothed her, made her ready to withstand more of his imaginative foreplay. "You're going to paint more on me?"

He gave a solemn shake of his head. "Not exactly."

"What does that mean?"

"Lay down and close your eyes."

This time, Mia didn't balk—she simply bit her lip and did it. This trading control back and forth had her on a plane of arousal she'd never experienced. She wanted to do everything with him, like their last encounter, but she was somehow more patient than before, eager to see what he had in store for her.

A few seconds later, a light, soft, feathery sensation started low on one breast, moving from the outer extremity in slow, teasing circles until finally it played about her nipple. "Oh," she whispered, "that's like heaven." Easing her eyes open, she found he'd located one of her unused brushes, her largest, softest—the red oxtail with white fluffy bristles. She'd never realized she worked with such erotic tools every single day.

With the paint on her body now dry, Rick performed the same sensual circling motions on the other breast with the oxtail brush. She didn't think she could climax from mere touches on her breasts, but there were moments when she wondered if she'd prove herself wrong. Soon he skimmed the brush down her side, tickly soft, before he spread her legs and, starting at one knee, grazed it up her inner thigh. By the time he reached her center, Mia was panting uncontrollably, and when he stroked it through her wet, sensitive flesh, she cried out at the sheer assault of pleasure, flowing through her rich and deep.

She parted her legs for him fully, and he took the invitation to rake the soft bristles up, then down, using full, long, languorous strokes that felt like hot velvet against her aching flesh. She moved against the brush without reservation, ready to take in every sensation Rick delivered.

"That's right, baby," he murmured above her, still stroking, brushing, bringing that sweet, swallowing pleasure, until finally he pushed two warm fingers inside her as well.

She whimpered at the sudden invasion, but it was oh-so-welcome, filling the emptiness as he lifted her higher and higher. His fingers moved as he worked the brush up above, and she became lost to the overwhelming bliss. "Almost," she murmured. "Almost."

And then she was flying—up, up, up—crying out as her body seemed to shoot through the night sky. And when the sweet, hot pulses finally began to subside, she opened her eyes to see . . . angels.

Trying to catch her breath, she pulled her gaze down to Rick and pretended she hadn't just had an out-of-body experience that made her want to hold him close and never let him go. "I . . . never suspected you were so good with a paintbrush."

He gave her a sexy wink. "Guess I'm just a different kind of artist."

Pushing up onto her knees, Mia moved to straddle him where he knelt. The time for teasing and hesitation was over, and they both seemed to know it. Maybe she *didn't* have to pretend—at least not about the depths of her passion.

They looked into each other's eyes as she lowered herself onto him, taking every glorious inch inside.

There was no more going slow after that. They kissed frantically and moved together; she rubbed her breasts against his chest and he held tight to her bottom. Pleasure and emotion swept through Mia's body—the pleasure she clung to, but the emotion she still tried to push aside.

"I want to make you come again," he breathed in her ear.

She pulled back just enough to look into his eyes. "Close," she whispered. "So close." That quick. The sweet, hot friction urged her onward and she rocked harder against him.

"God, I want to make you come so good, want to make you explode, want to make you—"

"Oh—*now*," she rasped as the waves of orgasm struck. "*Now*." And it was exactly as Rick had just hoped aloud: This time it came harder, rough flashes of heat and light, racking her body with intense spasms that made her moan and sob.

She was lost in her own private heaven until she heard his deep voice. "Don't stop, sweetheart, don't stop. God, here I come, too." He thrust powerfully up inside her, and she kept riding him just as urgently, wanting to give him every ounce of pleasure possible.

Afterward, they rolled off of each other and onto their backs, silent, staring at the ceiling. Mia noticed both their bodies were stained with sweaty paint that had mixed during sex, hers onto him, his onto her. The only sound for a long while was their labored breathing, finally softening.

"So, tell me about you and painting," Rick said without warning, his voice warm in the afterglow of sex.

She kept her eyes on the angels, same as him. "I've always painted, since I was a child. I tried to get noticed in New York, but it's a very hard business to break into, and it makes me sad that art becomes *about* business, decisions, money. And still, I yearn for my work to be seen, so it's a vicious circle. When I ran out of money, Aunt Clara was kind enough to invite me here." She turned her head toward him on the drop cloth. "I'm sorry I lied. About being the other kind of painter."

His glance was fleeting before it returned to the mural above, yet he reached out to lock his fingertips around hers. "It's okay."

They stayed silent then for a few minutes, until finally Rick spoke again. "How do you decide about the penises?"

Letting out a laugh, she turned to him, wide-eyed. "What?"

"The guy angels' penises." He pointed to the first angel she'd painted. "Seems like that guy got shortchanged. What did he do to deserve that?"

She giggled again, and found Rick smiling at her. "I just paint them as they come to me. I vary the way they look, like real people."

"I thought you told me once that they were supposed to be perfect." He concluded by arching one eyebrow.

"Perfection means different things to different individuals," she countered. "It's in the eye of the beholder."

His expression turned playful and sexy. "What if you were painting *me*?"

For a second, Mia feared he recognized himself in the dark angel toward the front of the room, but she realized that his gaze rested on her, not the ceiling, and that he was drifting back into a sensual frame of mind.

"Don't worry. If I was painting you, no one would think you have a small penis."

Rolling to face her, he rubbed it against her thigh. He'd already grown again and the sensation turned her insides to jelly. "So you like it?"

Their faces were only a few inches apart when Mia cast him a smile. "You have to ask?"

"I mean, it's big enough for you?" He seemed too confident for the question to be sincere, but it excited her that he wanted to hear it.

"Aren't you up on the latest?" she said, teasing. "Size doesn't matter."

A deep chuckle rumbled from his chest. "That's just a line to appease the guys who are little and the women who are stuck with them."

"You're bad," she said, giggling.

His eyes had turned glassy and hot on her again. "But am I big?"

"Yes, you're big. And bad."

"Why don't I show you just how big and bad I can be."

Chapter Seven

Rick grazed his palm across her smooth stomach, thinking, *I'm glad you lied about what you paint or I wouldn't be lying here with you right now.* Despite his admonitions and resolve, somewhere deep inside him he'd *known* that he couldn't stay away from her, that he had to have her again. She was so open, so cool, and so sexy, but it wasn't an act as he'd once thought—it was just Mia.

Every pore coursed with heated pleasure as he gazed on the arcs and curves of her paint-splotched skin, her breasts, her stomach. Parting her legs, he slid his hard length across her moisture until she moaned, then pushed himself deep into the hot, tight glove of her body. Who'd have thought he'd find heaven on a drop cloth spread across the floor of his bar?

Damn, this woman took him places he'd never been before. Even as he attempted to glide slowly in and out, to deliver long, thorough strokes that would let each of them savor the slick heat they created together, a sense of total abandon washed over him and made him pump into her harder, faster, with no restraint.

"Oh God, yes," she whispered. "Yes."

It was hardly the first time he'd heard such words from a woman's lips, but when Mia said them, they pushed him to the point of no return. Tremors racked him from head to toe as he came in her, groaning until the last ounce of pleasure melted away inside her.

When he opened his eyes afterward, he felt uncharacteristically sheepish. "That was . . . faster than I intended."

Her smile held a naughty edge. "Don't worry—I like it hard and fast."

If he could have come again, he would have.

Like before, Rick fought off the urge to sleep. It would have been painfully easy to give in, to pull her into his arms and drift off with her. But he couldn't. They were in his damn bar. And she . . . hell, she made him feel things. Things he simply wasn't going to let himself feel. His suspicions about her had died away, but that didn't mean she was safe. *Donna* was safe. A woman he could fuck and forget about was safe. Mia didn't fall into that category.

Although they lay side by side, facing each other, he let his gaze drift upward. When it landed on the bared breasts of one of the female angels, he forced his eyes back down, even though he didn't really want to look Mia in the face for what he was about to say. "I should probably tell you . . . I'm not looking for a relationship."

"I figured."

The quick, short reply caught him off guard. "Why?"

She shrugged, her paint-stained breasts jostling slightly. "I saw the way those women were mooning at you in here that first night. If you wanted to have a relationship, you'd have one, right?"

He stayed silent, painfully aware that he felt far differently about her than he did about those other women.

"By the way, are you sleeping with the leopard lady?"

"Huh?"

"The chick in the tight leopard-print dress last Friday night." When he hesitated, she added, "It's no biggie—I'm just curious."

"Sometimes. Occasionally," he replied. His gaze had wandered to her angels again, but he drew it back to her. "Not in a while."

She nodded, appearing content, but to his surprise, Rick somehow felt he owed her more, wanted to *give* her more.

"I was engaged once."

"Aunt Clara mentioned that. She said it didn't turn out well."

"Gina came from a rough background, abusive. Both her parents were alcoholics. What it came down to was that she needed . . . more than I could give her. Emotionally." He swallowed hard on the last word, one that didn't have occasion to leave his mouth often. "She needed someone to be sensitive and caring, someone to talk to and listen to her and come running every time she called . . . and I wasn't that guy."

Again, his paint-splotched lover gave a slight shrug. "I'm sure you were caring. And you seem to talk and listen okay."

He couldn't help laughing at her simple analysis. "This isn't exactly the norm for me."

"I gathered," she said, offering a grin. "So to what do I suddenly owe the privilege?"

He shook his head, then looked away, uncomfortable. "I'm not sure."

She stayed silent, acceptant. Again, he couldn't help thinking how incredibly unruffled she was—she took everything like it was nothing. Not exactly the hysterical, clingy woman he'd envisioned.

"The thing about Gina," he said, barreling forward for reasons he couldn't name, "is that when I couldn't give her whatever it was she needed, she started looking for it somewhere else. I found her in bed with my best friend."

She flinched, then met his eyes, hers shining with surprise and dismay. "God. I'm sorry."

He couldn't say why he'd volunteered the information, but the emotions surrounding those days came flooding back: the sense of betrayal, the utter shock, the anger . . . and the tears that had shown him something he hadn't liked facing, that he wasn't quite as tough as he liked to think. As tension gathered in his chest, he shoved all of it right back into the little box inside him where he'd kept it these last five years. "It was a long time ago," he said, working to keep his expression masked, his voice even.

She simply nodded, then kissed him, murmuring something to herself. Rick couldn't quite make it out, but it sounded like she said, "What a stupid girl."

An hour later, Rick lay on the drop cloth, looking up. Only now he was dressed, and alone. Mia had departed soon after his confession. Damn, what had gotten into him to go spilling that kind of stuff to her? Talk of an early day for both of them tomorrow, and her promise that she would have the ceiling finished within two days, had melted away the sexy mood and sent her on her way. He'd claimed he wanted to stay behind and check on a few things, but would be right behind her, turning out the lights and locking up.

He'd wanted her to go, was glad when she did, was glad when the intensity had ended.

Yet now he suffered the faint sensation of being left alone.

He hated dealing with these emotions, feeling as if there was something he wanted but just couldn't have. He hated that he'd told her about Gina. He hated that he'd even thought about it, that he'd let himself relive that ugly moment of walking into his fiancée's apartment and finding her naked with Rob.

Turned out the guy wasn't such a friend, and when Rick looked back on it now, it was clear Rob had really been more of a longtime buddy, a guy he'd hung out with since junior high, but not the kind of friend you counted on, the kind who was there for you in bad times, like his brothers were.

Now Rob and Gina lived up in Greenville; he'd heard they had a baby. He'd also heard that Rob stayed out late and drank a lot these days. Thinking of them being miserable with each other wasn't the consolation he thought it should be—it just made him all the more sour on the idea of one man, one woman, one life together.

As his eyes roamed the world Mia had created on the ceiling of his bar, Rick came to a conclusion: He and Mia were over, over before they'd really even begun, and it was for the best. He wouldn't weaken to her again.

Already his resolve felt stronger this time than before. And it wasn't that he'd had enough of her, not by a long shot. It was that he didn't think he'd *ever* get enough of her, not if he made love to her every day for a year, or ten years, or twenty. Ironically, she left him feeling the exact way he'd feared *her* to be: needy. And he wasn't going to live his life that way.

But as for the angels on his ceiling, there was simply no way he could cover them up. It made no sense to have them there—he was more conscious of that than ever before—yet he couldn't destroy the beauty she'd brought into a place that, quite frankly, didn't see much beauty. The kind that came from within, the kind that filled you up with something bigger than yourself each time you looked at it.

He couldn't give her romance, and he couldn't give her the need that burned inside him—but he could give her the angels on the ceiling.

And, well, maybe *one* thing more.

The next two days were pure torture for Mia. To paint was like bleeding. She still didn't know if he'd let her work stay there untouched, and even if he did . . . God, what had she done? How had she let herself get so wrapped up in this project, this man? The two seemed tied together in her heart now. When she thought of leaving Dawes, leaving the ceiling of the Rose Tavern behind, a strange, empty sadness overwhelmed her. But it was about more than leaving the ceiling—it was also about leaving Rick. To leave one was to leave the other, knowing she'd never see either again. It already felt like a chunk of her heart was missing.

The pièce de résistance on the ceiling came in the form of roses. In vibrant fuchsia and bold red, they were the punch of color the space needed. Only a few of them dotted the expanse of the sky, but in each curved corner, she painted a large brown basket from which a profusion of roses spilled down the wall. The angels were what gave the painting life, but the roses personalized it, connected it to Rick.

On Wednesday afternoon, nine days after starting the job and twelve days since meeting Rick Rose, she found the number of the feed store taped near the phone behind the bar.

A woman answered on the first ring. "Dawes Feed and Supply." Mia wondered if it was Rick's mother.

"Hi. Can I speak to Rick?"

"Hold on," she said, then returned a moment later. "I'm afraid he's unloading a truck right now. Can I take a message?"

Mia caught her breath, somehow both relieved and disappointed that he hadn't come to the phone. "Yes. Tell him the painting is finished at his bar if he'd like to come see it."

As usual, she'd forgotten lunch, so she wandered two doors down to the drugstore, where she bought a PayDay and a Coke. Upon returning, she boosted herself up onto the bar to eat the candy, and she'd just swallowed the last bite when Rick walked in. She felt her skin flush slightly at the sight of him.

His eyes fell to the wrapper still between her fingers. "Sweetheart, you've gotta start eating better."

She nodded. "I know. I will. I'll have more money soon." Because the job was over and he would pay her now. This was it. She had a feeling she'd never see Rick Rose again. Lest he witness the pain in her expression, she changed the subject. "Speaking of which, it's done. What do you think?" She held her arms wide and looked up, encouraging him to do the same.

He scanned the ceiling thoroughly, then drew his gaze back down. One corner of his mouth curved upward, threatening a smile. "You added roses."

She raised her eyebrows. "Get it? The Rose Tavern?"

As his smile came fully into being, she ached with how beautiful he was. "I like it," he said. "I like . . . the thought you put into it."

Her heart warmed and she bit her lip hopefully. "So . . . you're not going to make me paint over it?"

He shook his head and relief flooded her.

"Thank you."

At least it would always be here now—at least someone would see her art. And maybe every once in a while Rick would glance up at it and think of her and remember the passion they'd shared.

When the moment grew silent and awkward, she took a deep breath and forced out the next words. "Well, guess this is it."

His nod was slow, perfunctory. "Yeah." Then he reached in his pocket and extracted a check folded in half, slipping it into her hand. As her fingers passed over his to accept it, the payment felt hollow. Money mattered—it kept you alive, and she needed to have it—but being paid for what she'd created on this ceiling almost didn't make sense. It had been a labor of love, more than one kind.

"So . . . what's next for you? Moving on to someplace new?"

She thought it sounded like he wanted her to. And before a couple of days ago, she'd actually planned to stick around Dawes for at least a little while longer, to see if she could earn some more cash and hand some of it over to Aunt Clara. But recently, she'd decided she *couldn't* stay. She'd be looking for him everywhere. And if she saw him, her heart would break. Hell, it would break if she *didn't* see him. Either way, existing without him would surely be easier elsewhere.

"Yeah, I'll probably leave. It feels like time."

Liar. She didn't know how she'd fallen in love with him this fast, but that was exactly what she'd done. Leaving would be difficult, yet it seemed the only way to save herself from a life of hopeless infatuation.

"Listen, I've been thinking," he said, and a bolt of hope stabbed through her. Maybe he was going to say he'd changed his mind about relationships. Maybe he was going to ask her to stay. "My mother knows a guy who runs an art gallery in Charleston. I thought I'd ask him to come see the ceiling, see what he thinks. If he likes it, maybe he could help you out."

Mia's heart rose to her throat. She was at once devastated by the letdown and thrilled beyond her wildest dreams. Most of all, she was touched by his thoughtfulness. "That would be . . . wonderful. Thank you."

More than ever before, she wanted to throw herself into his arms, hold him close. At the very least, she wanted to kiss him good-bye.

But she couldn't. Because if she did, they'd likely end up on the floor or the bar, and despite her plan to take sex with Rick for whatever it was worth, she didn't think she could be that intimate with him again. It would only make parting even worse.

"I . . . should go," she said, pointing vaguely toward the door.

He gave a slight nod. His eyes said more, but she knew it wasn't enough. She knew she had to get the hell out of the Rose Tavern before she lost what remained of her heart.

So she turned and walked out, and it wasn't until after she'd gotten in her car and driven away that she permitted a few tears to roll down her cheeks.

The next week was a whirlwind for Mia. On Friday, John Brightman, owner of the Brightman Gallery on State Street in Charleston, had called Aunt Clara's house, asking to see some of Mia's canvases.

The small, tidy man arrived in a late-model Mercedes sedan, wore khakis with expensive Italian loafers, and sported a stylish goatee. She felt a bit odd greeting him in jeans and a T-shirt, but he'd seemed genuinely pleased to meet her and truly enthusiastic about her art when she invited him onto Aunt Clara's enclosed sun porch, where she'd been working.

"These are truly inspired, Mia," he'd said after studying the dozen paintings propped about the glassed porch. "And your mural at the tavern is breathtaking. If I'd had the time, I could have looked at it for hours."

She'd been absolutely speechless; no one besides Aunt Clara and a few of Mia's friends back in New York had ever seemed so taken by her work or handed out such overwhelming compliments. She couldn't help wondering if it was the emotions that had been coursing through her veins while she'd painted the mural that had given it enough passion to catch John Brightman's attention.

On the spot, he had offered her a showing, after which he'd also invited her to work for him. Clearly, Rick had filled the man in on her financial situation, and it so happened he was in need of an assistant for his growing business.

No matter how she looked at it, it was a dream come true. Not only would she finally get to show her work and maybe even sell some of it, but she also had a brand-new job in the field where her heart belonged. She sincerely liked John Brightman and thought she'd enjoy working with him.

After accepting his gracious offer, she'd begun to plan. She'd decided she would go to Charleston right away and use the money she'd made from Rick to get her new life started. She picked up a Charleston newspaper at the grocery store, and a day of phone calls netted her a furnished apartment that was ready to move into and required only a six-month lease. If she saved enough to buy some furniture by that time, she could find a new place. Once she arrived, she planned to spend a few days setting up house, then shopping for

have been before she arrived. "I promise to come see you every weekend. Or you can visit Charleston and see the sights. And, of course, you'll have to come to my showing next month." She lowered her voice slightly. "I love you. And I won't disappear from your life, ever. I promise."

The two women shared a warm hug; then Aunt Clara shut Mia into the old station wagon, packed to the gills with canvases and easels and clothing, most of which bore at least a few dots or smears of paint.

Her heart swelled in her chest as she pulled away, catching a last glimpse of her aunt's flowered dress in the rearview mirror, but she was determined not to cry. Tears were useless and she'd put them away long ago, having learned that you could cry an ocean and it wouldn't change anything.

As for the few she'd shed after leaving Rick for the last time, they were just as futile. As was pining for a man she couldn't ever really have. Having his body had been spectacular, but as she'd predicted would happen all along, she left wanting more. She was just glad she'd never let him know that. This way, she could remain a pleasant memory in his mind.

Why did that sound so empty, though? she wondered as she came to a stop sign. *A pleasant memory*—it sounded so vague, unimportant, seldom thought of.

A left turn led to Dawes, a right to her new life. For a brief second, she was sorely tempted to go looking for Rick, just to see him one last time. But just like tears, such a move would lead nowhere.

She turned right and resolved not to look back.

Chapter Eight

Rick dropped the rag he was using to wipe down the bar and went back to the note he'd left lying at one end. His eyes returned to the same handwritten words that kept sticking in his mind. *I won't forget them.* Meaning the experiences he and Mia had shared here beneath the angels. Damn, how he wanted to make himself believe it had been nothing more than sex, nothing more than two people following their physical urges and making each other feel good.

If that were truly the case, though, why was she still on his mind? Why had he picked up this note five times in the last hour since finding it waiting in the mailbox upon stopping in to check his liquor inventory? Why did his chest ache when he thought of her? And he'd been thinking of her long before receiving this card.

Setting it back down, Rick headed toward his desk to fill out a liquor order. And for the first time since unloading the back room of tables, chairs, and bar stools, he thought to empty the waste can near the door. That's when he noticed the torn blue panties, tossed away like they didn't matter. It wrenched his heart a little harder.

The note said that she'd gone to Charleston, was starting a whole new life, and that it was a dream come true. Jesus, she sounded happy—and it made him glad. Even if he felt a little lonely, too.

Since when do you feel lonely, for God's sake?

It was a totally new emotion for him. Even when all the shit with Gina and Rob had hit the fan, he'd never felt *lonely*. But the past couple of weeks had held a certain quality of . . . pointlessness. Life had begun to seem boring. Work had become drudgery. Even running the bar—something he usually enjoyed—had begun to seem a lot more like work than ever before.

It's all in your head.

Or maybe he was wrong and it was all in his *heart* instead.

Stepping back out into the barroom, he leaned back to look at the ceiling. He'd been concerned about how his customers would react, but his worries had been in vain. Some people had the same response as he and John Brightman—they sat and stared at it for a long while. And even those who weren't quite as drawn in seemed to find it sexy as hell. He didn't quite think some of his patrons understood they were looking at angels—but they read the passion loud and clear. And they liked the nudity, which gave him a laugh.

Mia had added so much here in such a short time. Why did it leave him feeling so damn empty?

Moving to the phone, he picked it up to call Jake, who'd just gotten off the road after a weeklong run and would likely be in no humor for his request, but that was too bad. As expected, his brother sounded groggy when he answered.

"I need a favor. I need you to tend bar for me tonight."

"Can't do it. Gotta get some sleep."

Rick took a deep breath. He didn't like to beg, but . . . "I need this, Jake. It's important."

Need. Lately his life was all about *need*, a concept he'd despised ever since Hurricane Gina had blown through his life.

Yet, to his surprise, he suddenly found himself thinking maybe need wasn't such a horrible thing.

Mia soaked in a bubble bath on Friday night, surrounded by the aromatherapy candles Aunt Clara had secretly packed for her. She'd just finished her first week at her new gallery job, where the work and atmosphere were exhilarating, but also tiring; she was exhausted and in need of a good long soak. She'd been pleased to discover her new apartment had an old white porcelain claw-foot tub much like Aunt Clara's.

Despite her fatigue, she felt great. Vital. Like someone who mattered, whose life was on the move, and certainly who was on the right track for a change. A few weeks ago, such feelings were unimaginable. Suddenly, turning thirty wasn't about counting failures and coming to grips with disappointment, but about discovering opportunity and finding a way to follow her heart, a quest that no longer seemed irresponsible or fruitless. Of course, her thoughts always came back to how she'd gotten here. Without Rick, she wouldn't have any of this.

She gave in to the urge to lean her head back. Her body felt as weary as her mind, yet she was still keyed up, too, finding it hard to relax despite the "mellow" labels on the candles. Sliding her palm up her thigh beneath the water, she followed the impulse to lift it to her breast. The sensation made her remember Rick's touch, his mouth, drinking at her nipple. She circled the hard bud with her fingertip, wondering how it felt on his tongue, and released a sigh as the crux of her thighs turned achy. Letting her eyes fall shut, she began to slip into a fantasy—or in this case, part memory. Rick's mouth gliding over her skin. His rough fingers fondling her where she was hot for him.

Stop it! The voice sounded from somewhere in her head. *Don't let yourself think of him like that anymore. It will only hurt worse that way.*

Because no matter how wonderfully she was doing, another part of her hurt so badly she couldn't bear to deal with it. Upon returning home from the gallery each night this week, she'd quickly thrown herself into painting, having relegated most of the living room to easels and canvases. She'd created new angels who wanted each other but couldn't touch; she'd thrown herself into her work so she wouldn't have time to think about the man beyond her grasp.

But wasn't thinking about wanting someone she couldn't have, if even through the eyes of her angels, the same as thinking about *him*?

The loud knock on the door startled her and she flinched, splashing water over the tub's edge. Who the hell could it be? She didn't have friends here yet, and though John had her address, she had no reason to think it was him.

"Who's there?" she yelled. This would have to be good to get her out of the tub.

"Mia, it's Rick."

Hearing his voice was like smashing into a brick wall and crumbling to pieces—nothing could have stunned her more. *Pull yourself together.* "Uh, it'll be a minute. I'm . . . in the bathtub."

She was about to push to her feet and reach for a towel when she heard the old brass knob turn with a click. A second later he came into view through an archway.

"You take a bath without locking your door?" His eyes widened in admonition.

Mia shook her head helplessly, still amid the bubbles. "I didn't realize. Totally irresponsible of me. A bad trait of mine."

But by the time she finished speaking, he'd come much closer, stopping at the entrance to the bathroom. Some misplaced sense of propriety made her cross her arms, covering her bare, soapy breasts.

"Sweetheart," he said, "I've seen them before."

Already, he was looking at her with a familiar heat burning in those dark, beautiful eyes, and she knew she was looking back exactly the same way. Her voice came out far breathier than she intended. "If you want to wait in the living room, I can get out and—"

"No, you don't need to get out. I just need to say some things to you."

"Wh-what?"

Mia finally let her hands fall from her breasts as he dropped to his knees next to the tub, bringing them eye to eye. "This isn't easy for me."

"What isn't easy?" She couldn't imagine what he'd come to say. Hadn't they already said everything?

"Mia, I shouldn't have let you leave town."

"Huh?" Her heart beat so hard in her chest that it hurt.

She watched as he lowered his gaze, drew in his breath, then looked back at her. "I thought I didn't want anyone to need me, but I was wrong. I want *you* to need me, Mia. I want you to need me like I need you."

She lifted one palm back to her chest, soapy fingers splayed in shock. "Rick, I . . . don't know what to say."

His expression turned from seductive to pained. He swallowed visibly, but never looked away this time. "That's okay. I . . . shouldn't have expected you to feel the same." He pushed to his feet. "I felt more than I was willing to admit, and I thought maybe you did, too, but . . ."

Mia's hand darted from the tub to grab his wrist and yank him back to his knees. He looked slightly alarmed, but she leaned close and said, "You're not going *anywhere*."

He looked thoroughly confused. "Why?"

"Because I crave you."

As he let out a ragged breath, the look in his eyes began transforming back to the hot, virile one she'd come to know.

"I crave you day and night. I long to have your hands on me. I long to kiss you, touch you. I long to have you inside me. I can't explain what you do to me or what it means, but leaving you was . . . way too hard." She slowed her pace then, lowered her voice. "I felt myself beginning to care for you, but I didn't let you know because I didn't think you wanted that."

His voice was like warm honey. "Well, I want it now."

Bending over the tub, Rick took Mia's face in his hands and delivered a sweet, tender kiss. It was far more gentle than any they'd shared before, yet the response it elicited in her body was like wildfire. "Oh," she whispered, stunned, "can we do that again?"

As his mouth moved over hers, his tongue eased between her lips, deepening the connection, deepening everything she felt. When the kiss ended, they were both breathless.

"So," he said, "do you think we can make this work—you here, me there?"

She offered a small smile. "It's a short drive."

"You're right. So if you decide to come back and live in Dawes, you wouldn't have far to go to the gallery," he concluded with a persuasive grin that melted her heart.

Dear God, he wanted her in Dawes, with him. And she wanted that, too, but she had to be smart, reasonable. Such resolve didn't prevent her voice from trembling when she spoke. "Maybe we should take one step at a time, but . . ."

"But?" He arched one brow.

"But that sounds like a distinct possibility, sometime in the . . . future."

His prodding grin returned. "The *near* future."

"You . . . realize we don't actually know each other very well," she felt the need to point out.

His eyes darkened with heat. "But when I'm inside you, it doesn't feel that way. Does it?"

She bit her lip and shook her head, unable to deny it. Then she couldn't help laughing. Everything in her life was suddenly too perfect to be believed. "Aunt Clara will be thrilled."

"She sounded happy when I called to get your address."

Mia tilted her head. "Sometimes I almost wonder if this wasn't her plan all along. She *knew* I didn't do that kind of painting. She has a secret side, you know."

He looked doubtful. "Clara? Nah."

But Mia nodded adamantly. "I think she has . . . secret passions."

"Like her niece?" he asked, suggestive expression in place.

Ignoring the warmth that ascended her cheeks, Mia cast him a sexy grin of her own. "Did I ever tell you I had a bathtub fantasy about you?"

"Uh, no," he replied, appearing utterly intrigued.

"Well, would you like to hear about it?"

"Actually, I'd rather just make it up as I go along," he said, kicking off his shoes behind him and reaching for his belt buckle.

Mia went weak, but found the strength to reach for the top button on his shirt.

Their gazes never left one another as, together, they undressed him, and he soon stepped into the tub, easing into the warm, bubbly water behind her. As she leaned back against his solid warmth, his hands came around to caress her breasts and he rained tiny kisses along her neck.

When his hard, beautiful length pressed into her from behind, Mia decided that lounging in the bathtub and thinking dirty thoughts about a man she didn't know had been an acceptable way to spend her birthday, but having the real thing was much, much better.

Thank God Rick was no angel.

Toni Blake knew she wanted to be a writer by the age of ten, when she penned her first novel—nineteen notebook pages long. Since then, Toni has become a multipublished author of contemporary romance novels, as well as had more than forty short stories and articles published. She has been a recipient of the Kentucky Women Writers' Fellowship and has also been honored with a nomination for the prestigious Pushcart Prize. Visit Toni on the Web at www.ToniBlake.com.